THE WORLD WON'T WAIT

Why Canada Needs to Rethink
Its International Policies

The need for an ambitious and forward-looking Canadian international strategy has never been greater. The worldwide changes that jeopardize Canadian security and prosperity are profound, ranging from the globalization of commerce, crime, and political extremism to the impact of climate change on the economy and environment. The reaction from Canada's policymakers, at least so far, has been underwhelming.

In *The World Won't Wait*, some of Canada's brightest thinkers respond. Covering both classic foreign policy issues, such as international security, human rights, and global institutions, and emerging issues like Internet governance, climate change, and sustainable development, their essays offer fresh and provocative responses to today's challenges and opportunities. The proposals are striking and the contributors diverse: Toronto's chief city planner makes the case that Canada needs a global urban agenda, while a prominent mining executive explains how to revitalize the country's position as a world leader in the sector. Their essays are sure to spark the kind of debate that Canada requires if its international policy is to evolve in the twenty-first century.

ROLAND PARIS is an associate professor and the director of the Centre for International Policy Studies at the University of Ottawa.

TAYLOR OWEN is an assistant professor in the Liu Institute for Global Issues and the Graduate School of Journalism at the University of British Columbia and a senior fellow at the Columbia Journalism School.

UTP insights

UTP Insights is an innovative collection of brief books offering accessible introductions to the ideas that shape our world. Each volume in the series focuses on a contemporary issue, offering a fresh perspective anchored in scholarship. Spanning a broad range of disciplines in the social sciences and humanities, the books in the UTP Insights series contribute to public discourse and debate and provide a valuable resource for instructors and students.

BOOKS IN THE SERIES

- Roland Paris and Taylor Owen (eds.), *The World Won't Wait: Why Canada Needs to Rethink Its International Policies*
- Stephen M. Saideman, *Adapting in the Dust: Lessons Learned from Canada's War in Afghanistan*
- Michael R. Marrus, *Lessons of the Holocaust*
- Bessma Momani, *Arab Dawn: Arab Youth and the Demographic Dividend They Will Bring*
- William Watson, *The Inequality Trap: Fighting Capitalism Instead of Poverty*
- Phil Ryan, *After the New Atheist Debate*
- Paul Evans, *Engaging China: Myth, Aspiration, and Strategy in Canadian Policy from Trudeau to Harper*

THE WORLD WON'T WAIT

Why Canada Needs to Rethink Its International Policies

Edited by Roland Paris and Taylor Owen

UNIVERSITY OF TORONTO PRESS
Toronto Buffalo London

© University of Toronto Press 2016
Toronto Buffalo London
www.utppublishing.com
Printed in the U.S.A.

ISBN 978-1-4426-4961-3 (cloth)
ISBN 978-1-4426-2697-3 (paper)

Printed on acid-free, 100% post-consumer recycled paper with vegetable-based inks.

Library and Archives Canada Cataloguing in Publication

The world won't wait : why Canada needs to rethink its international policies / edited by Roland Paris and Taylor Owen.

(UTP insights)
Includes bibliographical references and index.
ISBN 978-1-4426-4961-3 (cloth). – ISBN 978-1-4426-2697-3 (paper)

1. Canada – Foreign relations – 21st century.   I. Paris, Roland, 1967–, editor   II. Owen, Taylor, 1978–, editor   III. Series: UTP insights

FC242.W67 2015   327.71009'05   C2015-906246-2

University of Toronto Press acknowledges the financial assistance to its publishing program of the Canada Council for the Arts and the Ontario Arts Council, an agency of the Government of Ontario.

Canada Council
for the Arts

Conseil des Arts
du Canada

ONTARIO ARTS COUNCIL
CONSEIL DES ARTS DE L'ONTARIO
an Ontario government agency
un organisme du gouvernement de l'Ontario

Funded by the   Financé par le
Government   gouvernement
of Canada   du Canada

Contents

Preface

In a more complex, competitive, and crowded world, "standing still is falling behind." This was how Robert Greenhill, a particularly accomplished and globally networked Canadian, characterized the challenge facing our country today.[1] He was speaking at the inaugural Ottawa Forum, held in May 2014.[2] This book is the progeny of that conference, where some of the country's brightest "next generation" thinkers and most experienced policy practitioners gathered to brainstorm forward-looking options for Canada's international policy.

This volume was completed just before the October 2015 federal election, but its analysis and recommendations apply to any Canadian government emerging from the election. We are living through an era of fundamental change in world affairs. Many of the old assumptions and nostrums about Canadian foreign policy can no longer be taken for granted. Although the challenges facing Canada differ from one issue-area to the next, all the contributors to this book, who first presented their ideas at the Ottawa Forum and later refined them for publication, share the view that Canada needs to pursue a comprehensive, constructive, and ambitious international strategy. This volume explains why this is so. It provides a clear-eyed assessment of key transformations taking place in the world, explains how these changes impact eleven policy domains that matter to Canada, and answers the question "How can Canada best position itself to succeed in, and contribute to, the world that is now emerging, rather than the world we have known in the past?"

We owe many thanks to those who made this book's publication possible. The authors not only shared their insights but also did a superb job of revising their chapters in response to comments, challenges, and queries. Paul Heinbecker and Morris Rosenberg both read all the original Ottawa Forum papers and provided detailed and helpful reactions. Two anonymous reviewers of the ensuing book manuscript also offered comments that guided a second round of substantive revisions, yielding the volume you are now reading. Jennifer DiDomenico of the University of Toronto Press offered valuable advice in the preparation of this manuscript. We thank all of them. We also gratefully acknowledge the sponsors of the Ottawa Forum, who made this project possible: the Canadian International Council, the Centre for International Policy Studies at the University of Ottawa, the Bill Graham Centre for Contemporary International History, the Federation for the Humanities and Social Sciences, the Canadian Council of Chief Executives, the Graduate School of Public and International Affairs at the University of Ottawa, and the National Capital Branch of the Canadian International Council.

Roland Paris
Taylor Owen

THE WORLD WON'T WAIT

A Transforming World

ROLAND PARIS AND TAYLOR OWEN

Canada needs a more ambitious, forward-looking, and effective international strategy. Profound global changes are casting doubt on assumptions that have long underpinned Canada's foreign policy. No longer can the United States be relied upon either to drive Canadian economic growth or to single-handedly underwrite the global trading system and international security. Competition for markets, energy, and resources is intensifying. Communications technologies are collapsing distance and hierarchies, empowering new digital actors, but also raising new concerns about intrusive surveillance, cyberattacks, and violent radicalization across borders. Rising powers and non-state actors, from philanthropic foundations to terrorist networks, are playing a larger role on the global stage. Millions of people around the world are entering the global middle class for the first time, but other societies remain mired in cycles of poverty, poor governance, and conflict. The effects of climate change are multiplying, including in Canada's north, where sea ice is rapidly disappearing.

These and other transformations matter for Canada and for our future. They matter, in part, because Canadians have long believed that their country should play a constructive role in addressing global problems; we are not isolationists. They also matter because these changes have potentially serious implications for the prosperity, security, and well-being of Canadians. If we fail to maintain Canada's competitiveness, to address transnational threats to our security, or to deal with mounting global environmental problems, to name but a few examples, current and future generations of Canadians will end up worse off.

To understand the impact of these changes, however, we first need to remind ourselves of the core objectives of Canada's foreign policy. They are largely unchanging: to safeguard the security of Canada and Canadians; to create conditions for long-term economic growth at home; to protect and improve other aspects of Canadians' quality of life, from a healthy natural environment to a free and open Internet; and to work with others globally to strengthen the rules-based international order and to increase peace, human rights, pluralism, economic opportunity, and environmental sustainability around the world. Some might quibble with these objectives, but they vary little from decade to decade. Yet the international context in which Canada pursues these goals is undergoing significant change. Understanding this context is essential for determining what means and methods Canada should employ to realize its objectives.

But there's a problem: this kind of rethinking is barely occurring. Apart from a handful of books,[1] occasional position papers and research reports from the country's dwindling assortment of think tanks,[2] and periodic newspaper op-eds and blog posts,[3] debates about Canada's foreign policy rarely move beyond the news story du jour. We seem to have lost our national capacity for long-term strategic thinking about international policy. Instruments traditionally employed by previous governments to conduct such reviews – white papers and royal commissions – have fallen into disuse. Parliamentary committees produce substantial reports from time to time, but they tend to focus on relatively narrow issues (one recent example is cluster munitions) or Canada's policy towards specific countries (such as Ukraine or Syria), rather than on the broad directions of our international policy. Nor do academic foreign-policy specialists often examine these larger questions. They normally address more focused issues or the theoretical underpinnings of policy. This research can be fascinating and enlightening, but it ultimately offers little guidance for updating Canada's international policy in a world of breathtaking change.

Meanwhile, the very concept of foreign policy is being called into question as the boundary between domestic and international issues erodes. Nominally "domestic" matters such as economic competitiveness, social equity, innovation policy, post-secondary education, environmental protection, political radicalization, information security, labour market policy, critical infrastructure resilience, human trafficking, and maritime safety all require action at the international level as well. Conversely, the globalization of communications, technology, commerce, finance, and – more disturbingly – crime, extremist violence, and disease mean that international affairs is penetrating more deeply and widely into Canadian society than ever before. We are not the first to argue this point. Former Canadian diplomat George Haynal, for example, once described Canada's relations with the United States as "intermestic" – a blend of international and domestic – and a number of academics have made similar observations about Canadian foreign policy more broadly.[4] But the need to move beyond conventionally defined concepts of foreign policy has never been clearer.

In this book, we have therefore chosen to address Canada's "international strategy" rather than its "foreign policy." This terminological adjustment may seem minor, but it encompasses a wider variety of actors and issues. Canada's foreign ministry and its diplomats remain important players, but many other actors are also active on issues that transcend national boundaries. They include provincial and local governments, non-governmental organizations, advocacy groups, private companies, networked actors, and individuals. We need to adopt a more heterogeneous perspective on the issues and actors at play in international policy.

This volume represents one attempt to do just that. The authors of the following chapters are some of the brightest thinkers in the country. While some do not consider themselves foreign-policy experts, their expertise in related fields – from city planning to mining – broaden and enliven this discussion. The result, we believe, is a refreshingly diverse set of views on the future of Canada's international strategy. Indeed, we asked the authors to set aside old debates and settled wisdoms of Canadian foreign policy and to take a new look at eleven different international issues. They each had three tasks: first, to identify the main global trends bearing on their particular issue-area; second, to consider the positive and negative implications of these trends for Canada; and, finally, to set out a forward-looking strategy that will position Canada to capitalize on new opportunities while mitigating future risks.

As we shall see, although there are interesting points of disagreement between the authors, they arrive at strikingly similar prescriptions for the future directions of Canada's international policy. We describe these similarities in the Conclusion, and draw out their implications for the future of Canada's international strategy. For now, however, suffice it to say that there is broad agreement on the need for Canada to pursue a more comprehensive, constructive, and ambitious international strategy – more comprehensive in involving private actors and civil-society groups in the conception and implementation of policy; more constructive in working with other countries, non-government organizations, and multilateral institutions towards common goals; and more ambitious in placing Canada at the forefront of efforts to make the world safer, more prosperous, and healthier.

In the Conclusion, we go further, arguing that many of these prescriptions point to the necessary renewal of Canada's commitment to liberal internationalism, now updated to reflect the world that is emerging, rather than the world we have known. The label "liberal internationalism" can sometimes excite partisan passions, but it should not – at least, not in the way we are using it here. It refers not to the Liberal Party of Canada, but rather to the "small l" liberal belief in the value of diplomacy and international cooperation, institutions, and rules as means of securing Canadian interests and addressing global problems. This approach was at the core of Canada's largely non-partisan international policy for the better part of six decades following the Second World War, and its most successful practitioner in recent decades was arguably a (Progressive) Conservative prime minister, Brian Mulroney, who invested in diplomacy and the military while championing Canada's role in the United Nations, among other things. Although some of the contributors to this volume might not agree with this point, we believe that a refurbished liberal internationalism offers the basis for an effective, forward-looking policy – a policy that any Canadian government should embrace, regardless of its political stripe. But whereas liberal internationalism traditionally prized diplomacy in formal multilateral institutions, the contributors to this volume describe a more complex and diverse world in which a wider variety of actors (not just states) engage in more diverse and fluid forms of cooperation (not just multilateral organizations), among other changes. To be effective, Canada's international policy – whether or not it is rooted in a renewed liberal internationalism – must be informed by a clear-eyed assessment of the changes that are taking place in the world and how these changes impact specific issue-areas and Canada's interests. This book, we believe, provides such an analysis. We also hope that this volume will be equally at home in a university student's backpack, on a policy practitioner's desk, in a journalist's briefcase, and in the hands of anyone interested in Canada's current and future role in the world.

The Context: Eight Global Shifts

The chapters below examine eleven different areas of international policy, but the starting point for this discussion is the rapidly transforming global context. To observe that the "world is changing" might be the refrain of every generation, but we are struck by both the *acceleration* of change in international affairs in recent years as well as the *global scale* of these transformations, which together make it essential to reassess the goals and methods of Canadian policy. Eight transformations, or global shifts, stand out as particularly significant for Canada.

The first is the **rapid diffusion of economic power** in the international system from the Western industrialized democracies to emerging states. During the Cold War, the Western allies produced more than two-thirds of global economic output. Now they account for about half.[5] The speed of this transition is historically unprecedented. Two of the biggest emerging countries today, China and India, have experienced considerably higher rates of economic growth than previous rising powers did in their heyday. Britain took 154 years to double its per capita gross domestic product

Figure 0.1 Unprecedented growth

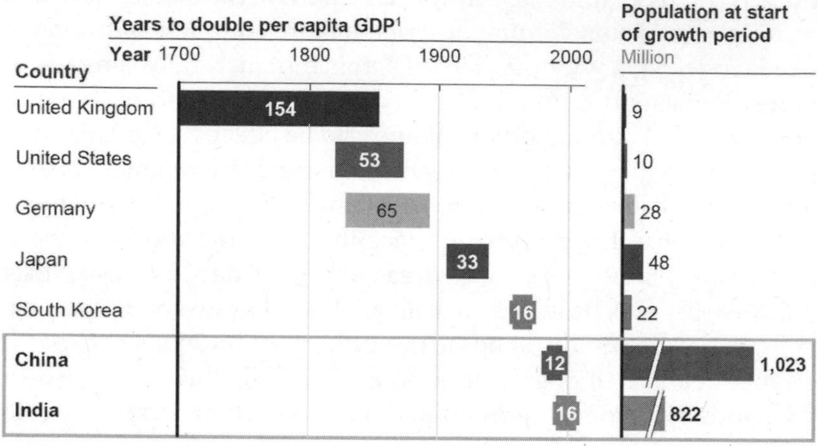

Country	Years to double per capita GDP[1] Year 1700 ... 1800 ... 1900 ... 2000				Population at start of growth period Million
United Kingdom	154				9
United States		53			10
Germany		65			28
Japan			33		48
South Korea				16	22
China				12	1,023
India				16	822

1 Time to increase per capita GDP (in PPP terms) from $1,300 to $2,600.

Source: Exhibit from "Resource Revolution: Meeting the World's Energy, Materials, Food and Water Needs," November 2011, McKinsey Global Institute, www.mckinsey.com/insights/mgi. Copyright © 2011 McKinsey & Company. All rights reserved. Reprinted by permission.

(GDP) from $1300 to $2600. The United States took 53 years. China and India achieved this milestone in 12 and 16 years, respectively, and with much larger populations (see figure 0.1). If current trends hold, China is expected to overtake the United States as the world's largest economy in about 2021.[6] Of course, linear projections can be misleading, and there is more to national power than economic output, but the disparity in growth rates between the West and emerging powers in South America, Africa, and especially Asia are so pronounced and sustained, other aspects of power seem bound to follow, including military capabilities and political influence.

The second global shift is the **diffusion of power from states to non-state actors**, in part owing to the advent of "disruptive" digital technologies. In nearly every aspect of international affairs, digitally enabled actors are challenging the institutions that once held a monopoly on power. Although states are, and are almost certain to remain, the most powerful actors in world affairs, new technologies are dramatically increasing the interconnectedness of individuals and enabling the growth of decentralized, networked forms of social and political organization. There is too often a disconnect between the norms, legal regimes, and institutions that were built to constrain and incentivize power in the twentieth century, and the actors and forms of behaviour that currently have power and influence online. As the US National Intelligence Council recently wrote, these changes "favour greater empowerment of individuals, small groups, and ad hoc coalitions" and the "increased power of non-state actors," from diaspora networks to advocacy groups and terrorist organizations.[7] The other side of this policy shift is that many of these same technologies can be exploited by states to increase surveillance and control of their citizens. The scale of the ambitions of both democratic and autocratic states in this regard is breathtaking. The struggle between hierarchical state power and distributed network power is likely to be a defining feature of global politics for the foreseeable future, but one thing is clear: states no longer dominate global affairs to the extent they once did. They now share the stage with non-state actors of all kinds, from the benign to the malign. In this more crowded world, effective international action will increasingly require forming coalitions and networks of like-minded states and non-state actors working towards common purposes – something that Canada has historically been good at doing.

The third shift – the **waning of US leadership** – is a partial consequence of the first two transformations. The diffusion of power makes it harder for the United States to influence global events to the extent that it did in the second half of the twentieth century. But declining American leadership is only partly due to changes in the international distribution of power. It also reflects US public opinion, which has expressed reservations about America continuing its global role, in numbers that have not been seen for a generation.[8] Barack Obama's foreign policy, which some view as restrained and others as overly cautious, has mirrored the mood of the American public. Although unforeseeable major events – black swans – have the potential to change Americans' attitudes about foreign policy once again, for now economic pressures at home and the legacy of two unpopular and costly wars in Iraq and Afghanistan appear to have diminished the will of Americans to continue playing the role of global policeman.

No one should write off the United States' potential for an economic revival and re-energized foreign policy, but the deference that used to be paid to the United States by other states – a reaction based in respect or fear of American power, or both – seems to be dwindling. This has potentially far-reaching implications for the international security and economic order, which seems likely to develop in directions that do not reflect American or Western preferences and values. New threats and challenges – but also new opportunities for cooperation – will emerge. Trade and commercial relationships will be reordered and may include a shift towards preferential or regionally-based trading blocks and a weakening of universal-membership multilateral arrangements. Access to the US market will remain a vital Canadian interest, but we can no longer rely on American economic growth as a driver of Canadian prosperity.

The remarkable **expansion of the global middle class**, however, creates important new importunities for Canadian investment and trade. This is the fourth global shift. As Robert Samuelson has pointed out, across the entire world, average per-capita incomes rose thirteen times from 1820 to 2010, but until recently these gains were concentrated in Western Europe and North America.[9] Now, the gap between rich and poor nations is narrowing as millions of people in developing countries enter the middle class (figure 0.2). According to one estimate, by 2030, two-thirds of the global middle class will be residents of the Asia-Pacific region.[10] Consumers in these countries are likely to become major drivers of global growth in the coming years – hence the importance of building trade and investment links with these economies. And these emerging markets are often driving new forms of consumption – leapfrogging many twentieth-century technologies and driving new global online marketplaces. Countries that do not develop extensive connections with these emerging markets will be at a disadvantage.[11] Meanwhile, global demand for natural resources to fuel these economies is likely to remain strong over the

Figure 0.2 Middle-class populations as a percentage of world total

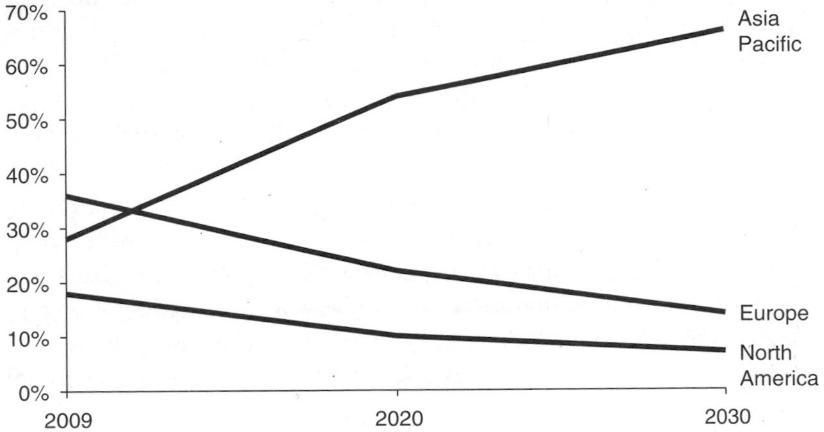

Data source: Homi Kharas, "The Emerging Middle Class in Developing Countries,"
Paris: OECD Development Centre, Working paper 285, 2010.

medium term, although short-term prices are subject to unpredict-
able fluctuations. Demand for educational services for the children
of the emerging middle class will likely also grow steadily. Less
salubriously, rapid industrialization and sharp increases in consumption will place even greater strains on the environment (see
below). Nor is it a given that all these countries will successfully
manage the social strains that accompany rapid economic change.
The expanding middle class may demand political reform, including democratization.

A fifth transformation is the **changing pattern of global energy
sources and flows**. With China becoming the world's largest importer of oil and India poised to become the world's largest importer of coal, global energy trade is reorienting itself from the Atlantic
basin to the Asia-Pacific region.[12] At the same time, technological
innovations that have made extracting shale gas and unconventional oil economically viable represent a "seismic development"
for the geopolitics of energy, with the United States becoming the
world's largest producer of oil and natural gas liquids, surpass-
ing even Saudi Arabia and Russia.[13] Based on current projections,

North America may become self-sufficient in energy during the 2020s.[14] These developments will have complex geopolitical effects. The United States may, for example, dramatically distance itself from the volatile Middle East, although its ability to do so may be limited by the fact that Middle East politics and policies will continue to shape the world price of oil. For Canada, the consequences of these shifts are also uncertain. Our oil is relatively expensive to produce, which is deeply problematic, including for provincial and federal finances, when prices drop. Alberta bitumen, in particular, has also come under criticism for the environmental costs associated with processing and transporting it. Nevertheless, Ottawa will almost certainly continue prioritizing the construction of infrastructure to ship landlocked oil to coastal terminals and to the United States.

The sixth global shift, related to the previous two, is **mounting pressure on the natural environment**, including climate change, arguably the most urgent global environmental challenge. Despite limited recent efforts to mitigate the causes of climate change, the most authoritative scientific information source on the subject, the Intergovernmental Panel on Climate Change (IPCC), reports that total human-caused greenhouse gas emissions were the highest in human history from 2000 to 2010.[15] Many ecosystems and societies are particularly vulnerable to extreme weather events linked to climate change, including heat waves, droughts, floods, cyclones, and wildfires, which can cause disruption of food and water supplies and damage to infrastructure and settlements, among other effects.[16] Closer to home, Arctic sea ice has been decreasing in recent years (figure 0.3) and is "very likely" to continue shrinking during the twenty-first century, according to the IPCC.[17] This will have significant implications for Canada's Arctic policies and the geopolitics of the Arctic region, as countries seek to exploit new commercial shipping and resource extraction opportunities.

The seventh transformation is **increasing volatility and turbulence in global politics**, including the unravelling of some states in the Middle East and North Africa, where initially hopeful Arab Spring protests morphed into intensified repression or ethno-religious bloodletting that has the potential to worsen and

Figure 0.3 Average monthly Arctic sea ice extent, April 1979–2015

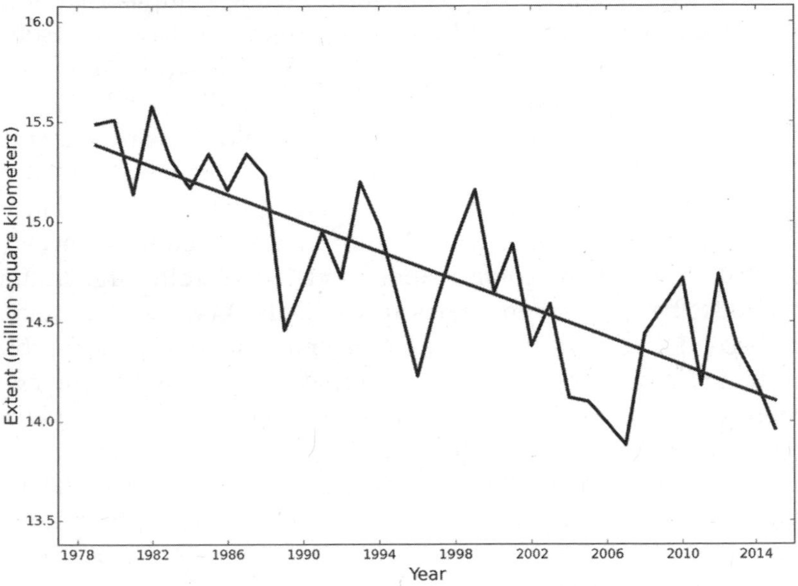

Source: National Snow and Ice Data Center

spread. Jihadist terrorism has become more diversified and de-centralized, and its tactics now include attempts to radicalize the citizens of Western countries. Russia's annexation of Crimea and its deployment of combat units to support separatist fighters in western Ukraine represent a threat to Europe's security that is unlike anything we have seen since the end of the Cold War. China, for its part, has become more assertive in its region, particularly in relation to its claims over parts of the South and East China Seas, heightening tensions with its neighbours. Overall, the world remains less dangerous than it has been for generations, but levels of violence are inching upwards and there appears to be a growing sense of disorder, magnified by the ubiquity and immediateness of social media that convey shocking, first-hand depictions of violence. There is reason to be concerned: some of these trends are genuinely disquieting.

The eighth and final shift is the increasingly **strained global governance system**. This system includes the complex panoply of formal and informal institutions and rules that have regulated international affairs since the end of the Second World War. As a moderately sized country particularly open to the world, Canada has always had an interest in helping to build and strengthen a rules-based international order. Even before Canada had its own independent foreign policy, it encouraged Britain and the United States to manage their North American disagreements through arbitration and joint commissions, and successfully argued for Canada to have a voice in these arrangements. A century later, after the Second World War, Canada played a modest but significant role in the negotiation of the San Francisco Treaty that led to the creation of the United Nations, and in discussions that established the global trading system and the North Atlantic Treaty Organization (NATO). Canadian governments used these and other multilateral arrangements to advance Canadian interests, ranging from commercial issues to arms control. Today, however, the "legacy institutions" of the post–Second World War era are failing to keep up with global power shifts or to address some of the world's most pressing problems, from climate change to regional security tensions. As noted above, multilateral trade arrangements seem to be giving way to regional and preferential blocks. Human rights and humanitarian law is increasingly being disregarded in brutal civil conflicts, and the International Criminal Court seems to be facing a crisis of effectiveness and legitimacy. Furthermore, a whole new generation of digitally enabled actors – be they hackers, global protest movements, or digital activists – sit outside these institutions and tend to subscribe to different norms of behaviour. The rule-based international order was always imperfect and partial, but today it seems to be fraying.

There are, of course, many other shifts under way in the world – from rapid urbanization to the robotization and automation of production and warfare, an increasing number of refugees and displaced persons, a reduction in biodiversity, growing water scarcity, and the depletion of fish stocks. We have chosen to highlight the eight shifts above because they seem most likely to impact

Canada's international policies. They also provide a global back-drop for the issue-specific chapters that follow.

Chapter Outline

The core of this book is a series of reflections on global change in eleven policy areas, and the implications of this change for Canada's international strategy.

In the first chapter, Danielle Goldfarb, associate director of the Global Commerce Centre at the Conference Board of Canada, describes major global economic shifts and their implications for Canada. The rise of emerging markets and globalized production, she argues, will both intensify competitive pressures and open up massive new opportunities for Canadian companies, but Ottawa will need to help these companies to "go global." Canadian firms are still too focused on the US market, and Canadian exports have flatlined in the face of rising Chinese competition. To achieve commercial success overseas, however, Canada needs to be an active and constructive global actor on non-economic issues, too, Goldfarb writes, because our trading partners "care about more than trade." There also need to be policy changes at home, including measures to help workers to transition to higher-skilled employment.

Jennifer Keesmaat, chief planner and executive director in the City of Toronto, focuses on the role of cities as incubators of Canada's knowledge and innovation economy. Cities are also critical to the successful integration of Canada's large number of immigrants and to addressing problems of public health and environmental sustainability, she writes. Keesmaat suggests that Ottawa pursue an urban agenda that cuts across domestic and international policy. At home, this would see the federal government adopting a national transit strategy and affordable housing plan as part of the urban agenda. Abroad, Canada would pursue an "international partnership framework for cities" to help other nations manage various problems associated with urbanization. Keesmaat's urban agenda thus addresses a number of policy domains – economic innovation, environmental sustainability, social cohesion and integration, and international development – while also drawing attention to the rising role of cities as global actors in their own right.

Andrea Mandel-Campbell, director of corporate communications for Kinross Gold Corporation, and previously a journalist and author of *Why Mexicans Don't Drink Molson*, makes the case that Canada needs to embrace its comparative advantage as a world leader in the mining sector and to see it as a space for innovation – an interesting contrast to Keesmaat's chapter. Natural resources, Mandel-Campbell contends, will remain an anchor of global economic growth and strategically important, and smart and sustainable resource development is fundamental to the future of the planet. Instead of trying to emulate Silicon Valley, she argues, Canada should instead develop "global mining hubs" in Toronto, Calgary, Montreal, and Vancouver and support a policy agenda that provides incentives for technical and social innovation as well as increased productivity in the mining sector.

Andrew Leach, Enbridge Professor of Energy Policy, Alberta School of Business at the University of Alberta, explores Canada's oil and gas sector, focusing in particular on our global competitiveness. Leach argues that the hydrocarbon industry must be seen not simply as resource producing, but rather as the next phase of development of Canada's manufacturing sector. As he puts it, we are moving into an era of "manufactured energy." Whereas Canada could once rely on cheap energy and skilled labour to build a manufacturing-based economy, we now need to shift our focus and innovation to the processing and moving of manufactured energy.

Stewart Elgie, director of the University of Ottawa's Institute of the Environment, also writes about natural resources, but focuses instead on Canada's carbon emissions and climate change policies. Canada, he points out, is a "high carbon emitter and producer in an increasingly carbon-constrained world," but the fact that we rely more heavily on natural resource production and refining than other industrialized countries can be viewed as an opportunity, rather than a threat. Specifically, Canada should position itself as an international leader in the growing clean-energy and clean-technology sectors as the engines of a new economy. Our niche should be that of the "most environmentally responsible and innovative producer of resource products," he argues, which will require placing a price on carbon, among other things. He also contends that Canada should play a more constructive role internationally in devising new governance arrangements in the area of climate change.

Mark Raymond, Wick Cary Assistant Professor of International Security at the University of Oklahoma, is also interested in global governance, but focuses on regulation of the Internet, arguing that the challenges of governing the Internet will increasingly extend to the social and economic constructions with which it interacts, including financial markets, privacy and security policy, and public safety. Canada has a clear interest in getting Internet governance right, he argues, and especially in maintaining an open, globally interoperable and responsibly managed Internet. Raymond maintains that in such a fluid policy space, Canada's first priority should be to ensure appropriate levels and kinds of policy learning, including both scientific research and policy experimentation. Further, Canada needs a patient, flexible approach to rule setting in relation to the Internet, which he calls a "soft law approach."

The Internet also features in the chapter by Jonathan Paquin, assistant professor of political science at Laval University, who addresses Canada's role in a rapidly changing global security environment. Paquin argues that traditional interstate relations are ill equipped to engage with fundamentally transnational contemporary global security threats such as cyberterrorism and climate change. The recent Canadian approach to this shifting security ecosystem, which he labels "tough-talk diplomacy," has been insufficient, Paquin maintains. He argues that Canada should instead renew its military commitment to NATO, while also promoting and investing in alternate mediation and dispute-resolution approaches such as "collective conflict management," and return to its role as a norm entrepreneur and international rule-builder, including on the issues of cyberespionage and lethal autonomous weapons systems.

David Petrasek, associate professor at the University of Ottawa and former special adviser to the secretary-general of Amnesty International, writes about human rights diplomacy. He argues that as the power and prestige of central state authorities decline, the role of sub-national and municipal governments in protecting human rights will grow in importance, as will the role of the private sector. Canada's "short-termism" and "erratic style" on human rights diplomacy has diminished its influence, he asserts. If Canada wants to make an impact, Petrasek writes, it must adopt a cross-party approach to human rights that can be sustained over time. Among other things, Canada should work to strengthen the UN's independent and expert human rights monitoring bodies, even as we actively nurture other and new venues to advance human rights issues. He also suggests addressing situations of mass atrocity and attacks on civilian populations, the rights of migrants, and – with a nod to Keesmaat's chapter – the human rights challenges arising from rapid urbanization in the developing world.

Emily Paddon, Rose Research Fellow in International Relations at Lady Margaret Hall, Oxford University, and Jennifer Welsh, professor in international relations at the European University Institute and the UN Secretary-General's Special Adviser on the Responsibility to Protect, consider the protection of civilians in conflict. Peacekeeping and humanitarian action have undergone radical transformations over the past fifteen years, they contend, and now typically include injunctions to protect civilians, but the sustainability of current practices is unclear. Canada could help improve the situation in three ways: by strengthening the role and functioning of UN's Special Committee on Peacekeeping Operations, by re-engaging on the implementation of the Responsibility to Protect, and by pioneering policy-focused research on the role of diaspora in responding to humanitarian emergencies.

John McArthur, a Canadian economist who is visiting fellow at the Brookings Institution and senior fellow with the United Nations Foundation, considers Canada's international development policies. He writes that Canada has been a weak performer in this area and that "global sustainable development" should be a centrepiece of Canada's international strategy, in part because it has implications for so many other issues, from security to climate change. Canadian policy needs to prioritize knowledge and training, leverage private resources, and establish long-term commitments to specific objectives backed by significant resources, rather than flitting from one set of priorities to another.

In the penultimate chapter, Yves Tiberghien, director of the Institute of Asian Research at the University of British Columbia, offers an analysis of the global institutional context that reinforces points made in many of the preceding chapters: namely, the need to devise more (and more creative) forms of multilateral cooperation for this "new period of intense change, technological shift, global competition, great multi-level risks, and high volatility." He argues that the existing apparatus of global governance is poorly equipped to manage "systemic risks" arising from globalization, particularly in the economic and environmental realms. Global connectivity has generated enormous benefits, he maintains, but it has also made the world more vulnerable to disruption and the "contagion" of instability. In his view, however, Canada is particularly well positioned to help stabilize the liberal economic order; it has the human capital and international connections to "nudge global institutions and catalyse new network formation between emerging and established powers." Investing in these efforts would benefit Canada – by placing us at the centre of new networks and institutions – while also contributing to the global public good of increased stability and predictability at a moment of multifaceted global change.

The book concludes with a chapter by Roland Paris and Taylor Owen in which we summarize the main points of commonality across the chapters and draw lessons from the authors' analyses and prescriptions. We then add some observations on the future of Canada's international policy – a future, we argue, that remains full of promise.

chapter one

Why Canada's Global Commerce Policy Needs to Lean In

DANIELLE GOLDFARB

Over the past decade – a period in which global trade has exploded – Canada's exports have mostly flatlined (figure 1.1). They have continued to focus mainly on the United States, where Canadian exporters face stiff and growing Chinese competition.[1] Given our relatively small domestic economy, we need more Canadian companies to "go global" and to tap into the world's fastest-growing markets in order to maintain our standard of living.

In this chapter, I investigate this problem and offer recommendations. First, I explore the key global shifts and challenges facing Canada as it tries to boost its global economic performance. I then outline several principles for policy action. Most importantly, Canada needs to be bold and creative. Policymakers can do this, for example, by making Canada the global standard for open markets and transparent rules. Strengthening Canada's long-term economic position also requires looking beyond economic interests, engaging deeply to help solve challenges important to both industrialized and emerging markets.

Canada Faces Rapid, Dramatic Global Economic Change

The global economy has undergone rapid and dramatic changes in recent decades, changes that are poised to accelerate, and that raise new possibilities and challenges for Canadians.

Chapter Summary

Key Transformations
- The rise of emerging markets has fundamentally reshaped the global economy and will continue to do so.
- China's growth created a dramatic resource boom, but commodity prices are moderating and subject to wild swings.
- The ability to digitize information and communicate rapidly has accelerated the rise of traded services and the globalization of production, making the global economy even more integrated than before.
- Despite all this dramatic change, geography does and will continue to matter.

Implications for Canada
- The rise of emerging markets and globalized production will both intensify competitive pressures and open up massive new opportunities for Canadian companies.
- Canadian governments and businesses cannot count on high or stable prices for commodities going forward.
- Canada has opportunities to sell not only its products and resources globally, but also its less visible commercial services.
- Despite rapid growth in the emerging world, Canada's geographic realities mean its commerce will still be mostly focused on the relatively slower-growth US market.

Recommendations
- Canada should set the global standard for market openness and transparent rules, including those that smooth the path for traded services.
- Policymakers should address policy gaps at home, including aligning infrastructure with expected demand and helping workers to transition to higher-skilled employment.
- Policymakers should continue to open doors to large emerging economic powerhouses, while advancing a "next generation" proposal to the United States that goes far beyond moving products.
- Canada should engage deeply with others' problems, beyond short-term economic interests.

Figure 1.1 Canada's sub-par export performance*

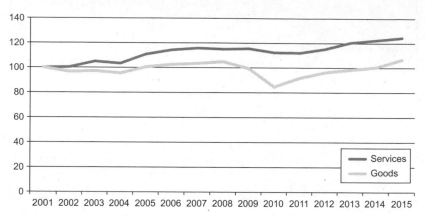

* Real export index, 2000q1 = 1
Source: Statistics Canada, Conference Board of Canada

Emerging Markets

Developing-country markets now represent a full half of the global economy, compared with one-third of a much smaller global economy in 1990, according to the International Monetary Fund.[2] Developing countries now account for roughly half of world trade and attracted more than half of world foreign direct investment in 2013.[3] Emerging markets also accounted for a record almost 40 per cent of global outward foreign direct investments in 2013.[4]

The conversation has shifted away from discussing "poor" countries towards the growth prospects of emerging markets. Business leaders and policymakers have focused their attention on the large economic powerhouses of India, China, and Brazil. Other "next-tier" markets in Southeast Asia, Latin America, Africa, and Eastern Europe have also come onto the radar screen. Even with the recent slowdown from rapid growth over the past decade, emerging markets represent much higher growth potential than do Canada's traditional trade partners.[5] And emerging market growth (not the Canadian dollar's value, as is commonly argued) is likely to be the most important factor affecting Canada's future commerce (figure 1.2).[6] Emerging markets face long-term and serious energy, water, and food challenges. Canada has expertise and products or technologies in all of these areas, including related services such as engineering.

Figure 1.2 Emerging market growth driving Canada's future trade*

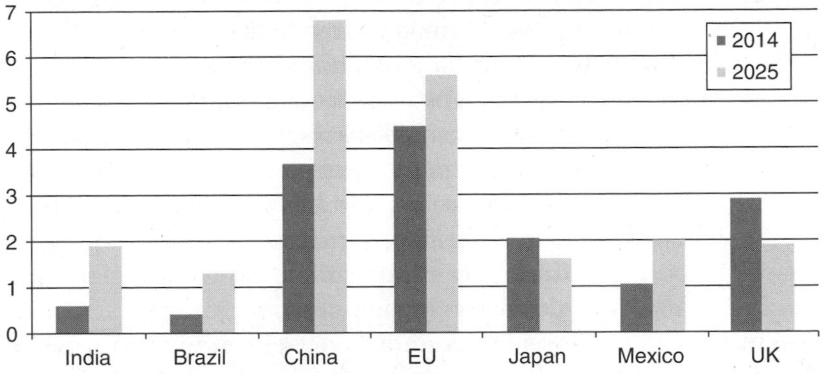

* Canada's goods exports, share of total (exports to US excluded)
Source: Industry Canada, Conference Board of Canada

China's Rise

China's economic rise is dramatically reshaping the global economy. Canadians may not yet appreciate how dramatically it is reshaping our own economy. For one thing, China appears to be largely responsible for Canada's lost market share in the United States. This loss is widespread across almost all Canadian sectors. Moreover, Chinese companies are now moving up the value chain, beyond lower-end manufacturing. In the future, Canadian companies are likely to face more intense competition at all stages of the supply chain.

While opportunities are being squeezed in the United States, the scale and growth potential of opportunities on offer in China and other emerging markets is massive. China and other emerging markets can, however, be extremely challenging places in which to do business,[7] and are very different from Canada's traditional markets. The gap between high-performing Canadian companies and weak performers is wide in these markets – those that were prepared did well, while others have lost badly.[8]

Resource Boom and Bust

China's – and other emerging markets' – rapid economic growth also created a surge in demand for Canada's natural resources.

These include energy, minerals, forest products, and agricultural products (e.g., wheat, canola, lentils). The resulting boost in commodity prices has increased Canada's wealth and living standards. Alberta, Saskatchewan, and Newfoundland have all experienced energy and resource booms. The impact has been far-reaching and dramatic. For example, it intensified shortages for specific skill sets, led to an intense focus on getting energy products and other resources to high-demand markets, and heightened concerns about the pace of oil sands extraction and related carbon emissions. It also raised difficult questions about impacts on the environment, aboriginal communities, and public safety as more oil travels by rail.

While prices for Canada's resources have been high for several years, the only future guarantee is that these prices are likely to fluctuate – and potentially wildly. The most dramatic recent example was the fall in world crude oil prices in 2014.[9] The price drop meant a negative shock to the overall Canadian economy, hitting the federal budget and some provincial budgets (Alberta, Saskatchewan, Newfoundland) hard, and throwing major oil sands projects into question.[10] As the commodity super-cycle draws to a close, Canada can no longer count on the high prices it has been reaping for its other resources either.

Globalized Production

Declining communication costs and the ability to digitize production have made global coordination easier and more attractive. Companies have been rapidly accelerating their use of global inputs and services. A related trend is the rapid acceleration of direct investments abroad, boosted by the emergence of developing economies as key investment players. These trends mean that competition at each stage of the supply chain has intensified. Canadian companies need to have a world-leading product or service to be able to succeed in global markets. Even Canadian companies that sell only at home often face global competition. Cheaper global communication and digitization of production also mean that Canadian companies have the potential to access the best and most cost-effective technologies, services, and products the world has to offer, in turn making our own products and services more globally competitive.

As a result, Canada now has a greater stake in the effective functioning of the global economy and in adopting policies that reinforce global growth. The 2008–9 recession is a good example. Deep global linkages helped pull Canada and the world more deeply into recession than would otherwise have been the case. But these interconnections may have helped blunt the protectionist response that would have pulled the global economy even further down.[11] In the face of cross-border supply chains, a country that shuts out imported inputs hurts its own interests. Globalized production also makes us vulnerable. Canadian companies are now deeply intertwined with countries that have different norms than our own. Companies need to ensure that their entire supply chain meets reasonable working conditions and ethical standards, at the least to protect their reputations, which can be easily and quickly destroyed. And they need to innovate constantly, and find local partners they can trust to protect their ideas and products from intellectual-property theft both in person and in cyberspace.

Technological Advance and "Invisible" Services Trade

Traditionally, customers only bought services locally. But research shows that distance now matters less for selling services than it once did. The ability to digitize information and communicate globally has made it easier and more attractive to sell many kinds of services in global markets. Traded services are not merely an afterthought; they represent close to half of Canada's total trade (when trade is measured according to the value it adds).[12] Despite the image many have of trucks crossing the Canada-US border and the intense public and policy attention to oil and other resources, some less-visible services exports also account for some of Canada's strongest trade growth (figure 1.3). There are massive and growing markets for Canadian services in both traditional and emerging economies. For example, emerging markets have huge infrastructure needs, and Canada has proven strengths in engineering and architecture services.

Technological advance has also and will continue to create new types of products and services that may challenge our traditional

Figure 1.3 Services trade is real and growing*

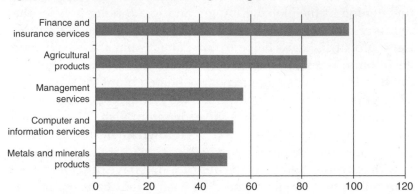

* Fastest growing inflation-adjusted Canadian exports; per cent change 2003–13
Source: Statistics Canada, The Conference Board of Canada

economic assumptions. For example, 3D-printed customized manufactures produced close to the customer can cost as little as those
that are mass-produced. Technological advance also creates a
premium for skilled labour, leaving less skilled workers behind.
Moreover, technological advance also opens up possibilities for
cybertheft of Canadian company intellectual property.

Geography's Pull

Canadian companies remain and will continue to remain focused
on the United States. Living next to the large, dynamic US market
represents a huge economic advantage for Canada. It has given
Canadian companies a massive, sophisticated market right next
door, dramatically boosting Canadian living standards. Though
US economic growth potential is likely to be modest compared
with that of many emerging markets, it represents stronger potential than Canada's domestic market, or Europe and Japan. The
United States is an ideal place to test out and establish a reputation
for products and services, which can serve as a springboard for
sales elsewhere. Moreover, the United States is also a conduit to
the rest of the world. Supplying to US multinationals represents

one pathway to take advantage of emerging market growth, at lower risk than going directly to those markets.

Being so reliant on the United States also raises challenges. Canada's exports have been mostly flat over the past decade precisely because our companies are primarily focused in the slower-growth US market. The relative ease of access to the US market may obscure Canada's view of opportunities in a rapidly changing Mexico[13] and to both emerging and industrialized markets beyond.

Leaning In

A robust global-commerce policy framework is critical to advancing Canada's public interests, such as improved living standards, equity, safety, and security. Governments have a role to play in opening doors to global commercial activity, and providing support where markets are inadequate. Rather than protecting Canadians from global change, governments should prepare citizens to both seize the benefits of and mitigate the risks of such change. As a relatively small global economic player, Canada will fail to advance its public interests if it takes middle-of-the-road policy steps, making discrete contributions related to its short-term economic needs. Leaders instead need to be proactive and ambitious. Here are eight policy principles that respond to the key shifts outlined above, and that could advance Canada's interests.

Set the Global Standard for Market Openness and Transparent Rules

A transparent and clear-cut policy would eliminate Canada's barriers to international commerce. A good start would be eliminating all duties on imports, and committing to not introduce new ones.[14] While tariffs provide some government revenue, they come at an economic cost. They penalize Canadian companies' global competitiveness, making it more difficult to access the best global technologies, funding, ideas, products, services, and inputs at the best prices. They make little sense in the context of globalized production. The greatest gains come from all countries adopting such a policy. Accordingly, any unilateral changes should complement rather than replace global, regional, and bilateral trade talks. Still, unilateral change could be both economically important and entirely within the government's control.

Canada's actions would be noticed, and could have a domino effect. In turn, this could boost global growth and stability, in which Canada has a large stake. Moreover, such a policy could give Canada a central role at the table in future and current trade negotiations. At present, Canada is in the uncomfortable and not very effective position of arguing for greater access to global markets while having to explain why we charge, for example, over 200 per cent tariffs on most dairy products. A clear-cut no-tariff policy would restore equity: the same policy would apply across industries. This would send a powerful signal from governments about equal treatment and the need for all to prepare to both take advantage of and manage the risks of the global economy. A more open policy would also help bring developing country markets more fully into the global economy, and particularly help women in those economies gain income by participating in the more lucrative export sectors. Governments also would have a role to play in helping individuals and companies transition out of areas that have been long protected.

Address Gaps at Home

OECD evidence suggests that changes that Canada makes to its own policies – including domestic policies – are more likely to result in greater Canadians trade and investment gains than are policy changes in other countries. Domestic policy actions may not draw as much public attention as signing trade deals or sending trade missions, but they are no less critical, and perhaps even more so.

Among other things, to make Canada more economically successful in the world, we need to address regulatory differences between the provinces and provincial government purchasing restrictions. We need to prepare the entire workforce (not just those involved in exporting) for global shifts and opportunities. As an increasingly competitive global market widens the gap between skilled and unskilled workers, governments should do more to help workers transition towards higher-skilled, higher-demand work. Governments should also consider preparing Canadians for short-burst work patterns that are a feature of resource booms and busts.[15]

Canada also needs to align today's infrastructure (rail, air, ports, roads, and pipelines) with anticipated future growth in trade with emerging markets. Canadian governments at all levels should work together to address existing and expected transportation and infrastructure gaps – through long-term planning rather than quick fixes. This includes finding a workable compromise that addresses environmental concerns and those of aboriginal communities.

Location Is an Advantage, but Don't Let It Constrain

The US market is and will remain Canada's "bread and butter" for the foreseeable future, despite Canada's loss of some US market share. Policies need to continue to recognize the significant advantage this relationship provides Canada, even as we seek to expand Canada's commercial links elsewhere. To maintain (and, ideally, enhance) Canada's access to the US market, creativity is crucial. As the smaller partner in this bilateral relationship, Canada has traditionally had to come up with new policy ideas and then get buy-in from the US administration. Canadian policymakers should put forward a leading-edge "next generation" proposal that goes beyond movement of goods to future-oriented issues including enhancing the flows of services and ideas. It must hit at the heart of US interests (physical security, cybersecurity, environment, economics, etc.) to ensure sustained US attention. And when the United States is involved in multiparty trade talks, Canada should be at the table in order to secure its interests in, and access to, the US market, as well as other markets.

Canadian governments should also continue to open doors to the large emerging economic powerhouses in Asia and elsewhere, as well as large developed-country markets, including Europe.

Canadian trade negotiators should focus on large markets with the most promising growth opportunities, rather than any country that expresses an interest in negotiating with Canada. This may mean dropping some negotiations under way, or not starting others. However, opening doors to markets requires more than trade negotiations. Governments could also continue to help to address information gaps. This is particularly important in emerging markets that can raise challenges different from those in Canada's traditional markets. For example, trusted local relationships can be especially important in protecting companies from intellectual property theft.

The federal government's 2013 global markets strategy focused on doubling the number of small companies in emerging markets, and highlights priority sectors. Since some small companies do very well in emerging markets and others perform poorly, rather than focus on sector or company size, governments should devote more resources to those businesses that are prepared for emerging markets with innovative products and services, that have connections or are prepared to invest in understanding market needs, and that are prepared for the challenges.

Make It about More than Money

To achieve commercial success, Canada also needs to be an active and constructive global actor on *non*-economic issues, including on matters such as advancing global stability and security, reducing poverty, improving labour standards, reducing corruption, addressing environmental issues, bolstering cyber- and physical security, and addressing intellectual property theft. Why? For one thing, Canada's trading partners care about more than trade. If Canada is present and demonstrating constructive leadership, others will be more interested in developing long-term relationships that extend to a range of issues, including trade. Also, setting high standards and engaging deeply in international discussions could earn Canada an influential role in terms of global standard-setting. It could also nudge emerging markets to raise their standards across a range of issues, helping them converge to standards closer to Canada's.

Another advantage of setting high standards and deeply engaging on these issues is that it has the potential to inoculate Canada against negative charges that can derail our commercial interests. When Canadian companies are linked with corruption, terrible working conditions, and environmental degradation, it can highjack Canada's longer-term commercial interests. Rather than "playing defence," Canada can advance its commercial interests (not to mention other public interests) by effectively neutralizing these issues, including by setting exemplary standards and by presenting positive alternatives. This might mean investing even more heavily to make Canada the global leader in responsible resource extraction, for example, including demonstrating technological leadership in this field. It could entail applying carbon taxes so that oil sands companies internalize the environmental costs they are imposing. It could mean taking a stronger leadership role in advancing working conditions in and opening doors to the poorest countries. Canada then becomes associated with responsible, secure, safe, and high-quality products and services – a winning strategy, at home and abroad.

It's about You, Not Me

Canada's global commerce policies typically focus on sectors of historical Canadian strength. This can certainly benefit Canadian businesses today. But it may not provide a good framework for future success. Canada's strengths can and have changed rapidly, and they may not align with the best growth opportunities elsewhere. A more effective and forward-looking strategy could flip the focus onto others' needs. Naturally, business – not government – needs to identify what other markets need. But governments can take the lead in identifying broad areas in which both emerging and developed market partners have long-term problems. Then they can more effectively make the case for Canada to have better access to investment and trade opportunities to help solve those problems over the long term. This could be a pragmatic way to make progress when comprehensive deals are not in the cards.

One example is the intense energy needs of many Asian markets, particularly China and India. Long-term access for Canada's energy-efficient products and related expertise and services could meet the needs of Canada and these emerging markets. Other examples could be infrastructure problems, exploding demand for telecommunications and education services, technology needs, and demand for food products in the emerging world. Safety and security are other problem areas in both emerging and developed country markets.

Recognize Canada's Full Potential

Canada's policies need to seize Canada's full international potential by aligning with the realities of globally integrated production. Past policies focused on removing tariff barriers. Tomorrow's policies need to be broader to address global production and new kinds of trade, opening the door not only to exports as they often do, but also to imports that benefit both consumers and the ability of Canadian companies to compete globally. Policies more in line with global production would transition Canada to become more fully open to two-way investment, while still employing transparent, pre-defined criteria that protect key national interests, including security. A broader, future-oriented policy would also ensure traded services are given weight in line with their economic potential. Traded commercial services represent some of Canada's fastest-growing exports, but are relatively invisible, and get much less policy and public attention than do resources and manufactures (both of which also matter for Canadian living standards). The risk is that more visible trade can crowd out attention that should be paid to smoothing the path for services. And, among other benefits, selling high-value services globally can help buffer the impact of commodity price gyrations affecting Canada's resource trade.

Barriers to traded services are more challenging than tariffs on products. Services are often sold via setting up an affiliate abroad, or travelling abroad. So restrictions on moving people (e.g., via visas, air access, work permits), information flows, or investment can impede global commercial-service sales. Fortunately, the next generation of Canada's trade agreements is already starting to address these kinds of barriers. Government agencies that provide loans to exporters also need to continue to reframe their thinking to incorporate knowledge-based activities. The traditional approach is to value manufacturing plants as assets or collateral for loans. Forward-looking policies need to view intellectual property as an asset. Governments may have a role to play here where markets under-provide loans for companies that aren't selling a physical product.

Further, we need to reconsider existing methods of measuring Canada's global commercial activities. Governments base policies, in part, on what they measure, but official statistics have evolved slowly in response to global economic change. These statistics tend to over-weight both Canada's trade with the United States vis-à-vis the world, and trade in products or raw materials compared with traded services. They don't adequately capture the role of sales via Canadian affiliates in global markets. Governments should examine new sources of data and creative ways to capture these activities.

Conclusion

The stakes are high. Canadian companies need to be able to find growth opportunities to support rising or sustained living standards. Other countries are ahead of Canada's government in taking aggressive actions to help their companies gain an edge. Tomorrow's global commerce policy needs to be clear-eyed in measuring, recognizing, and addressing head-on the hyper-linked, hyper-competitive reality that Canada faces. The job of the policymaker is to show leadership, educate, and create a framework so that Canadians can best seize the benefits of the global economy, while preparing them for the inevitable challenges and vulnerabilities it presents.

As a relatively small economic player, Canada needs to be creative and bold. It needs to model openness at home and abroad. This would both yield economic gains and strengthen Canada's influence in trade negotiations. Policy weight needs to be shifted in line with economic potential and realities. This means making infrastructure investments today in line with expected future demand. It also means ensuring that attention paid to resources trade does not crowd out attention to other issues, such as Canada's less visible services trade, or longer-term interests.

Canada's geographic realities require it to propose new ideas to protect and advance legitimate Canada-US trade. But the pull of geography should not constrain Canada's actions to open doors in other important industrialized and emerging markets. Finally, Canada should engage deeply with others' problems and look beyond short-term economic interests. Not taking bold and creative action to do so puts at risk Canada's future living standards.

chapter two

Towards an International Strategy for Liveable Cities

JENNIFER KEESMAAT

More than half of the global population lives in cities – and this number continues to climb by 60 million people a year, according to the World Health Organization.[1] It may seem that as we embrace becoming a more urban world, moving from rural, agricultural societies to cities, the places where we live, work, and play will inevitably – and naturally – become beacons of innovation, prosperity, sustainability, and civility. Cities, after all, represent progress. The urbanization of our world, in this view, is a sign of our evolution as a species.

There are some places in the world where our cities mostly work: places where the mix of uses, amount of density, and variety of natural and public spaces combine with high-quality design and infrastructure to create a liveable city. These cities are resilient during economic downturns; their walkable and transit-supported communities are built at densities that facilitate local economic development, entrepreneurialism, and meaningful work. These cities value access to education and cultural institutions, as much as they value access to clean land, air, and water. These cities are places in which it is possible to arrive as a newcomer and comfortably transition, in just one generation, into the middle class, because all the amenities one needs to do so, such as libraries, access to recreation, and affordable housing, are at one's fingertips. These cities are not only a point of pride for their nations; they also drive foreign investment, the gross domestic product, and therefore shared prosperity.

However, by global standards, such cities are relatively rare. The vast majority of cities in our world need to be fixed, not emulated. Many are characterized by high unemployment, environmental decline, and substandard housing. They are hindered by poor city design resulting in long commutes, lost productivity, and limited access to the natural systems that sustain human life, such as food and water. Alarmingly, the world's poorest, most vulnerable, and least resilient cities are also the fastest growing.[2] This rapid pace of urbanization continues to strain the infrastructure of cities around the world. Lack of capacity to provide basic services, such as access to clean water and electricity, poses threats to human health and stifles economic potential.

Chapter Summary

Key Transformations

- More than half of the world's population lives in cities; this number is set to double by 2050.
- But a vast majority of global cities need to be fixed, rather than emulated. High unemployment, environmental decline, and substandard housing characterize many of the world's largest cities, which are hindered by poor city design resulting in long commutes, lost productivity, and limited access to the natural systems that sustain human life, such as food and water.
- For many of the transnational problems that the world faces today, such as poverty, migration, crime, climate change, and intolerance of pluralism, cities occupy centre stage.
- As the world rapidly becomes an urban place, humanity faces new threats and challenges that will demand new collaborations, innovations, and new approaches to city building.

Implications for Canada

- Canadian cities are leaders, consistently outperforming cities around the globe, according to third-party indices in liveability, economic competitiveness, and resilience.
- Three key functions of our city building align with the Canadian Charter of Rights and Freedoms, and therefore ought to be central to our domestic policy: (1) our ability to welcome, respect, and integrate newcomers; (2) our capacity to attract talent as the basis of

a knowledge and innovation economy; and (3) our continued commitment to designing for long-term health and sustainability.

• However, we require a clearly articulated national urban agenda to ensure that governance models and priorities inform a domestic policy that supports and enhances our city building.

• In the absence of domestic policy, we are beginning to lag behind in our infrastructure investments.

Recommendations

• If cities are to be effective actors on an international stage in an age of mass migration, new mechanisms are required to facilitate how cities act – and interact.

• Central to a transnational urban strategy should be the sharing of information, knowledge, and best practices as critical to lessening disparity, mitigating climate change, and improving quality of life.

• The Canadian government, as part of its domestic agenda, should embrace a central role in advancing an international-partnership framework for cities.

• This framework presents the opportunity to make a critical contribution to international development. Canadian leadership, rooted in our values and our evolving best practices, would facilitate social justice on a global scale.

In absolute terms, in the period for 1990–2010, the number of people in urban areas without an improved source of water has actually increased, despite the push to upgrade existing infrastructure.[3] While access to electricity is improving in the rapidly industrializing countries of Asia, it remains stubbornly low in many less-developed countries.[4] Nigeria, whose capital of Lagos is experiencing explosive, chaotic growth and by some estimates has a metropolitan population of over 21 million people, provides reliable access to clean drinking water, electricity, and waste disposal for only one out of three residents.[5] Projected growth will similarly challenge sanitation services.[6]

Using cities as a tool to meet basic human needs, such as providing access to clean land, air, water, and sanitation is, in and of itself, a worthy goal of transnational city building. But doing so is linked to another reason for a renewed emphasis on justice and equity in cities: a direct, positive correlation between geopolitical stability and pluralistic societies that value diversity and differ-ence. For example, countries where residents have trust in the po-litical, legal, and police systems (i.e., where there is a high level of trust in institutional power) are more tolerant of immigrants. Similarly, people who have a more positive expectation of their future well-being, and whose attitudes to socio-economic risks are lower, are also more likely to welcome immigrants. Conversely, unstable places tend to be much less tolerant of immigrants.[7] In an age that will be defined by global migration and integration (or lack thereof), fostering cities as places that welcome immigrants is a critical, transnational issue, and the effective provision of basic services underlies all efforts to achieve this goal.

Successful places of the future will be characterized by access to full participation in society. Where you were born, or where you come from, will be valued as an asset and will not determine, or compromise, future citizenship or employment. This city-building model is viable to the extent that our cities transition from resource-extraction-based economies, which are finite, to creative, knowledge-based economies – which hold limitless potential to grow as people are enabled to thrive. In the "old" model, which exists in most of the world today, immigrants are unwelcome (un-less there is a surplus of employment) due to scarcity, with the as-sumption being that economic growth is tied to finite resources. In the new model, governance systems are designed to empower learning, creativity, and growth, as opposed to primarily manag-ing people and their impacts. People, themselves, are viewed as a resource and an asset.

Whereas Andrea Mandel-Campbell, in her chapter, argues for the potential of mining to lead our international competitiveness, she con-cedes that it will only do so if we embrace entrepreneurial drive and technological innovation – characteristics of Silicon Valley that are not inherent to our mining industry, but are facilitated in our most urban centres as an outcome of a concentration of talent. Toronto is, indeed, one of the world's leading mining hubs in terms of head offices and mining finance, but not in terms of mining technological innovation. Herein lies the opportunity – to advance creative, knowledge-based technologies and to link them to various industries, whether resource-or knowledge-based. Healthy cities are essential to advancing the knowledge-based, creative work that Mandel-Campbell envisions as indispensable to advancing Canadian mining in the future. Our ongoing capacity to educate, attract, and retain people *in general* will be critical to all sectors. Toronto's cluster of firms and institutions help facilitate access to capital for the mining industry – but many of these firms have no operations in Canada, according to the Canadian Chamber of Commerce.

In some places on our planet, cities are manifestations of our highest intelligence and our capacity for innovation. It is no coincidence that great universities are, frequently, associated with great cities. In other cities, however, the future is fundamentally compromised, and redesign and investment are required if they are to become welcoming, resilient, sustainable, and just. These places are fragile, politically unstable, and incomplete; survival, rather than a high quality of life, is the goal. For a sense of the scale of this challenge, consider this: Despite the continuing economic growth of cities, over 850 million people in urban areas around the world live in informal housing settlements.[8] Without a doubt, *how* we approach our final, global migration, from rural agricultural societies to urban places, will define the future of our species. In this sense, cities will either foster or undermine global stability.

Cities as Actors on the International Stage

Canadian cities were enabled, through the Baldwin Act of 1849, to raise taxes and create by-laws such that the provision of roads, waste management, town planning, and policing and fire services could be administered at the local level. As people began to congregate around natural resources (such as waterways) to facilitate commerce, new governance was required to manage shared interests. These structural changes permitted cities to become key actors in solving some of the biggest issues facing humanity with respect to public health at the time. In the mid-1800s, for example, following reoccurring cholera outbreaks in London, England, an extensive underground sewage system was designed to divert waste from the Thames River – at the behest of Parliament, and as a result of new domestic policy.

In Canada over the past 150 years, cities have evolved, yet these initial, rudimentary government powers have not kept pace. Urban poverty has grown, demanding new processes and considerations. As density has increased, new movement and waste management systems have been required. It could easily be argued that cities have always been at the centre of where we live, work, and play – and, for that matter, at the centre of crime, poverty, commerce, and immigration. But as the balance of the world population has shifted from primarily agrarian societies to urban ones, and as cities have increasingly shifted from resource-extraction-based economies to knowledge-based economies, our interest in improving quality of life for all through urban development has, in our most advanced societies, grown as well.

For many of the transnational problems that the world faces today, such as poverty, migration, crime, climate change, and intolerance of pluralism, cities occupy centre stage as a key contributor, making these issues worse. At the same time, other cities have embraced comprehensive approaches to unlocking tangible solutions to improve quality of life. The extent to which we are able to share information, knowledge, and best practices between cities is increasingly key to lessening this disparity, and ought to be central in our transnational strategy.

Individually, many large cities are broadening their own functions by tackling these challenges through new approaches to municipal governance, public-private partnerships, and progressive approaches to land-use planning and design, and by embracing interdisciplinary frameworks and collaborations with new partners, such as businesses, the not-for-profit sector, and universities. Canadian cities, over 150 years ago, were enabled to exist. Today, new instruments – both domestically and transitionally – are needed for them to thrive.

Linking Domestic and International Policy

As articulated in the Canadian Charter of Rights and Freedoms, our values include the celebration of our diversity and multiculturalism, the protection and promotion of human rights and freedoms, respect for democracy, and opportunity for all. These values manifest in the ways we live our daily lives in cities. The extent to which we live side by side in diverse communities, respecting and celebrating inter-culturalism, is distinct to Canadian cities.

If we consider the critical elements that determine the progressive success of a city in providing a sustainable, liveable, prosperous place for people to thrive, three key functions come to mind that are consistent with and central to these Canadian values that solidify our identity as a nation:

1. *Welcoming, respecting, and integrating newcomers*: Fundamental to our current global wave of migration is the need to successfully transition newcomers into cities in a way that capitalizes on their interests, assets, and potential contributions to the new society they are joining. Well-designed transit-oriented communities are central to accessing education, employment, and ensuring affordable movement options. Providing access and opportunity for integration – essentially creating an inclusive city – mitigates the potential for crime and social unrest.
2. *Attracting talent – and in particular echo boomers – as the basis of a knowledge and innovation economy*: In this wave of global migration, cities will thrive to the extent that they are able to appeal to the creative class – those diverse, agile, and entrepreneurial types who are always creating, who bring new ideas and energy to urban places. If the conditions are welcoming, this group brings employment with them. This cohort chooses liveability over excess, placing a greater emphasis than past generations did on access to culture, meaning, and community life.
3. *Designing for long-term health and sustainability*: It is no longer sufficient to pave over paradise and hope for the best. Changing weather patterns demand new approaches to infrastructure investment and consideration of the food, energy, and water systems that are necessary to sustain the flourishing of life.

Prior to fully participating in transnational conversations about excellence in city building, we need to refine our domestic urban agenda by identifying, making explicit, and recognizing in federal policy our national shared interest in great city building. While a funded national transit strategy and affordable housing plan are two significant places to begin, it is vital to acknowledge that cities drive our GDP, facilitate our direct foreign investment, *and* assimilate new immigrants. It is our large cities that are taking leadership on climate change. As such, an urban agenda at the federal level must be pervasive, seeking to reorient the ways in which we view, understand, plan for, and administer our cities and their economies–precisely because the presence of our cities in everyday life and the building of our national economy and identity is so far-reaching.

Infusing all aspects of federal governance with an urban agenda, as a fundamental lens through which to extrapolate urban values, would both ensure progressive city building and leverage our successes to gain international exposure and help Canada strengthen its presence globally. This idea sits in contrast to the notion of creating a "department of urban affairs," or simply a fund, such as the New Build Canada Fund, which is disconnected from a larger mandate for the advancement of global urbanism in both domestic and international policy.

An urban agenda must be driven by the recognition that all aspects of governance – whether related to health or crime or immigration or infrastructure investments – can be positioned to further stronger cities and a comprehensive, advanced, sustainable urbanism, or will, inevitably, act in opposition to it. When considering new policy or new funding, the federal government could employ evaluative criteria that align with clear, consistent, city-building objectives. The three key functions of our city building outlined above – welcoming, respecting, and integrating newcomers; attracting talent as the basis of a knowledge and innovation economy; and designing for long-term health and sustainability – could provide the basis, in broad terms, for establishing a new way of thinking about domestic policy as critical to the future of Canada.

An International Strategy for Canada: A Partnership Framework

If cities are to be effective actors on an international stage in an age of mass migration, new mechanisms are required to facilitate how they act, and interact. Just as the G20 was established as a forum for cooperation and consultation on matters pertaining to the international financial system, cities require transnational organizational infrastructure to support shared learning, information and knowledge exchange, and the building of partnerships pertaining to city building. Various options have emerged over the past decade to underpin such a network of cities, and yet no formalized, active model has been put in place.

In the context of the growing global exploration of urban sustainability, prosperity, and liveability, the Canadian government's domestic agenda should embrace a central role in advancing this partnership framework – just as the G20 was proposed by former prime minister Paul Martin. This is why: While far from perfect, Canada's largest cities consistently rank near the top of studies benchmarking best practices in urban liveability, resilience, and economic growth. In the domain of city building, our credibility precedes us. According to the Economist Intelligence Unit's *2013 Liveability Report*, Vancouver, Toronto, and Calgary rank among the world's top five most liveable cities.[9] Toronto is considered as among the world's most "youthful" cities by the *2014 YouthfulCities Index*, a study that analyses quality of life and economic opportunity indicators valued as important by youth.[10] Toronto also leads globally in the *Resilient Cities* index, followed by Vancouver and Calgary in second and third respectively.[11] According to the *American Cities of the Future 2013/14* report, Canadian cities of all sizes rank highly on indices comparing economic potential, human resources, business friendliness, and foreign direct investment.[12]

As a counterpoint, it could easily be argued that our cities are thriving today as a result of "legacy infrastructure" (subways, parks, schools, affordable housing) built upon visionary contributions to city building made by past generations. It could be suggested that this legacy – which is soon to run dry – is why we are favoured by third-party rankings. Our cities, according to this view, work well today as a result of investments made a generation ago. Indeed, the data supports this analysis: Currently, the collective infrastructure deficit of Canadian cities stands at $171.8 billion dollars, or the equivalent of $13,813 for every household.[13] In addition, our largest cities, including Toronto, Vancouver, Calgary, and Edmonton, some of which consistently rank as having the longest commute times in North America, all have multi-billion-dollar transit plans that remain unfunded.

Nevertheless, we are trending upwards in most measures. Canadian city builders continue to lead best practices, including through progressive planning and by setting aggressive targets to both advance and measure change through strong public policy. Consider two examples, the first pertaining to global migration. In this new way of thinking about municipal roles, transit systems are recognized as *critical* infrastructure that supports abundant access to education and employment opportunities, facilitating migration and the integration of newcomers into the middle class. The City of Toronto's Immigration Portal builds on the presence of these hard services by providing the soft infrastructure required for people to find jobs, homes, health care, and services in their own language.[14] Toronto, as a result, is recognized as a world leader with respect to integrating newcomers. In *Arrival City*, Doug Saunders documents this last wave of global migration as it is unfolding across the world and describes Thorncliffe Park, a Toronto neighbourhood, as an international model for transitioning newcomers successfully into the middle class within one generation.[15]

Successful global migration hinges on providing people with the tools they need to work, play, and live. Cities, when we plan mixed-use walkable communities, are a critical tool to lift people from poverty, as has been well documented and studied in relation to the St Lawrence Neighbourhood, in the emerging and redesigned Regent Park, or through programs such as Streets to Homes. Further, activities within cities, or the way that cities choose to act, will continue to define climate change – a quintessential transnational issue. According to UN Habitat, although "cities cover less than 2 per cent of the earth's surface, they consume 78% of the world's energy and produce more than 60% of all carbon dioxide and significant amounts of other greenhouse gas emissions, mainly through energy generation, vehicles, industry, and biomass use."[16] The design of walkable, transit-oriented communities, coupled with "green" policies and standards targeted at reducing the environmental footprint of people, businesses, and the buildings they occupy, is vital to the future of the planet. Both the design of cities, which impacts whether walking or transit is a viable way to move, and policies pertaining to the "greening" of buildings, are municipal in jurisdiction.

A second example: The City of Vancouver, through its Greenest City 2020 action plan, has set ambitious goals with respect to carbon, waste, and ecosystems, requiring carbon-neutral buildings, planning green space in such a way as to ensure everyone lives within a five-minute walk of a park, and reducing the amount of solid waste destined for land fill. Vancouver – despite any international protocol that the Canadian government might or might not sign – is able through its organization, policy, and operations to have a measurable impact on a global issue: climate change. City building, it turns out, presents itself as an effective platform to address climate change through progressive "green" policies that result in the remediation of brownfield sites, the improvement of air quality through green roof policies, and the reduction of our energy consumption through the implementation of green standards, such as the Canada Green Building Council's Leadership in Energy and Environmental Design (LEED).

An international-partnership framework for cities in light of worldwide urbanization presents the opportunity to position our prominence and growing expertise in city building as a critical contribution to international development. Our leadership, rooted in Canadian values and our evolving best practices, could serve to facilitate social justice on a global scale. As articulated in our Charter of Rights and Freedoms, these values include the celebration of our diversity and multiculturalism, the protection and promotion of human rights and freedoms, respect for democracy, and opportunity for all.

These values manifest themselves in the ways we live our daily lives. The extent to which we live side by side in diverse communities, respecting and celebrating inter-culturalism, is a distinctive feature of Canadian cities. The provision of basic infrastructure and services that provide opportunity and access to full participation in Canadian society is an outcome of the way we organize our cities and their services. And importantly, the civility with which we recognize our differences and negotiate our values through local democracy is also contingent on the access to participation provided in cities.

Finally, sustainable cities of the future will provide healthy places for diverse members of society to thrive. According to the Economic Intelligence Unit, the quality of a city's physical infrastructure is highly correlated with its overall competitiveness on a global level.[17]

This urban agenda – both at home and abroad – should focus on the core elements that support liveability: housing, transit, the environment, long-term infrastructure, and incubating innovation. Our cities will define our future as a nation. They also have the capability to position us to become global leaders in urban excellence. In this sense, Canada's domestic and international approaches to urban issues can be complementary and mutually reinforcing. We should be supporting and facilitating great cities, both at home and abroad.

chapter three

Make Canada the World Leader in Mining Innovation

ANDREA MANDEL-CAMPBELL

At a young age Canadians learn about the almost mythic boun-
ty of our natural resources; from the forests of British Columbia,
Alberta oil, and the mighty wheat fields of the Prairies, to the
copper and nickel mines of Central Canada and the fisheries of
Atlantic Canada. What they are not taught in social studies class
is that global competition has taken its toll on Canada's resource
prowess. Fast-growing forests in South America and massive new
Chinese pulp mills have left a trail of empty towns and closed
mills from BC to New Brunswick. The Atlantic fishery is now a
shadow of its former self, while the storied mining giants Inco,
Falconbridge, and Noranda have been swallowed whole by a new
breed of global mining behemoths.

Some Canadians are undoubtedly happy to see resource companies go, discomfited by our image as simple drawers of water
and hewers of wood. The epithet, after all, traces its origins to a
biblical curse in which a wayward tribe is condemned to slavery
as woodcutters and water-toters. Such a lowly fate doesn't sit well
with our ideal of Canada as a modern, progressive, and innovative country. As the online editor of the *Huffington Post* asked in a
2013 interview with a federal minister working to advance a mining mega-project in Northern Ontario: "Why would you want to
promote mining in Northern Ontario? Mining is so vintage!"

For many looking to wean Canada off its hardscrabble, lumber-
jack past, the answer to ghost towns and fallen resource icons is to
focus on the sexy new technologies of the future; the next Google

glass, app, clean tech, or nanotech breakthrough. It is not a unique-ly Canadian phenomenon. Since Apple's blockbuster $1.3-billion initial public offering in 1980, Silicon Valley has become a byword for innovation and, by association, prosperity. Cities and countries around the world have tried to replicate the Valley's alchemy of universities, entrepreneurs, and venture capital, in an effort to launch leading-edge industrial clusters that are seen as the best de-fence in an increasingly competitive and crowded global economy.

According to a 2012 report by British bank HSBC, nineteen of the world's top thirty economies in 2050 will be "new emergers." These include not only China and India, but countries like Nigeria, Peru, Mexico, Turkey, and the Philippines, which barely registered on the global economic radar a decade ago. HSBC maintains that as the global balance of power shifts, stable and aging countries like Canada, with little material gains to be made through improved education or rule of law, will "need to operate at the frontier, driv-ing technological change" to boost productivity and maintain their standard of living.[1]

Chapter Summary

Key Transformations
- There has been a shift in economic balance of power as "new emergers" from China and India to Nigeria, Peru, Mexico, Turkey, and the Philippines will dominate world's top thirty economies in coming decades.
- Pressure is mounting on stable and aging countries like Canada to emphasize innovation if they are to boost productivity and main-tain their standard of living.
- Natural resources will remain an anchor of global GDP and strategi-cally important; and smart and sustainable resource development is fundamental to the future of the planet.

Implications for Canada
- Canada's rich resource endowment positions us well to capitalize on the evolving changes in the global economy.
- Mining in particular is "Canada's Silicon Valley," combining a rich resource endowment, first-mover advantage, scale, scope, and in-novation.

- Canada's position as a leading global mining hub is being challenged on a number of fronts; deteriorating market conditions, increased social and environmental pressures, increased competition from "new emergers" and more aggressive peer countries, insufficient investment in innovation, and a lack of strategic focus domestically.

Recommendations
- Drop the silos, pool resources and collaborate, collaborate, collaborate – including equipment manufacturers and suppliers, industry, academia, and government; consider contracting out management of certain government research labs to private companies.
- Significantly reduce the number of government funding programs, which are currently estimated at 4500, and design funding mechanisms that revolve around industry needs, not academic research.
- Stop assuming things will go on forever as they always have; as a country we need to get strategic, understand the mining industry, measure it, embrace it and develop comprehensive strategies (not ad hoc tactics) to maintain it.
- Invest in Canada's next generation of mining talent – companies need to commit to consistent student hires and universities need to stop burying mining-related studies within more politically correct disciplines and provide leading-edge curricula.

A key question for Canada is whether we burnish our international competitiveness by directing government policy and finite tax dollars to support myriad new, politically palatable industries and clusters, or do we build on our comparative and competitive advantages? A renewed focus on the historically strong and naturally endowed elements of the Canadian economy is compelling, particularly when considering the basic economic laws of supply and demand; as the "new emergers" expand their economies and draw more of their populations into the middle class, they will need natural resources in much the same way Chinese mass urbanization over the past decade has fuelled a commodities super-cycle.

As Mark Cutifani, the CEO of South African mining giant Anglo American, pointed out in a 2013 speech to the World Mining Congress in Montreal, mining and petroleum, including payments to their service providers and spin-off benefits to other industries from agriculture to manufacturing, energy, and construction, contribute more than 45 per cent of global GDP, making the sector "the most important industrial activity on the face of the planet."[2] In other words, natural resources are in high demand and strategic. And the good news is that Canada, despite some serious challenges, not only has the resources, but also the talent, know-how and institutional capacity to deliver.

This is not what everyone, especially urban Canadians who feel little or no connection to the country's resource endowment, want to hear. For Jennifer Keesmaat, Chief Planner for the City of Toronto – which also happens to be one of the world's leading mining hubs – resource development and cities have little in common. "Our cities provide the impetus for knowledge-based, creative-based industries where the sky's the limit," Keesmaat told a 2014 meeting of the Ottawa Forum. "I could never compare mining to Silicon Valley because Silicon Valley is about innovation and knowledge-based development, which is fundamentally, ideologically, different from resource extraction."

But is it? What naysayers fail to realize is that resource development is intrinsically technology-driven – its future growth predicated on innovation, whether it be incremental or transformative. As a 2012 Public Policy Forum report on natural resources and innovation concluded, resource innovation is arguably where Canada will get the biggest bang for its productivity buck as demand (and competition) from emerging economies continues to grow.[3] And while, as I will argue below, the Canadian resource sector needs to up its innovative game, smart and sustainable resource development is fundamental to the future of the planet. According to the same report: "There is an imperative to innovate in this sector because the stakes are higher – not just for sustainable economic growth, but for solutions to the very real challenges facing humanity and the planet we all share."[4]

Canada's Silicon Valley

To illustrate both the opportunities and the challenges for Canada's natural resources sector, this chapter will use, as a case study, the closest approximation to a Silicon Valley that this country has:

the mining industry. While this analogy may seem antithetical to some, it is important to understand the origins of Silicon Valley's success as well as the size and breadth of the Canadian mining industry. In simple terms, the Valley represents a critical mass of human capital and companies, built on technology and entrepreneurial drive. Its dominance is predicated on its first-mover advantage; in the 1940s and 1950s it was a hub for the burgeoning semi-conductor industry and the newly established Hewlett Packard Company. "There is a reason why there is only one Silicon Valley," explains Piotr Pikul, a principal in the Toronto office of McKinsey & Company, a consultancy. "It was the first place to get enough scale and it became unbeatable. In Canada that hub is mining."[5]

As with the Valley, Canada's mining prowess is based on a number of key first principles: a rich resource endowment, a long mining history, and scale. Canada is a top-five global producer of eleven metals and minerals, from potash and uranium to diamonds and nickel, with mining operations in virtually every province and territory.[6] We also boast the largest concentration of junior miners in the world – the risk-taking start-ups of the sector – and represent 30 per cent of the mid-range producers with market capitalizations in the $5–$30-billion range, including the lion's share of the world's gold miners. These companies flock to the Toronto Stock Exchange, with its savvy mining investors and cluster of specialized bankers, lawyers, and accountants, to list their stock and earn the highest price-to-earnings multiples in the world.

And while Toronto is recognized as a global mining hub, with the TSX accounting for 57 per cent of the world's publicly traded mining companies,[7] and the city home to more than 400 mining and exploration offices and several hundred suppliers,[8] what makes the sector truly unique is its scope. Not only is mining thoroughly pan-Canadian, it bridges the rural-urban divide with its remote operations and corporate headquarters in Montreal, Toronto, and Vancouver. It is also the most global of Canadian sectors, with more than half of the industry's assets held abroad. "You won't find another Canadian sector that is so dominant internationally as mining," says Jon Baird, managing director for the Canadian Association of Mining Equipment Services for Export (CAMESE).[9] It generates 20 per cent of the country's exports and represents

10 per cent of Canadian foreign investment abroad.[10] In addition to heavyweights like Barrick Gold, Goldcorp, Potash Corp, and Teck, there are more than 800 Canadian exploration companies in more than 100 countries, representing a third of global exploration spending.[11]

Despite the sector's importance, however, its overall contribution to the Canadian economy is unclear; its substantial contingent of service suppliers, from engineering consultants and technology vendors to securities lawyers and bankers, has never been quantified. The Conference Board of Canada in fact calls mining supply one of the largest "hidden" industries in Canada.[12] It's a remarkable omission that speaks to some of the strategic challenges tackled later in this chapter. Nevertheless, mining and its downstream production alone contributes, on average, 4 per cent to Canada's GDP and employs an estimated 420,000 people.[13] It's also the largest employer of First Nations in the country. Mining jobs, which include highly educated engineers, geoscientists, and geologists, are skilled and well paid, with wages on average 36 to 57 per cent higher than in sectors ranging from manufacturing to forestry, construction, and finance.[14] As the Canadian Chamber of Commerce summed up in its 2013 "Mining Capital" report: "[Mining] is one of the few sectors in which we have the expertise, capital and capacity to be world leaders."[15]

The Slow Boiling Frog

While the Canadian policy community has often fretted over an industrial strategy that "picks winners," when it comes to bulking up Canada's international competitiveness, championing mining seems an obvious choice. This is all the more compelling given that mining, both as a global industry and here in Canada, is facing some fundamental challenges that require a coordinated and strategic response.

The mining industry has undergone a dramatic transformation in the past three decades as small, high-grade, easy-to-access underground mines are exhausted and producers have been forced to go deeper and further afield to mine lower-grade reserves that are more costly and complicated to process. To compensate for the higher costs and lower returns, mines have moved to super-sized open-pit operations that have, in turn, increased environmental pressures, strained corporate finances, and stirred opposition from anti-mining activists and local communities.

A classic example of these growing challenges is Barrick Gold's now suspended Pascua-Lama project straddling the Altiplano of the Chile-Argentina border. A massive open-pit copper-gold project located 4500 metres above sea level, Pascua-Lama's construction costs quickly ballooned from US$3 billion in 2009 to an estimated US$8.5 billion, while its proximity to pristine glaciers in Chile, a country already suffering from severe water shortages, fuelled heavy opposition. Environmental authorities called a halt to the project in 2013 and slapped Barrick with a $16.4 million fine for violations before Barrick, struggling under heavy debt and plummeting gold prices, suspended the project.[16]

Like Barrick, many miners are literally caught between a rock and a hard place; grappling with intense pressure to reduce operating costs and their environmental footprint while in a financially weakened position. A sharp drop in commodity prices following a slowdown in Chinese growth saddled many with debt, and high-cost, unprofitable mines. According to PricewaterhouseCoopers, the world's forty largest miners took nearly US$100 billion in asset write-downs in 2012–13 alone.[17] At the same time, many host countries, under financial pressure themselves, are demanding a larger share of mining profits, introducing windfall profit taxes and upping royalty rates.

To break the deadlock of diminishing returns and meet the demands for a more sustainable approach to mining, industry observers agree, there needs to be a greater emphasis and investment in innovation, technological as well as social. The challenge, however, is that while mining is very capital-intensive, it can also be a slow adopter and culturally resistant to change. As Mark Cutifani of Anglo American noted in his 2013 Montreal speech, the industry spends 80 per cent less on technology and innovation than the petroleum sector. "We, as an industry, are woefully under-spending on innovation and business-improvement programs given the state of extraction challenges," he said.[18]

Indeed, there has not been a major technological breakthrough in mining in decades, while many of the industry's most widely used processing technologies, like ball mills and flotation cells, are more than 100 years old. When mines got bigger, the technology simply got bigger with them; in the case of ball mills, for example, just 2 to 3 per cent of the energy that is consumed is for grinding the ore to a fine powder – the rest is needed to run the massive machines. Says Cutifani: "Our current models for innovation and change are out-dated and they are simply not delivering what society needs from us."[19]

Within this global context, the Canadian industry is grappling with its own set of challenges. There is a widespread belief that Canada is falling behind traditional peers like Australia and new, emerging market entrants in Brazil, China, and India, which for the first time now make up the bulk of the world's top forty miners.[20] "When I started my career in the mid-80s we were powerhouse in the world," says John Bianchini, CEO of Toronto-based engineering firm Hatch. "We have certainly lost ground to the mining industry in other parts of the world. The Australians really ate our lunch in the last decade. And now the Chinese are emerging with a lot of capital and their mandate is clear; they want to find resources wherever they can."[21]

The Canadian industry took a major hit in 2006 when two of its largest, anchor companies – Inco and Falconbridge – were acquired by Brazil's Vale and Swiss-based Xstrata. The historic miners, pioneers of the industry's global expansion, had nearly 200 years of mining experience between them. In 2007, another Canadian icon, Alcan, was bought by Anglo-Australian miner Rio Tinto. The wave of consolidation produced a new global hierarchy of mining "super-majors" from which Canada is notably absent.[22] Large and diversified, the super-majors are like the coral reefs of the industry, providing the capital and R&D dollars on which service providers and smaller miners feed.

When Inco and Falconbridge were acquired, their in-house R&D laboratories, which had supported much of the technological innovation of the last century, were downsized or closed. Other companies have followed suit, says Engin Özberk, who retired as the vice-president of technology for Saskatchewan uranium miner Cameco in 2013, and was not replaced. "Things have changed very significantly in mining and processing and I don't think it's fully appreciated," says Özberk. "If we are not renewing ourselves, not innovating, we are going to be dinosaurs."[23]

In contrast, Australia, home to super-majors BHP Billiton and Rio Tinto, is seen as an industry leader when it comes to innovation.[24] Both miners have opened real-time remote data centres in Perth that allow them to track and direct massive iron ore operations 1500 kilometres away, including the deployment of autonomous trucks, drills, and, eventually, trains. According to the OECD, Australian miners spend over three times more on R&D than their Canadian counterparts.[25] The increased investment is supported by an unparalleled collaborative framework linking industry, academia, and government that pools research and innovation dollars to greater effect. Some specific examples will be cited later in this chapter, but what is striking is how un-strategic and scattershot Canada appears in comparison.

While in Australia there is one well-funded federal agency, the Commonwealth Scientific and Industrial Research Organization (CSIRO), that is the focal point for innovation funding and collaboration, in Canada investments are made through one or more of some 4500 government programs, according to Carl Weatherell, the CEO of the Canadian Mining Innovation Council (CMIC). The funding is overwhelmingly channelled through academia or must follow the same guidelines as university researchers, while in Australia the government directly earmarks funding for long-term industry challenges. "In essence, innovation in Canada is equated to university research in academia," explains Weatherell.[26] The result is often a disconnect between academia and industry as professors pursue individual research that may have little connection to industry needs.

"Australia is a Commonwealth, and all institutions are funded by the same national body. They speak the same language and there is a unity of endeavour in Australia that you don't see in

Canada, which is a Federation," explains Andrew Bamber, the CEO and founder of MineSense Technologies, a Vancouver-based start-up that has developed real-time sensor technology to sort and grade ore in the mine pit. The technology, which reduces the amount of ore and waste rock that needs to be transported either to the mill or the waste dump, came out of Bamber's PhD work at the University of British Columbia. The company has received some federal funding, but Bamber admits that he's been tempted to relocate his company Down Under. "The ecosystem I'd like to belong to doesn't exist here," he says. "There should be 100 MineSenses in Canada (but there are not). What's missing is a cohesive, sustained and serious effort at the national level."[27]

It's an observation that has been made time and again in a host of sectors. Where Canada fails and Australia succeeds is in the ability to recognize key strengths and execute industry-led initiatives and strategies with a singularity of purpose by pooling resources, collaborating, and branding at a national level. In Canada, we do not buy wine from New South Wales, we buy wine from Australia. And yet Ontario will lead a trade mission of mining service suppliers to Mexico, which may very well be followed a few days later by a federal delegation and one from Quebec a week later. Jon Baird of CAMESE has long envied the professional, custom-built Australian, Swedish, and German trade show pavilions. The Canadians, in comparison, rely on the standard nondescript government hoardings and whatever CAMESE can scrounge up. "There is simply no system in place," says Baird. "Everyone is on his own."[28]

It's an odd approach for a small, trade-reliant country like Canada. While there are some important instances, like oil sands development, where prescient, early-stage government support helped to spawn one of this country's key sources of wealth, there is an unnerving habit of waiting until a major industry goes into complete collapse before trying to douse the political outcry with taxpayer dollars. Such was the case with the forestry sector, now much diminished by international competition. Carl Weatherell of CMIC worries the same thing might happen to mining, although his analysis could apply to other sectors. "We treat mining like a utility. It's just there, nobody thinks about it," he says. "Only when someone shuts off the lights will people freak out."[29]

Mind the Gap

There is a lot that Canada has gotten right when it comes to mining: innovative financial and reporting instruments and an avoidance of some of the ownership and marketing limitations that have hamstrung the competitiveness of industries from telecommunications and agriculture to beer. But there is plenty we could be doing better, specifically as it relates to technological and social innovation, which are key elements of the industry's international competitiveness. The observations here can, in many ways, be applied to other sectors. And, while it's tempting for Toronto's chief planner to muse about building new "knowledge-based, creative-based industries," such as those housed in the MaRS complex – a grandiose technology accelerator cum white elephant occupying prime real estate in downtown Toronto, bailed out by the Ontario government (read taxpayers) to the tune of $309 million, its more than half-empty new extension consigned to becoming high-end offices for bureaucrats[30] – if we can't get the basics right, then we are doomed to repeat our past mistakes.

Faced with low productivity, operational inefficiencies, and an environmental imperative to reduce its footprint, mining has a huge opportunity to make significant gains through technological innovation. The question is how? Industry players are notoriously unwilling to share intellectual property. But with corporate balance sheets stretched and in-house labs closed or downsized, the answer increasingly points to different forms of collaboration. "We are more and more convinced going it alone is not the answer," says Andrew Bamber of MineSense. "The consortium approach is the way to finally be able to commercialize and disseminate technology."[31]

Dundee Precious Metals, the small, Toronto-headquartered gold miner, has gained international attention for the out-of-the-box way it has applied the consortium model. The company brought together half-a-dozen service providers, from tech giant Cisco to software developers and equipment suppliers, to wire its Soviet-era Chelopech underground mine in Bulgaria with Wifi and radio tagging devices. The mine is able to track its operations in real time and the return, while difficult to quantify, is significant. Since the network was installed, production has doubled and costs have been cut by almost half, says Dundee CEO Rick Howes. Total investment: $2 million by Dundee and $8 million in in-kind contributions from vendors who can now market their capabilities to other customers.

"Technology is clearly no longer the barrier anymore," says Howes, a former mine manager with Inco and Falconbridge, who spent years "banging his head" against a Canadian industry "moving way too slow." For Howes, the key to innovating in such a high risk, complex industry is "bite-sized" improvements using proven technology. "There are many things you can do before taking the big leap," he says. "There's still a need to invest in R&D, but many companies don't think 15 years out. I'm on the much more practical side. You can transform yourself in small steps."[32]

But while operators are looking for digestible, real-time improvements that don't require betting the company, it is not the transformative step that technologists say is necessary to meet the challenges of the future. "The industry is fantastic at incremental change, but it's fighting a losing battle," says John Thompson, a consultant and former vice-president of technology at Teck Resources. "The sheer amount of rock they have to move is beating them. We need to attack these issues before they get the better of us."[33] Traditionally, governments have stepped in to support longer-term research for the broader, universal benefit of industry and society, but financial pressures have forced governments to retrench as well.

There is one model, however, that is widely recognized for bridging the divide between longer-term research and immediate industry needs. AMIRA International was founded in 1959 by a group of Australian mining CEOs as a vehicle to tackle common industry challenges through collaboration. The not-for-profit group, which has expanded its membership to include miners from around the world, works with a global network of researchers, universities, consultants, and suppliers on research programs, leveraging both corporate and government funding. It currently manages twenty-five projects worth $55 million. One such project has brought together researchers from Australia, France, South

Africa, Ghana, and Burkina Faso to map the geology of West Africa. The Australian government provided aid funding to cover the capacity-building component of the project, including training for local university students and geological surveys, which ultimately supports Australian (and Canadian) mining companies exploring in the region.

AMIRA has also helped to spawn some half-a-dozen Cooperative Research Centres (CRCs), an Australian government program launched in 1990 which brings together industry, universities, and the CSIRO "to deliver significant economic, environmental and social benefits across Australia" through user-driven collaborative research ventures. The Deep Exploration Technology (DET) CRC, launched in 2010 and the product of an AMIRA road-mapping exercise focussed on future drilling technology, is the world's largest independent initiative of its kind, garnering AUS$145 million in private-public funding, including, to the consternation of some, from Canadian miners like Barrick Gold. As Pierre Gratton, CEO of the Mining Association of Canada, notes: "If Canada had a better option, the companies would be here not there, but it's too much trouble to navigate the system."[34]

In 2007 Canada launched its own version of AMIRA – the Canadian Mining Innovation Council, CMIC. The council has struggled to gain traction and it wasn't until 2013 that it sealed its first collaborative project, a modest, five-year, $13-million exploration initiative involving 54 organizations, including 30 companies and 24 Canadian universities. The consortium is led by the chief geologist for Barrick Gold and is the largest collaboration in the history of Natural Sciences and Engineering Research Council of Canada. The federal government has invested $5.1 million. "If it were up to me, I'd like to see corporate and government money flowing into CIMC in a less judgmental fashion," says Andrew Bamber. "We need to stop moving chairs around and get things going."[35]

John Bianchini, the CEO of engineering firm Hatch, is naturally more circumspect about the merits of open-source consortia. Technology development has increasingly migrated to service providers and Hatch owns hundreds of its own patents. Nevertheless, Bianchini is convinced of the need for partnerships and closer ties to government and universities. The head of one of the country's leading engineering firms recently invited himself on a two-day tour of Natural Resources Canada's Canmet lab. He was amazed by the talent and work being done – work he had no idea about. "I came out of there with 20 ideas," said Bianchini. "These guys work in a vacuum. They are doing a lot of interesting work that I think is being wasted. When I asked them how they share their research, they told me they have a conference and publish."

Contrast that to how government labs in the United States are run. The US Department of Energy laboratories, for example, are operated by private-sector organizations under contract with the DOE. US engineering firms Aecom and URS, which announced in July 2014 they will be merging to form the world's largest engineering company, are both involved with managing several large DOE facilities. The merged group, which will be double the size of its next closest rival, Worley Parsons of Australia, has no doubt benefited from the combined public-private muscle.

Could Canada contemplate something so radical? It's pretty bold, but as Serge Dupont, deputy minister for Natural Resources Canada told an industry gathering before leaving on a fact-finding mission to Australia in mid-2014: "We can't afford complacency. This is an historic opportunity for the Canadian resource industry and innovation is the starting point."

Glenn Dobby and his partner Glenn Kosick are arguably among the most successful mining technology entrepreneurs in Canada. After selling their first company, MinnovEX, to Swiss multinational SGS in 2005, the Toronto-based duo are now on to their next venture: a potentially transformative technology that reduces the footprint and energy consumption of massive processing equipment, known as froth flotation cells, by 40 to 50 per cent. The "two Glenns," as they are known, used proceeds from the sale of MinnovEX to buy a stake in a Newfoundland mine, where they tested the new technology and spent a year cobbling together a consortium of nine mining companies that have committed funding and technical staff to a pilot project at a mine site in northern Brazil owned by Vale, one of the world's largest miners. "It's a very unique project," said Dobby just before embarking on a five-week trip to Brazil. "I don't know if there is anything like it in the industry."[36]

The "two Glenns" are themselves a rare commodity; both a product of mining's "golden age" in Canada, Dobby, sixty-four, is a former associate professor in the Department of Metallurgy and Materials Science at the University of Toronto. He has a PhD in metallurgical engineering from McGill University and is a leading expert in flotation technology. He got his start in the industry with a university scholarship from Inco, followed by a summer job at Inco's in-house technology group. "It was a great team – you don't see that anymore," says Dobby, whose PhD was partially funded by the likes of Inco and other companies that "mostly don't exist anymore." Kosick, a former mineral processing engineer with Cominco,[37] is a dogged salesman. The combination of technical strength and entrepreneurship, together with their long track record and deep connections, has allowed them to break through the industry's natural reticence.

The danger for Canada and the mining industry is that the pair's innovative alchemy may not be replicated after they, and their generation, retire in the coming years. Some 40 per cent of the industry is fifty years old or more, with one-third of the workforce is set to retire by 2015.[38] The industry lost an entire generation between the mid-1980s and the early 2000s amidst sinking metal prices and a growing environmental backlash. Companies stopped hiring and Canadian universities looking to scrub the industry's "dirty" image buried extractive metallurgy – the study of extracting metals from ore – within their material sciences departments. The global industry bounced back in the early 2000s, but mining's place within Canadian universities did not.

The upshot is that while Canada remains a major global player in the mining industry, it is facing a significant skills shortage in the coming years and lacks a well-defined and visibly promoted educational foundation to fill the gap. With a few exceptions, universities are weak in teaching the fundamentals of mining and metallurgy, say observers, and there are just six Canada Research chairs (out of 2000) dedicated to mining and mineral processing.[39] "This is huge – these are the people who sustain operations," explains John Thompson, who is also the chair of GeoScience BC.[40] "Universities need to get rid of old-school thinking and get the pizzazz back into mining, with a greater emphasis and visibility. They need to make the case for innovation and career opportunities."[41]

Thompson's call to action could also apply to Canada's approach to social innovation, which has become a key element in its ability to operate successfully overseas. With local opposition to some projects capturing headlines and governments in developing countries struggling to regulate the industry and manage newfound resource revenues, both companies and their governments have come under immense pressure to develop comprehensive standards and practices around corporate social responsibility. Yet Canada's slower response to the fast moving and at times volatile issues surrounding corporate social responsibility (CSR) has arguably left the industry open to greater attack.

In March 2009 the federal government unveiled its "Corporate Social Responsibility Strategy for the Canadian International Extractive Sector," aimed at improving the industry's competitive advantage by "enhancing its ability to manage social and environmental risk." It followed a 2005 House of Commons Standing Committee report on "Mining in Developing Countries" and national roundtable consultations in 2006, and came six years after a landmark decision by Calgary-based Talisman Energy, the target of a high-profile international boycott campaign, to pull out of war-ravaged Sudan.

The strategy, however, has met with rather mixed results. Its centrepiece – a CSR counsellor mandated to support the resolution of disputes between companies and stakeholders, has been the target of widespread criticism by NGOs and industry. NGOs complained the office was all bark and no bite as it could not force companies to come to the table to resolve disputes, while companies felt the process was stacked against them. The first appointee stepped down in October 2013, one year before her five-year mandate was up, and the post remained vacant until March 2015, when Jeffrey Davidson, a Queen's University mining professor and thirty-five-year CSR veteran, was named as replacement.

Other pillars of the CSR strategy have also garnered less than optimal results; the CSR centre of excellence, created to provide stakeholders with access to CSR resources and best practices, is essentially defunct. A third plank, which looks to coordinate government aid projects with mining operations, follows a long-standing practice in the United States, United Kingdom, and elsewhere of linking aid and economic interests,[42] yet has been controversial since it was introduced in 2011. "It's such a big deal in Canada," notes one industry observer, "but frankly we're a bit late to the game."

To a large degree, the CSR strategy was hamstrung before it ever got off the ground. It was pre-empted by Bill C-300, a highly contentious private member's bill introduced in the House of Commons in February 2009, which drew on brewing opposition to overseas mining among activists, and proposed giving Ottawa a sweeping extraterritorial mandate to investigate, report on, and punish companies found to be acting outside CSR standards. The bill was ultimately defeated, but left a lingering expectation and belief that the industry needed to be policed.

In response to continuing pressure and criticism, in November 2014 the federal government unveiled a 2.0 refresh of its strategy, dubbed Canada's Enhanced CSR Strategy: *Doing Business the Canadian Way: A Strategy to Advance Corporate Social Responsibility in Canada's Extractive Sector Abroad*. The revamped effort looks to balance the calls by NGOs for greater enforcement measures with recognition that the CSR counsellor might not be the appropriate arbiter for resolving certain disputes. The carrot-and-stick approach includes refocusing the counsellor's role on early detection and prevention of disputes while emphasizing the OECD's National Contact Point as a recognized vehicle for dispute settlement. For the first time, the government will also withdraw federal funding if a company refuses to participate in a dispute-resolution process, be it through the CSR counsellor or the National Contact Point.[43]

While it is too early to assess how effective the revamped strategy will be, it is interesting to contrast it with the Australian experience. While we tie ourselves up in knots in Canada, Australia has no ombudsman, nor have there been legislative attempts akin to Bill C-300. One of the key reasons, according to Davidson, Canada's newly named CSR counsellor, who has worked in both Canada and Australia, is because the Australian industry and academia moved early on to find innovative solutions to social challenges. The Minerals Council of Australia and its member companies actively sought a vehicle for training employees in CSR and a deal was struck with the University of Queensland's Centre for Social Responsibility in Mining, a world-leading institute established in 2001, to coordinate the development of a post-graduate distance-learning program. In 2007 Davidson was seconded by Australian miner Rio Tinto to help get the program off the ground, while the industry, through the mining council, subsidized the development of the curriculum and guaranteed enrolment for five years. "Because the industry was invested from the start, they made a big effort to send people," says Davidson. "And it worked; the program is quite successful.[44]

Davidson's efforts to set up a similar program at Queen's University, where he has been a professor, have not met with the same success due to lack of corporate commitment. In 2013 there were six students enrolled in the school's Community Relations Graduate Certificate program. "The problem in Canada is these things are not organically grown or occur in a collaborative way," he says. "Everybody is doing their own thing." At the same time, Davidson adds, Australian miner Rio Tinto "was innovative and a leader and really pushed the agenda," while Canada has been content to "let others pioneer and see how it goes."

There is a cost, however, to being a follower. When it comes to companies' social licence, or community approval to operate, they risk reputational damage and increasing opposition to their operations. The image of the industry as "vintage" and antithetical to knowledge becomes accepted wisdom and young Canadians see mining as a threat rather than an important contributor to Canada's prosperity or as a potential career opportunity. At the University of British Columbia, for example, the newly established Canadian International Institute for Extractive Industries and Development (CIIEID)[45] is still not fully operational, yet it is already facing a student-led campaign to "Stop the Institute," which it decries as a "tool to legitimize Canada's predatory mining extractive model."[46]

It's no different with technological innovation. Those that invest themselves in the development of new technology – versus simply buying it off the shelf – influence how it's developed, get the technology earlier, and are able to use it more effectively. "Fast followers don't exist," says Hatch CEO John Bianchini. "Fast followers get left behind. You are either a leader or a follower when it comes to innovation. And it's more important now than in the past because mines are getting poorer and more remote and to make the business case stick you are going to need new ideas and game-changing innovative technologies."[47]

There is plenty that can be done to keep Canada in the game. It starts with making a choice to recognize the industry as key to the country's prosperity, and a willingness to collaborate when it comes to university scholarships and summer jobs, investing in technological innovation, and in CSR initiatives and training, and to communicating the industry's benefits, successes and challenges. It's a step-change the industry can't afford not to make, says John Thompson. "We need to do this from a production, margin sustainability, and social licence point of view."[48]

But the initiative must begin with the industry itself, says Rick Howes of Dundee Precious Metals: "In order for Canada to lead in the mining sector, there needs to be the willingness from top management in order to drive this change. Government and university participation is based on the willingness of companies to welcome the advancement. If the Canadian mining sector wants to be a leader, the companies have to drive the change. We have to be the change."[49]

chapter four

Canadian Hydrocarbon Resources in an Era of Manufactured Energy

ANDREW LEACH

Canada has a long history of competitiveness in manufacturing, smelting, assembly, and fabrication, much of it underpinned by our resource wealth. In Ontario and Quebec, cheap electricity prices relative to regional and global competitors combined with a skilled and productive labour force to drive Canadian economic growth. Today, this narrative is being turned upside down as a new story of Canadian growth emerges. In the decades to come, it will be our manufacturing and processing skills which determine the value of our energy resources, and our role in global energy markets. We are entering a new era of manufactured energy – will Canada be in a position to lead?

The era of manufactured energy in Canada will likely be defined initially by the success (or lack thereof) of two hydrocarbon industries, oil sands and liquefied natural gas, but the logic presented in this chapter extends to the production and installation of renewable energy components, to renewable fuels, and even to the automation of demand-side responses. As we move into this era, the lines between an energy business, a technology business, a manufacturing business, and a construction business will become increasingly blurred and Canada will need contributions from all these sectors in order to realize the maximum value for our energy resources.

The Canadian steel industry, centred in south-western Ontario, has been one of the symbols of Canadian manufacturing but has fallen on hard times. Today, Canadian production of rolled steel is lower by 30 per cent compared to 2004, and the levels have fallen for decades from peaks in the 1980s.[1] Traditional manufacturing in Canada, including steel production, has been hurt by increased costs of energy, increased real wages, and a higher Canadian dollar. Steel production is part of the value chain leading from iron-ore mining through to final products such as buildings, pipelines, automobiles, and railways. It is clear, at least in the way the data are presented by Statistics Canada, that the line between mining and manufacturing, or between the resource industry and the so-called value-added sector, occurs at the mine mouth, and that distinction is easier in the case of steel because steel production tended to occur at locations distant from the mine mouth. This distinction has made it easier to vilify the resource sector in discussions of the "Dutch disease," and to point the finger at other regions' growth for the decline in manufacturing in central Canada.

The distinction between what is resource production and what is manufacturing is not so obvious for some of Canada's key hydrocarbon resources, but how we choose to draw that distinction will be important for perception of the resource industries as we move into a Canadian era of *manufactured energy*. Is oil sands extraction manufacturing or energy? What about shale gas? Are mechanical transformations different because they occur in the subsurface versus a factory? Whether you consider different parts of the resource supply chain as part of the energy sector or the manufacturing sector is a matter of semantics, but the importance of what once would have clearly been thought of as a manufacturing industry to the value of the resource itself cannot be ignored.

When you look at forecasts of the future of Canadian hydrocarbon energy, the upside is tied to two key markets – crude oil and related products derived from oil sands and liquefied natural gas. Both of these industries differ substantially from the traditional resource industry – each looks more like manufacturing than drilling for oil. Both industries also depend on global competitiveness – as energy exporters, Canadian oil and natural gas will have to compete with products from other jurisdictions, net of transportation costs, in American, Asian, and European markets. For these reasons, the success of Canada's hydrocarbon industries

---

Chapter Summary

Key Transformations
- We are entering an era of manufactured energy – synthetic products derived from oil sands, liquefied natural gas, and renewable power all rely on what we would have traditionally thought of as manufacturing expertise.
- Success in this era will require devotion to enhanced productivity, and avoiding the temptations to maintain the status quo in the structure of our manufacturing industry.

Implications for Canada
- Although Canada's energy resources remain world-scale and a great source of natural wealth, the long-run value of these resources will be determined not just by their physical size, but by the technology and productivity we can bring to bear in extracting and shipping them.

Recommendations
- Allow the lines between energy and manufacturing to blur and avoid false differentiations or policies that seek to maintain the market share in either space.
- Prepare our energy industries for future carbon policy; do not prepare carbon policy to suit the existing energy industry.
- Avoid the temptation to force more manufacturing through discounted energy resources; conceive of the products of energy production as value-added products in themselves.

---

will depend as much on our manufacturing expertise as on our resource endowments.

Canada's oil sands resource is immense, with current estimates placing the quantity of *original oil in place* at approximately two trillion barrels, with approximately 10–15 per cent of that quantity currently classified as recoverable.[2] Oil sands will be extracted by one of two means – in situ technologies that extract the bitumen from the ore using steam or other media injected via wells drilled into the deposits, and the more traditional mining operations that have been the mainstay of oil sands development since the late 1960s. Today, approximately one-half of oil sands production is tied to each of these broad categories of extraction technology. Each of these requires substantial inputs of fixed capital and labour, as well as energy, to transform the raw resource into a useable, marketable product. In that sense, it can be argued that the definition of manufacturing versus resource appears to be one of location (mine vs. dedicated facility, surface vs. subsurface, etc.) rather than substance.

Natural gas, in a globalizing market, presents an even more compelling case for the era of manufactured energy and a substantial opportunity for Canada. Canada has, as of 2014, 66.7 trillion cubic feet of natural gas reserves – potential future production that is economically viable with today's prices and technology, representing over 20 years' worth of current consumption.[3] Two technological changes, one global and one local, have begun to take hold in gas markets and have led to natural-gas-reserve growth in Canada to levels not seen since the late 1990s. The first and most obvious is the combination of horizontal drilling and multistage fracturing, which has unlocked natural gas resources long thought to be inaccessible in shale deposits. Since 2005, this innovation alone has led to an increase of approximately 50 per cent in natural gas reserves in the United States and Canada, during a period in which prices fell in inflation-adjusted terms. The second change, relatively new to North America and a growing influence in the world, is liquefied natural gas. Like oil sands, the future of Canadian natural gas production, at least at the margin, looks to be based on the potential to sell natural gas to Europe and to Asia, again via a process much more akin to traditional manufacturing – large, coastal liquefaction facilities.

Success in these two areas, each of which is discussed below, depends on a set of common elements. First, each requires substantial up-front capital investment as well as significant construction labour, generally in relatively remote locations. Second, each represents a long-term investment in commodity markets, with financial conditions more akin to refining or traditional manufacturing than to traditional resource industries. Third, each depends significantly on efficient infrastructure and predictable regulation here in Canada, since these factors will each weigh on the manufacturing margins for what are global commodities and the long time-horizons involved make future regulations a much more important risk than might be the case in some resource extraction plays.[4] For example, both industries involve significant exposure to future climate change policies, which are the subject of another chapter in this volume and so are not discussed in great detail here. Finally, and perhaps most importantly in the domestic market, growing these industries will involve a significant shift of Canada's manufacturing base away from both traditional areas and traditional industries towards manufacturing energy commodities.

The era of manufactured energy does not end with hydrocarbon energy. When you hear people talk about renewable energy, at least for wind and solar, you will hear them discuss an energy source where the fuel is free for the taking, renewable, and in practical terms inexhaustible. However, the cost of getting a system built and mounted remains significant. Again, as with hydrocarbon energy, success in renewables will not come to those with the resources but to those who can most effectively create and install the means to capture those resources and convert them to useful energy and link that energy to the highest-value markets.

Oil Sands

Imagine a different reality than what we see today. Instead of seeing bitumen production of two million barrels per day from the oil sands region, imagine we were shipping oil sands ore. It takes approximately 1.7 tonnes of oil sands ore to produce a barrel of bitumen, so to produce two million barrels per day of bitumen, you would have to process upwards of one billion tonnes of oil sands ore per year – that would be 10 million rail cars per year of ore leaving Northern Alberta. It would be quite a sight! Now, imagine all those rail cars bound for a manufacturing facility in Southern Ontario – the industrial capacity required for processing would be substantial. There would also be no question that the impact would be described as a manufacturing renaissance if all that ore were processed and transformed into higher-value bitumen in central Canada.

Of course, that's not what we have today. Today, we have two sorts of bitumen extraction: mining and in situ, each of which are, in their own rights, means of ore processing. Oil sands deposits are deposits of sand, clay, bitumen, and water, mixed with small amounts of other contaminants, but the extraction of bitumen from the oil sands deposits occurs entirely in Alberta, as does some additional processing known as upgrading through which bitumen is chemically transformed into synthetic crude oil. Unlike other oil resources, the challenge is not in the finding of the oil sands, but in the manufacture of useful energy from them. Despite significant process improvements in the last forty years, bitumen production costs have risen substantially in Alberta, and these inflated costs represent one of the most significant threats to Alberta's (and to a lesser degree Canada's) potential to profit from this resource wealth.

In discussions of the future role of Canada's energy resources in a global market, we've recently been concerned mostly with pipelines. Yes, it's true that new infrastructure providing low-cost access to premium markets for oil sands production will be important to increasing the value of that resource for Canadians. However, the ability to extract bitumen from oil sands at a competitive cost, and with lower resource use, may be even more important.

First, with respect to pipelines and price discounts, oil markets in North America have changed. As figure 4.1 shows, Canadian heavy oil (Western Canada Select, or WCS) used to trade at par, or at least closer to it, in Canadian dollar terms with Maya crude, a similar grade traded on the US Gulf Coast. Since 2010, the North American crude market has changed significantly, and as a result, the value of Canadian crude has decreased. Increasing production in the US Midwest and in Canada combined with flat demand have led to a situation where what used to be a premium market, in and around Chicago, has become a discounted market as producers try to move crude to the coast. Canada's oil has gone from trading at or even above global prices because of our proximity to this premium market to trading at steep discounts. A crucial step

Figure 4.1 Prices in Canadian dollars for Western Canada Select (WCS), Arab Heavy for Asia delivery, and Maya heavy crudes traded at Hardisty, AB, Singapore, and in the Gulf of Mexico, respectively.

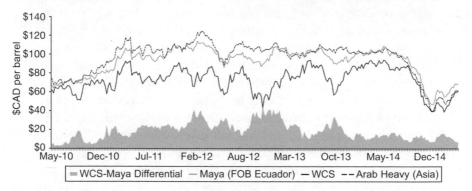

Source: Bloomberg terminal data (online). Author's graphic.

to realizing value for Canadian energy resources is allowing them access to the highest-price markets in the world via the shortest routes possible, and today this means pipelines to the west coast. It may be that such pipelines are not feasible, but it should be understood that this comes at a cost of devaluing our natural resources by forcing on them more expensive transportation.

Alberta oil will see a higher value when shipped to the coasts, given this new market reality, than when it is shipped to or through traditional destinations in the US mid-continent. Looking ahead, however, maximizing the value of the resource is not as easy as that. As the last oil sands boom was gathering steam in 2006, the Canadian Association of Petroleum Producers forecast that oil sands production would reach four million barrels per day by 2020, and this under a forecast which still considered oil prices above $70 per barrel to be a temporary feature soon to disappear.[5] In CAPP's 2014 forecast, that same forecast methodology led to forecasts 20 per cent lower, even with oil prices stuck near $100 per barrel, after having exceeded consensus forecasts in just about every year of the last decade. So why, in an environment where prices increased twofold, has production lagged forecasts? As a

Figure 4.2 Oil sands growth forecasts

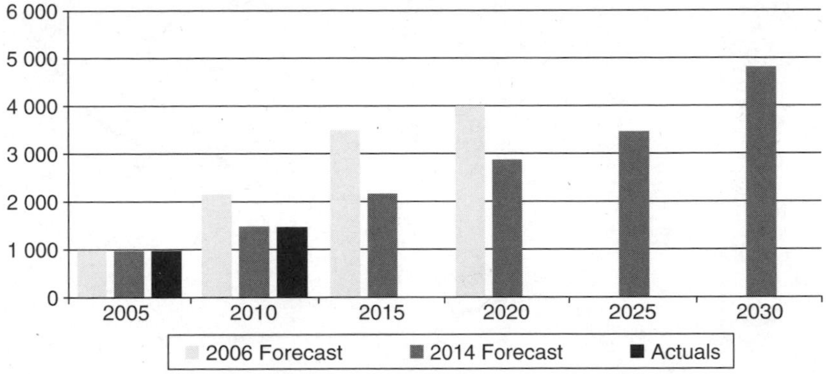

Source: Canadian Association of Petroleum Producers (2006 and 2014). Author's graphic.

result of low productivity and high construction costs. It's easy to blame the financial crisis for this lag, but as figure 4.2 shows, production was lagging forecasts at the height of the boom, well before the crisis hit. The same is true today, in another period of low oil prices – production was lagging forecasts and projects were being reconsidered due to high costs long before the drop in prices.

In fact, as one can see clearly from figure 4.2, oil sands production has lagged earlier forecasts significantly, despite an environment in which prices have increased far above expectations and the costs of natural gas, a key input to production, have been much lower than expected. What has happened? Oil sands plants have become much more expensive to build and to operate than anyone would have predicted at the time the boom began, as shown in figure 4.3.

There is a long history of expecting things to get better, or of forgetting why they've gotten worse. In October 2000 the National Energy Board reported that "industry analysts anticipate that ... operating costs [in dollars of the day] for integrated mining/upgrading plants [will come down] to $10 per barrel as early as 2004, with further improvement to the $8 to $9 per barrel level by 2015."[6] In 2006, the NEB reported that operating costs for integrated mining

Figure 4.3 Oil sands operating costs for select projects and companies

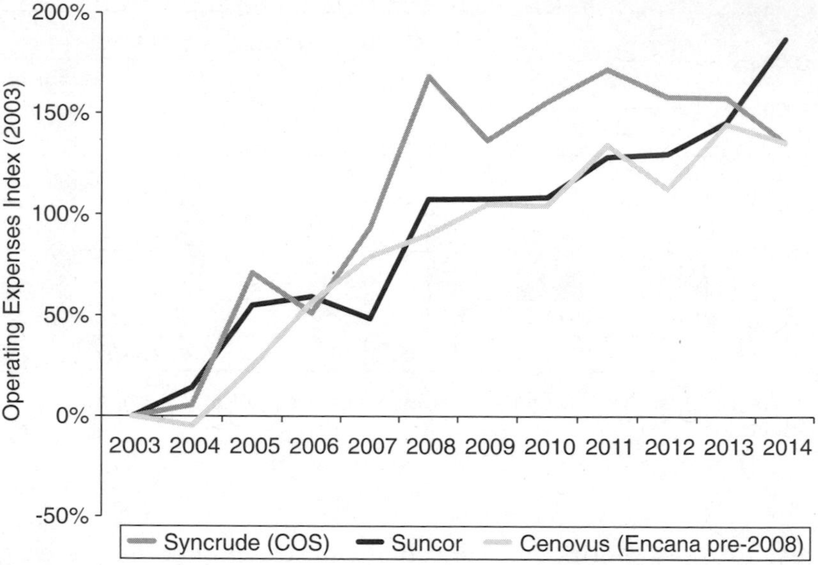

Sources: Company reports, Raymond James Financial, Bloomberg, Yahoo! Finance. Author's graphic.

and upgrading projects had jumped to $18–$22 per barrel, but with increased oil prices, the NEB's oil sands production forecast had been updated to 3 million barrels per day in 2015.[7] By 2009, the NEB had increased its *break-even price* for new oil sands projects to US$55–$70 per barrel WTI, and these were increased again to $85–$95 per barrel in 2011. Today, those break-even prices have decreased by about 20 per cent, largely as a result of the devalued Canadian dollar, and partially due to reduced natural-gas price outlooks.

Besides cost and market access, the other major factor in determining the role for Canada's oil in the world market is going to be climate change and the policies implemented to combat it, both at home and abroad. While the topic of climate change is addressed separately within this volume by Stewart Elgie, it is worth considering in the context of the era of manufactured energy. In the most widely cited forecast of world energy markets under stringent climate change policies, the International Energy Agency's 450 parts per million scenario, two things change which impact Canadian oil sands – first, the price of oil decreases relative to a case with less aggressive policies; and second, production emissions face higher greenhouse gas penalties. Each of these will hurt oil sands resource values more the poorer the performance is in terms of bitumen extraction.

The impact of the stringency of policies imposed in the IEA 450 ppm scenario over the life of a prototypical in situ oil sands extraction project built today is significant. Based on a prototypical project model, cash flows are reduced from $129.20 per barrel of bitumen (in inflation-adjusted 2014 dollars) to $76.20, and operating costs increase by $3.22 per barrel largely as a result of greenhouse gas compliance costs. This reduces the rate of return from the project significantly, although importantly the project remains bankable as a result of higher underlying oil prices in the IEA 450 ppm scenario published in 2014 – about $100 per barrel in inflation-adjusted terms.[8]

In an era of more stringent greenhouse gas policies, there will still be significant oil consumption, potentially at prices comparable to today's: the IEA forecast sees prices above $100 per barrel in inflation-adjusted terms and oil production of 76 million barrels per day under their 450 ppm scenario through 2035. The question for Canada is whether our ability to manufacture energy will allow us to remain competitive in a world where high-cost and high-emissions oil will be penalized. In order to ensure this is the case, Canada's policies must be designed to prepare our oil industry for a carbon-constrained world, and not designed in an ill-conceived attempt to protect the industry from such a world – this means pricing carbon, or imposing equivalent policies, consistent with global action on climate change and thus ensuring that not only the lowest cost but also the lowest-emissions oil sands resources are those which are produced.

Natural Gas

The other area in which Canada's capacity for manufactured energy will be tested is in the global natural-gas business. Natural gas had, traditionally, been a local market in North America, with only isolated trade in liquefied natural gas on the margins into and out of the United States. Over the past decade, we have seen a 180-degree shift in thinking as to the role of LNG in the future of the North American energy market.

In the 2000s, it was generally accepted that North American natural gas supplies were declining and that the market would become increasingly reliant on imports of LNG. While Canada was still expected to remain a net exporter of gas, only 15 per cent of its domestic production was expected to be exported by 2030, according to the 2006 International Energy Outlook produced by the US Energy Information Administration.[9] At that time, it was generally expected that the United States would be a major importer (up to 4 trillion cubic feet per year) of LNG by 2030.

That world has been completely turned on its head over the past decade, thanks to the so-called shale gas revolution. The ability to extract natural gas from shale using a combination of horizontal drilling and multi-stage hydraulic fracturing has led to significant increases in North American gas reserves and expected future production. Rather than being a net importer of over four trillion cubic feet per day of LNG in 2030, the EIA's 2014 analysis suggests that North America will export approximately four trillion cubic feet of natural gas in 2030, and that the figure will increase further by 2040.[10]

Of course, Canada and the United States are not alone in either the expansion of shale gas or the development of LNG technology. The Canadian Energy Research Institute (CERI) has forecast an increasing of LNG supply to Asia, with potential US and Canadian LNG competing with volumes from Australia and East Africa as well as existing supplies from the Middle East.[11] There are three primary factors which will determine the degree to which Canadian LNG can compete in these markets: the capital costs for liquefaction facilities, operating costs of liquefaction, and well-head costs of Canadian gas. What's crucial here is that any potential increase in value for Canadian resources (the gas in the ground) will come from manufacturing and subsurface extraction productivity – lower costs equals higher rents.

That relationship is discussed in CERI's 2013 report, which shows that assuming that facilities generate their liquefaction power from natural gas, up to $5 per million British Thermal Units (MMBtu) of the cost of the delivered LNG would be in liquefaction. As CERI's long-run price analysis is based upon an Asian LNG contract of $10.50 per MMBtu, the margins for Canadian LNG on that basis look perilously thin, if not negative. Even using a Japanese-crude-cocktail-linked gas price, which yields an extra $3 per MMBtu at early 2014s prices, the margin available for Canadian gas would be approximately $2 per MMBtu. After the collapse in oil prices, with natural gas in Asia trading much lower today than in 2014, the economics of export projects look even more speculative. Any additional capital or operating costs in liquefaction place the Canadian industry at significant risk.

The world LNG market is changing – historically, the business model involved long-term offtake contracts for supplies of gas, priced based on oil. The contracts largely protected the projects from downside risks – the project had a minimum, built-in margin which would pay for the costs of liquefaction under most circumstances.

Two models are expected to take hold on Canada's west coast – first, one whereby shippers or buyers would agree to long-term liquefaction contracts with merchant LNG plants (Kitimat LNG, for example), and the second involving vertically integrated projects like LNG Canada, which links Shell's upstream assets to downstream markets. The majority of the proposed plants on the west coast are now either owned by, or joint ventures of, companies with large gas-producing asset positions as well, which effectively creates a well-to-tanker supply chain. This implies that the value of the natural gas in BC and in Alberta is intrinsically linked not only to the LNG spot or contract price these facilities can negotiate, but also to the capital and operating efficiency of liquefaction. LNG produced on the BC coast will have to compete with other LNG producers such as Qatar and Australia, but also with land-based Asian sources as the shale gas revolution becomes more global. The first sign of this local competition emerged in 2014 as Russia announced a massive natural-gas-supply deal with China.

In the case of natural gas, unlike the oil sands, the manufacturing component (processing and liquefaction) is directly linked to access to world markets. However, the fact that the capacity for manufacturing will determine the value of the underlying resource remains the same. Natural gas also differs from oil in that, while it is a carbon-based fuel, it is also a less carbon-intensive substitute for coal, and potentially for oil, in power generation and transportation. The International Energy Agency predicts a decline in natural gas demand relative to a scenario with no climate change policies; but there is more scope for global natural gas markets to grow from today's levels under global greenhouse-gas constraints consistent with a 450 ppm or 2 degrees Celsius trajectory.

Renewables

Over the history of Canadian manufacturing, as mentioned earlier, Canada was able to compete globally due to the immense hydro-electric resources which allowed electricity to be made available cheaply while the costs of generation are still recovered, at least on average. Today's renewable energy growth is in other sources – wind and solar – both of which have far broader resource distribution and relative lack of exploitation compared to reservoir hydroelectricity. What will determine success in the renewable energy markets of tomorrow is the ability to manufacture energy, and by extension the ability to manufacture energy-manufacturing technology. Canada's non-hydro renewable energy market is still growing and relatively new, but at this point there are significant challenges.

From a solar energy perspective, Canada's latitude means that our resource availability is relatively poor and highly seasonal. Furthermore, with the exception of Southern Ontario, our best solar resources are in the Prairie provinces, where populations are sparse. As a result, the supply chain for manufactured energy from solar radiation is long and expensive. Given the mobility of technology, it is hard to see how Canada's market could evolve in this space in any meaningful way, relative to the global market; but it may still prove an important source of domestic electricity supply.

Wind energy faces some of the same conditions in Canada – our best wind resources are in remote, northern areas, in the western mountains, in the great lakes, and on the east coast. Perhaps the most potential for growth is in the North, where excellence in manufactured energy from wind – with effective storage for cold climates – could provide a real advantage for northern communities now reliant on expensive fossil fuels. There is also significant potential in the densely populated areas around the Great Lakes, and in Alberta and British Columbia.

Conclusions and Policy Recommendations

While Canada's history has seen us rely on cheap energy and a skilled labour force to build a manufacturing-based economy, we could see the tables turned on us. Canada is blessed with a world-scale endowment of resources, but getting those resources to market in useable form is going to depend on our ability to manufacture energy. If we are unable to process our resources, converting them to products which can reach world markets, we will see this tremendous resource wealth devalued. This is not, by any means, a case of forcing more processing in Canada – quite the opposite. The largest barrier to realizing Canada's resource promise is the cost of extracting those resources and moving them to world markets. It is hardly a solution to that problem to demand more costly processing. In fact, what we need in order to realize the rents from these resources are the lowest-cost means of extraction, processing, transportation, and, where necessary, upgrading these resources. The more we are able to do so, the more value Canada will realize from its energy resources in an era of manufactured energy.

What policies will allow Canada to realize this potential? First and foremost, a *lack* of policies which seek to maintain existing sectors' market shares or to shift resources away from sectors which can make the most use of them. A mandate to keep labour in auto manufacturing versus oil sands or a mandate to maintain the size of the oil and gas sector at the expense of renewables will result in long-term losses. Second, excellence in manufacturing is not

synonymous with forcing more of it – while we may see significant advantages in increasing productivity in oil sands extraction,
we could also erode that advantage by forcing further processing
to synthetic crude of refine products here at home. Finally, as has
been mentioned above and in other chapters in this volume, we
must prepare Canada's industry for a carbon-constrained world –
this means a carbon policy for Canada which, if applied globally,
would reach global goals. We must cease to look at carbon policy
through a lens of maintaining our existing industries, and ask what
industries would thrive under well-designed carbon policies. With
these changes in place, Canada's resource sector will be positioned
to thrive in an era of manufactured energy.

chapter five

Brown Meets Green: How Can Canada's Resource-Intensive Economy Prosper in a Low-Carbon World?

STEWART ELGIE

The world is moving towards a low-carbon, "greener" economy. Companies (and countries) that are energy efficient, low polluting, eco-innovative, and that conserve scarce natural capital will prosper in this emerging economy. We expect to hear such forecasts from traditional "green" voices. But in recent years that prediction, phrased in different ways, has come from many of the world's most respected economic and business authorities, such as the OECD,[1] World Bank,[2] International Energy Agency,[3] McKinsey & Co.,[4] and the Canadian Council of Chief Executives.[5] They are not alone. Over 90 per cent of global CEOs believe "sustainability will be important to the future success of their business."[6] Some are even calling this shift the "next industrial revolution." The World Business Council for Sustainable Development, in a report by twenty-nine major global CEOs from fourteen sectors, says: "The transformation ahead represents vast opportunities in a broad range of business segments as the global challenges of growth, urbanization, scarcity and environmental change become the key strategic drivers for business in the coming decade."[7]

Of course, predicting the future is an inexact science. Reasonable people can (and do) debate the *pace* of this economic shift towards sustainability, but there is ample evidence that this shift is already under way. For example, renewable energy, hybrid and electric cars, clean technology, and many other environmental sub-sectors have been growing much faster than both the rest of their sectors and overall GDP in recent years.[8] Even traditional resource industries – such as oil, forestry, and fisheries – have experienced unprecedented market pressures to improve their sustainability performance, or pay an economic price.

This chapter starts from the premise that this shift towards greener growth is a likely scenario for the world's economic trajectory in coming decades, and that countries would be wise to prepare for it. If this is so, then what does it mean for Canada? Should we see this change more as a threat (as some of our leaders do) or an opportunity? Is it possible for a resource-intensive ("brown") economy to prosper in a greening world?

This chapter argues that it *is* possible, and that Canada should pursue this opportunity – albeit in a strategic way, based on our comparative advantages. But doing so will require a different policy approach, one that moves away from our traditional, cumbersome regulatory tools and uses more flexible tools that can better harness market forces to drive cleaner production and innovation. Economists have a pretty good idea what those tools are (like pricing pollution); the challenge will be mustering the political will to use them. The prospects for this happening at the federal level have seemed dim in recent years, but there are promising signs of provincial leadership, and history shows us that policy leadership in Canada often starts with the provinces, then migrates to Ottawa.

Drivers of the Global Green Economic Shift

Why do so many globally respected economic and business authorities think that we are shifting towards low-carbon, greener growth? And what are its underlying drivers? While many factors affect the world's economy, this shift is being driven largely by two realities. First, global population and GDP have both reached record levels and continue to grow, especially in the developing world. Second, this growth, and the associated economic demand, is placing an unprecedented strain on the planet's finite ecosystems and natural resources. Simply put, economic and population growth are running into environmental and resource scarcity, more than ever before in human history. Scarcity, in turn, drives value

Chapter Summary

Key Global Transformations
- The world is moving towards a low-carbon, "greener" economy; companies (and countries) that are energy efficient, low polluting, and eco-innovative, and that conserve scarce natural capital will prosper in this emerging economy.
- This shift is being driven largely by two conflating realities: first, global population and GDP have both reached record levels, and continue to grow, especially in the developing world; and second, this growth, and the associated economic demand, is placing an unprecedented strain on the planet's finite ecosystems and natural resources.
- Companies that find innovative ways to respond to this growing environmental and resource scarcity – by producing goods and services with a lower environmental and more efficient use of natural resources – will gain a competitive edge.

Implications for Canada
- The key challenge is that Canada has a fairly high-carbon, resource-intensive economy in an increasingly low-carbon, resource-efficient world.
- Canada should see the global shift not as a threat but as an economic opportunity, and respond by crafting our own vision of what it means to be both a green *and* a resource-intensive economy.
- This vision should include building strategic strengths in emerging clean-energy and tech sectors, but also taking advantage of our wealth of natural resources by building a niche as the most environmentally responsible producer.
- Doing this will push our industries to become more efficient and innovative in how they extract and process resources, manufacture products, and manage wastes; innovating around low-impact resource extraction and processing (and related skills and services) could be a great niche for Canada.
- Also, the wealth derived from our resources can be a vital source of funds to help bolster investment in a more diversified, advanced, cleaner economy that is less vulnerable to the volatility of commodity prices (as we have experienced).

Recommendations

- To position Canada for success in this changing global economy requires creating incentives that will drive corporate investment towards cleaner energy, technologies, and processes, and nudge consumers towards lower-carbon choices for homes, transportation, and appliances.
- The key goal is to decouple economic growth from environmental harm; doing this will require a mix of public policies and investments, including:
  - Integrated planning across government
  - Pricing carbon (and eliminating fossil fuel subsidies)
  - Public investment/incentives for clean energy and tech
  - Low-carbon infrastructure (energy grid, transportation, etc.)
  - Research (emphasizing clean innovation)
  - Smart regulation (e.g., energy-efficiency codes for buildings, cars, appliances)
  - Information (labelling, corporate reporting, green national accounts, etc.)
  - Training and skills (for a lower-carbon economy)
- Carbon pricing is an essential starting point; it is the most cost-effective way to reduce greenhouse gas emissions and accelerate clean innovation across the economy.
- While the federal government has resisted carbon pricing to date, provinces are taking the lead; several provinces have brought in their own regimes, and others may soon follow.
- This is consistent with many other historical examples (like medicare) of policy leadership starting in the provinces, then migrating to Ottawa, and with the global trend towards climate policy leadership coming from sub-national governments.

– a basic law of economics. Companies that find innovative ways to respond to this environmental and resource scarcity – by producing goods and services with a lower environmental and more efficient use of natural resources – will gain a competitive edge.

Of course, not all resources are becoming scarce and not all environmental problems are hitting critical thresholds, but more and more are. The widely cited Millennium Ecosystem Assessment concluded (conservatively) in 2005 that "more than 60 per cent of the Earth's ecosystem services are being degraded or used unsustainably."[9] For example, greenhouse gas (GHG) emissions, freshwater use, biodiversity loss, and deforestation are all at or approaching critical threshold levels across much of the planet. At the same time, overall commodity (resource) prices have roughly doubled in past fifteen years after a century of general decline (see figure 5.1). Though some cyclicality will no doubt remain (as we've seen recently with oil prices), this lengthy, atypical trend of rising resource prices is a strong sign of growing overall resource scarcity – and, in many cases, indicates that accessing the remaining resources is becoming more costly and difficult (e.g., oil sands, arctic offshore oil, remote forests).

This growing environmental and resource scarcity means that natural capital is increasingly becoming a limiting factor to economic growth on a wide scale. And we will respond to this natural capital scarcity much the same way we have to human capital (labour) scarcity: with a growing emphasis on finding more efficient, innovative, and productive ways to use these limited resources. Those that do better at this will win the competitiveness race.

What Does This Low-Carbon Global Shift Mean for Canada?

Let us start by naming the elephant in the room: Canada is a high carbon emitter and producer in an increasingly carbon-constrained world. We have an economy that, relative to other developed nations, (a) is heavy on oil, gas, and natural resource production, and (b) ranks near the highest in terms of carbon emissions, air pollution, and material consumption per capita among OECD countries.[10] Simply put, we have a fairly brown economy in a greening world. Given our economic mix, how should Canada respond to the growing global focus on sustainability – not just the environmental challenges, but also the economic ones? In particular, how can we reconcile these seemingly contradictory pulls, of mounting environmental stresses and rising resource demand (and value)?

Our current national conversation juxtaposes two different schools of thought on this question. One (advocated by some environmental groups) calls for a swift transition to a green, low-carbon economy that emphasizes clean energy, electric cars, and other clean technologies, while phasing out fossil fuels.[11] The other

Figure 5.1 Resource prices have increased significantly since the turn of the century*

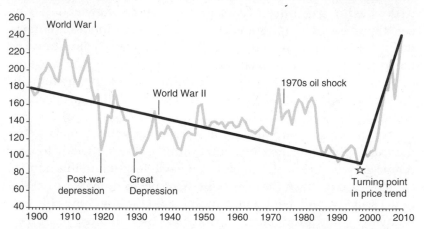

* McKinsey Commodity Price Index (years 1991–2001 = 100), based on arithmetic average of four commodity sub-indexes: food, non-food agricultural raw materials, metals, and energy
Source: McKinsey Global Institute, *Resource Revolution: Tracking Global Commodity Market-trends Survey 2013*, http://www.mckinsey.com/insights/energy_resources_materials/resource_revolution_tracking_global_commodity_markets. Reprinted with permission.

proposes boosting our production and export of natural resources, particularly oil, even in the face of rising environmental and aboriginal concerns (more or less the view of the Harper government).[12] These two paths tend to be seen as contradictory: a binary choice between green growth and conventional (brown) growth. But they need not be. If done right, the two can be mutually reinforcing strategies to position Canada for economic and environmental success in a greening global marketplace.

We should aim to accelerate the growth of Canada's clean technology sectors – building on our educated workforce, research and development capacity, and other advantages. But those sectors, even with rapid growth, will probably remain fairly small parts of the economy, at least for the next few decades. Moreover, many bigger countries – such as the United States, China, and Germany – are trying to be leaders in this same space. Canada needs to be realistic about identifying our best niches. At the same time, it is in Canada's economic interest to take advantage of the growing global demand for our energy and natural resources, but not by giving short shrift to the environment.

While some may argue that streamlining environmental rules and resisting new ones – like carbon pricing – is an economically expedient strategy, this view is dangerously short-sighted, for two main reasons. First, Canada's increasingly imperilled environmental reputation is becoming a growing economic risk, as evidenced by the stalled Keystone pipeline (costing us $10–$20 billion annually in lost revenues).[13] Meanwhile, our failure to price carbon is impeding investment in promising low-carbon solutions. For example, TransAlta pulled out of a $1.4 billion carbon-capture project in 2012 because of a carbon price insufficient to make it viable.[14] Second, that approach misunderstands Canada's comparative advantage in global resource markets. Our niche is not to be the fastest, cheapest producer of oil, minerals, or forest products. Other less developed (and less democratic) countries will out-compete us for low wages, low environmental standards, and speedy project approval. The better opportunity – one that we can realistically achieve – is to *position ourselves as the most environmentally responsible and innovative producer of resource products, including oil.* This is a great niche for Canada. It aligns with the way the world already wants to see us – as a "green" country. In marketing terms, it plays to our "brand" (which we have not been doing) and positions us where global markets are going.

To be clear, we must be mindful that the world as a whole will need to limit the extraction of oil and some other scarce resources (e.g., wild fish stocks). Canada should support such global efforts. However, to the extent that the world consumes oil (as it will for at least several decades) and other resources, Canada should position itself as the most environmentally responsible producer – setting an example for how to do it right.

Canada's forest industry has already realized this opportunity. Back in the 1990s, it was the global environmental piñata, as the oil sands are now. After more than a decade of economic bloodshed, the industry decided to change its basic economic model and to see sustainability as an opportunity rather than a threat. Many Canadian firms have since become global leaders in sustainable forestry, and environmental non-governmental organizations (NGOs) that once fought them now help to promote their products.[15]

In short, Canada should regard the global shift towards a low-carbon, resource efficient economy not as a threat, but as an economic opportunity. We should craft our own vision of what it means to be a green *and* resource-intensive economy. This includes building strategic strengths in emerging clean energy and tech sectors. It also means taking advantage of our wealth of natural resources, by building a niche as the most environmentally responsible producer. Doing this will push our industries to become more efficient and innovative in how they extract and process resources, manufacture products, and manage wastes. Those innovations themselves will create value, which can yield jobs and exports. Innovating around low-impact resource extraction and processing (and related manufacturing, skills, and services) could be a great niche for Canada. Moreover, the wealth derived from our resources can be a vital source of funds to help bolster investment in a more diversified, advanced, cleaner economy that is less vulnerable to the volatility of commodity prices.

What Should Canada Do to Position Itself for a Low-Carbon Global Economy?

What kinds of policies are needed to build a cleaner Canadian economy that is positioned for success in changing global markets? A full answer to that question goes beyond this space, but in a nutshell, it requires creating incentives that will drive corporate investment towards cleaner energy, technologies, and processes, and will nudge consumers towards lower-carbon choices for homes, transportation, and appliances. The key policy goal must be to decouple economic growth from environmental harm. While we tend to equate economic growth with greater environmental harm, but that does not have to be the case. For instance, by shifting towards energy from renewable sources, electric cars, or recycled paper, an economy can generate products and services that meet the same needs, but with much lower environmental and resource impacts.

No country has yet fully achieved decoupling, or tried in earnest to do so, yet there are many examples of limited successes in which countries (including Canada) have managed to significantly reduce certain types of environmental harm without impeding economic growth. For example:

- From 1990 to 2010, Canada cut SO_2 and NO_x emissions, which cause acid rain, by over 60 per cent[16] – from energy, manufacturing, and transportation – while experiencing robust economic growth.
- From 2005 to 2012, Ontario reduced its GHG emissions by 19 per cent,[17] mainly by shutting its coal power plants, while its GDP grew by almost 10 per cent.
- From 2001 to 2009, Australia reduced water consumption by 40 per cent, while GDP grew by more than 30 per cent.[18]
- From 1990 to 2010, Western European countries reduced GHG emissions by 11 per cent, and even slightly reduced total material consumption, while their economy grew by 39 per cent.[19]

These limited successes (which resulted from limited efforts) suggest that decoupling growth from carbon emissions and other environmental harm on a broader, longer scale *is* possible, with a genuine effort and the right policies. Which policies? There are many recent studies and reports on this question (see page 81) yielding a fair amount of agreement on the answer. The list of key policy tools includes the following, with the optimal mix varying by issue and other factors:

- Integrated planning across government (with goals and benchmarks).
- Pricing carbon (and eliminating fossil fuel subsidies).
- Public investment/incentives for clean energy and tech (to correct market failures).
- Low-carbon infrastructure (energy grid, transportation, etc.).
- Research (emphasize low-carbon innovation).
- Smart regulation (e.g., energy-efficiency codes for buildings, cars, appliances).

- Information (labelling, corporate reporting, green national accounts, etc.).
- Training and skills (for a lower-carbon economy).

While all these tools – and their mix – are important, most studies say that carbon pricing is particularly critical as the foundation for a low-carbon transition.[20]

Carbon Pricing

Broadly speaking, there are many benefits to using more flexible regulatory tools – as opposed to the prescriptive, "one size fits all" approaches that have dominated environmental policy in Canada and the United States since the 1970s (often called "command and control"). Particularly effective are environmental fees, taxes, emissions trading, and other market-based instruments. In the words of the International Monetary Fund: "Fiscal instruments (carbon taxes or similar) are the most effective policies for reflecting environmental costs in energy prices and promoting development of cleaner technologies."[21] These instruments correct the fact that markets fail to put a price on carbon pollution (and most environmental harm). This fundamental market failure – long recognized by economists – is probably the main cause of unsustainable behaviour.

Well-designed market-based instruments (MBIs) have three main advantages over conventional "command and control" regulations.[22] First, they can achieve environmental goals at the *lowest cost*. A price on carbon gives firms and households the flexibility to decide where, when, and how to make carbon-reducing changes, and so they will be done as cost-effectively as possible. (And if the price is set right, it can achieve the desired environmental goals.) For example, the projected US costs of reducing GHGs through a carbon price are 90 per cent lower than through conventional regulation.[23]

Second, MBIs are much better at spurring *clean innovation* – which will be critical to success in a low-carbon global economy. A conventional, across-the-board emission limit motivates firms only to reach that standard; much like a speed limit, there is no incentive to go further. When carbon is priced, firms get an extra reward for every tonne they reduce, and there is an incentive to find new, lower-cost ways to keep cutting emissions, because the firm will make more money. Whereas conventional regulatory approaches engage the compliance side of a firm, market-based instruments tap into the profit-generating, innovative part of a firm. They can unleash the effort and creative genius of the market towards solving environmental problems.

Third, MBIs are more nimble and far-reaching than regulation. A carbon price ripples through the economy, influencing a vast array of choices by firms and households. To try to reach all those activities by conventional regulation, one at a time, would be practically impossible.

There is a broad base of evidence supporting the benefits of market-based instruments. A prime example, close to home, is British Columbia's carbon tax, which came into force in July 2008. It started at a low price ($10 per tonne of CO_2) and ramped up gradually, reaching $30 per tonne (about 7 cents per litre of gas) in 2012, where it now stands. Also, all the revenues from the carbon tax, by law, must be offset by cuts to corporate and personal income taxes. Plus, BC gives additional breaks to low-income and rural residents, who are disproportionately affected by the tax.

In its first five years, the tax shift seems to have been remarkably effective at reducing the use of fossil fuels (whose combustion emits greenhouse gases).[24] Since it came into effect, BC's per capita use of fuels covered by the tax has declined by 16.1 per cent – while it went *up* by 3 per cent in the rest of Canada (see figure 5.2). While it is premature to firmly conclude that the carbon tax caused all these changes, the evidence indicates that it is a major driver of BC's fuel-efficiency gains.

Furthermore, the policy does not appear to have hurt the economy. Since the tax came in, BC's GDP growth has slightly outpaced the rest of Canada's (by 0.47 per cent from 2008 to 2013). And by using the carbon revenues to finance other tax cuts, the province now has Canada's lowest income tax rate and one of the lowest corporate rates in North America. In effect, the carbon tax shift has enabled BC to successfully decouple economic growth from fuel use and carbon emissions.

Figure 5.2 Sales of fuels subject to BC carbon tax (2000–2013)

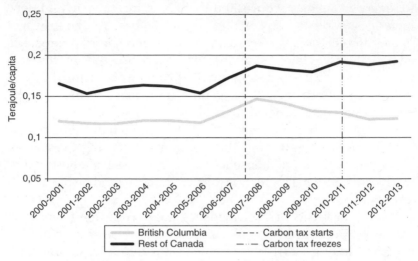

Source: Elgie, "Just the Facts" (2014)

These results are not surprising. Similar changes happened in six European countries that have brought in similar carbon-tax shifts over the past two decades. A major econometric study, funded by the European Union, found that in all six cases the tax shift led to GHG reductions (up to 6 per cent) and had a small, *positive* overall effect on GDP.[25]

The other main carbon pricing instrument is cap and trade. Quebec has recently implemented such a system – too recently to evaluate its effects – but well-designed cap and trade systems can be very effective. For example, the US Acid Rain program, the world's first large-scale emissions trading experiment, achieved 25 per cent greater reductions of SO_2 and NO_x at about half the cost of conventional regulations – saving over $1 billion per year.[26] By contrast, Europe's carbon trading system has experienced major price volatility[27] due to design flaws, which weakens long-term investment in low-carbon technologies and products (and it remains unclear if those investments will pay off with such a variable carbon price). This problem, however, can be minimized with smart policy design, such as a price floor and/or ceiling, as in Quebec's system.[28]

Figure 5.3 Environmentally related tax revenue in OECD countries and select others (2012)

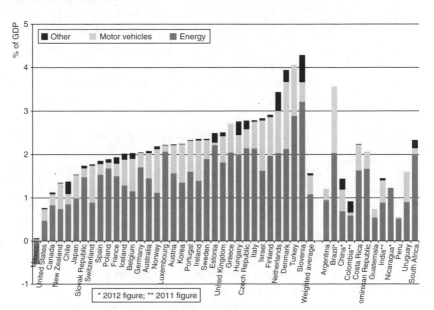

Source: OECD, *Green Growth Indicators 2014*, OECD Green Growth Studies (OECD Publishing, 2014). http://www.oecd-ilibrary.org/environment/green-growth-indicators-2013_9789264202030-en

In short, well-designed market-based instruments are a critical policy tool for building a prosperous, low-carbon economy. However, Canada lags behind other most other developed countries (and many developing ones) in their use, as figure 5.3 shows. The OECD regularly criticizes Canada for this shortcoming.[29]

There are many reasons why these tools have been used so sparingly by Canadian governments. One is simply policy inertia. Canada built up its environmental regulatory system around a mostly "command and control" approach in the 1970s, when such tools were in vogue, and has been resistant to change that path since then, with limited exceptions. By contrast, other nations with similar path dependence have been better at overcoming it, including European countries (with greater use of eco-taxes) and the United States (with greater use of pollution markets).

Another, more recent cause is the perception that carbon taxes are a political non-starter. This perception is fuelled, in large part by the (incorrect) belief that Stéphane Dion lost the 2008 federal election because of his carbon-tax-shift proposal. However, this perception is at odds with real-world experience. In BC – the place that actually passed a carbon tax – it caused no political harm. Gordon Campbell's Liberals were re-elected in 2009 with a small increase in seats, as many pro-environment voters deserted the NDP over its vigorous opposition to the carbon tax ("axe the tax"). That tax has since enjoyed a solid majority of public support, in a province not known for its love of new taxes.[30] Moreover, in the other two provinces that have put a price on carbon – Alberta and Quebec – the policies were not even particularly controversial.

Thus, the real-world experience in Canada gives no evidence that carbon pricing policies (if brought in sensibly) are likely to be politically harmful. Polls continue to show that a majority of Canadians support a carbon price.[31] Moreover, many prominent business and economic voices[32] have been calling for a carbon price, including major banks (e.g., TD), oil companies (e.g., Suncor), the Canadian Council of Chief Executives (in its "Clean Growth" report), and hundreds of Canadian economists.[33]

What, then, explains Canada's carbon pricing inertia? Oft-heard explanations are that we have a large fossil fuel industry and that our major trading partner has not priced carbon. While both of these factors are true, other countries facing similar challenges have successfully priced carbon, including Norway, which has had a large carbon tax since 1991, and Mexico. As noted, moreover, the province most affected by these factors, Alberta, also has a carbon price (albeit a modest one).

Rather, a major reason for Canada's inaction seems to be that our federal government has been ideologically resistant to carbon pricing. In 2008, the Conservatives under Stephen Harper fought and won an election opposing it. Although the Harper government briefly flirted with the idea of a carbon price (via a technology fund) in 2007 when it was in a minority and public concern for climate change was at its peak.[34] As the economic downturn of 2008–9 and subsequent shaky recovery pushed climate concerns down the public priority list, the Harper government again dug in its heels against a carbon price – saying it would "destroy jobs and growth."[35] (It did, however, impose carbon limits on cars and coal power plants, consistent with its stated aim of aligning with US regulations.).

As the economy's health returns, governments are again turning their attention to climate policy. In Canada, this is happening mainly at the provincial and local levels. In particular, Ontario has indicated that it will soon bring in carbon pricing.[36] If that were to happen, Canada's four largest provinces would have a carbon price – and others might soon join them. The provincial premiers, in summer 2014, committed to develop a coordinated, Canada-wide climate and energy strategy.[37]

This provincial climate policy leadership, in part, reflects the policy vacuum that has been left by the federal government on this issue. But Canada is not alone in this situation. In the United States and Australia, state-level carbon pricing policies preceded federal action (and in Australia's case, outlasted it). The same is now happening in China and Japan, with large cities moving first with cap-and-trade systems. Even in the European Union, a handful of individual countries moved first, introducing carbon taxes before the EU-wide carbon trading system came in.

On one hand, this preponderance of sub-national (or sub-EU) policy leadership may seem less than ideal, given that climate change is a quintessentially global problem. It also results in an uneven patchwork of standards and approaches, with gaps. On the other hand, this regional (and local) leadership may, at least in part, reflect the fact that climate policy is fundamentally about an economic transition – a transition of energy, industrial, and urban systems and the related infrastructure.[38] In Canada, as in the United States, Australia, and Europe, these energy, industrial, and urban systems tend to differ by region, often greatly. For example, provinces dependent on coal power face very different challenges in shifting to a low-carbon economy than ones with abundant hydropower. Moreover, control over these systems tends to rest mainly with provinces or states, either though ownership (of fossil fuels, energy utilities) or regulatory authority (over energy, cities, and most industrial activity).

In short, the fact that a low-carbon transition mainly involves systems of great regional importance, and is subject to regional differences and control, may help to explain why there has been such regional leadership. Even though national governments have authority to regulate greenhouse gas emissions, the political economy of the issue lends itself to regionally tailored solutions, at least initially.

It is also worth noting that such provincial leadership has occurred in other areas of environmental law, such as environmental assessment and endangered species, and on other issues, such as public medicare. In those cases, several provinces moved first and tested different policy approaches, after which the federal government came in with a law, filling in regional gaps and setting a national base level of protection, without crowding out provincial laws. Such an approach could work well for carbon pricing. A federal law could ensure a coordinated national approach, with no regional gaps, designed to meet Canada's overall target, but also allow for provincial variation in approaches (e.g., tax, trade, or other systems).

The bigger issue, regardless of what level of government leads, is whether Canada will make the fundamental policy changes needed for our economy to prosper in an increasingly low-carbon, resource-efficient global marketplace. It will not be easy. Economic transitions never are. But there are some good historical examples to draw on. In the late 1980s and 1990s, Canadian governments took far-sighted policy action to get out ahead of the global shifts towards free trade and deficit reduction. Those actions were not politically easy, but they gave Canada a solid economic foundation that helped us to weather, and to prosper in, the ensuing two decades of global economic change.

Preparing for a low-carbon future is an analogous challenge – perhaps even greater, since it goes to the core energy source that has fuelled our modern industrial economy. What lessons can we learn from these previous examples? Can our governments muster the same kind of policy leadership we saw in the 1990s, and do so in a time when governments seem much less inclined (and able) to lead on major policy change?

chapter six

Meeting Global Demand for Institutional Innovation in Internet Governance

MARK RAYMOND

It is commonplace to acknowledge that the rapid adoption and development of information and communications technologies (ICTs) is reconfiguring many, if not most, areas of human life. These technologies, and the social disruptions they create, are generating demand for institutional innovation at the domestic, regional, and global levels. This chapter surveys challenges associated with meeting global demand for institutional innovation in both traditional questions of technical Internet governance and broader issues of Internet-related public policy. This distinction recognizes the difficulties created by the increasing integration of Internet technologies into every area of human society. It will become increasingly difficult to govern the Internet without effectively governing financial markets, privacy, and public safety – just as it will be increasingly difficult to govern these essential issue areas without at least potentially affecting the stability and interoperability of the Internet itself.

Across a range of policy issues, from Internet naming and numbering to cybersecurity and privacy, the basic challenge is to effectively apply and alter social rules. The analysis in this chapter therefore applies to those areas, as well as to others such as competition policy and international trade. As I will suggest, however, there are grounds to expect these rule-making exercises will remain complex and contentious. Dealing effectively and intelligently with these complications will require a particular kind of Canadian international strategy. This strategy should begin with a concerted effort to generate and disseminate knowledge about the governance implications of ICTs. It should also entail a patient, flexible approach to rule-making that privileges soft-law instruments.

Chapter Summary

Key Transformations
- Rapid development of Information and Communications Technologies (ICTs) will disrupt most areas of human life over the next several decades.
- These disruptions will lead to increasing demand for institutional innovation, from multiple actors and in numerous fora.

Implications for Canada
- Actors, including states, will need to participate in complex and contentious processes of global rule making, interpretation, and application in order to update institutions in light of technological disruption.
- They will need to do so in the face of serious legitimacy and trust deficits.

Recommendations
- Invest in a sustained process bringing together experts on ICTs and international relations with government officials (from Canada and beyond) for an intensive learning process about the governance implications both of ICTs and of particular potential institutional responses.
- Adopt a patient, flexible approach to rule making that privileges soft-law instruments, in order to allow procedural innovation and to maximize the ability to adapt to future developments.
- Work to establish baseline agreement among all actors on the principle of doing no harm to global Internet interoperability.
- Work to establish baseline agreement among all actors on the secondary principle of a "responsibility to troubleshoot" in the event of negative externalities for global Internet interoperability.

Global Demand for Institutional Innovation

Internet penetration is proceeding rapidly throughout the developing world. While the "digital divide" will persist, the centre of gravity of the global Internet user base is shifting south and east along with the centre of gravity of the global economy.[1] In the short term, these new Internet users are highly likely to retain their pre-existing (non-Western) values; there is no guarantee of cultural convergence. As the Internet is a product of the perspectives of the users who create much of its content, the Internet's future will be unlike its past. To the extent that Internet governance retains its distributed, privatized nature, decisions about how the Internet should be governed are also likely to reflect these values. This is not to say that digital authoritarianism is predestined. Generalizing about the political views of Internet users in the developing world is an impossible task, and there are staunch advocates of an open Internet throughout the world. However, the rapid expansion of Internet access in states with large populations and weak democratic traditions suggests that changes in the demographic composition of Internet users may reinforce troubling trends with respect to online freedom.

Internet technology is also changing rapidly. These technologies are notable for their potential to increase economic productivity, enhance public safety, and facilitate real-time monitoring of human rights abuses, among many other potential benefits.[2] However, they are also capable of undermining privacy, placing a great deal of sensitive information in the hands of large firms, and creating attractive targets for cybercriminals.

These underlying technological and demographic trends are not susceptible to change as a result of policy initiatives by any single state, let alone a small state such as Canada. However, they are also indeterminate. Demography is not destiny, and the social implications of any new technology depend on the uses to which it is put. As a result, it is impossible to move directly from observations of these trends to conclusions about policy. Instead, it is necessary to examine relevant political trends.

The dominant political trend relevant to Internet governance and Internet-related public policy is an increasing number of demands for institutional innovation. An array of actors has already begun to act on these demands. Examples include the negotiation of new regulations for international telephony at the World Congress on International Telecommunications (WCIT); the work of the United Nations Group of Governmental Experts on cybersecurity; the efforts of the Internet Corporation for Assigned Names and Numbers (ICANN) and the German and Brazilian governments, culminating in NETmundial; the WSIS+10 preparatory process; and Internet-related dimensions of ongoing international trade negotiations, such as the Trans-Pacific Partnership (TPP) and the US-EU free trade talks. Some of these processes are still ongoing, and it remains premature to make conclusions about their success or failure. Crucially, though, there is no reason to believe that efforts to make international rules for Internet governance or Internet-related aspects of public policy will cease in the near future. One example is the recent NETmundial meeting, where the most that could be attained was a hortatory document that outlined a "roadmap for the future evolution" of Internet governance.[3]

Obstacles to Meeting Global Demand for Institutional Innovation

There are also good reasons to expect such rule-making efforts to be complex and conflict-prone. In this section, I briefly outline some relevant observations from social science. The policy implications of these findings will be discussed in the conclusion. The first such observation is the increasing incidence of distributional conflict between parties. These kinds of problems exist at both the domestic and international levels, and governments often find themselves attempting to strike bargains that balance the interests of parties at both levels.[4] Given the importance of the Internet to daily life, and the potential for national decisions about Internet regulation to have negative externalities for the effective operation of a globally interoperable network of networks, it is highly likely that policymakers will routinely face complex bargaining scenarios involving foreign and domestic actors.

The severity of distributional conflicts varies across issue areas and over time. Some situations are characterized by more tractable problems involving the development and implementation of shared standards, while others are characterized by the possibility of exploiting cooperative players in order to maximize short-term gains.[5] Issues with the former structure have lower levels of conflict and more robust cooperation. They are also often governed by, or have substantial input from, transnational expert networks.[6] Examples include the International Postal Union and the International Civil Aviation Organization.

The Internet has essentially been governed in this manner for most of its history. These legacy governance arrangements reflect its origins in academic research conducted primarily in the United States, and the fact that it initially had no obvious mass social purpose; few parties had clear interests in specific Internet governance outcomes.[7] These conditions no longer obtain.

As it grew in importance, the Internet became too important to leave entirely to technologists, prompting increased interest from firms and from states. Accordingly, Internet governance and Internet-related public policy issues are increasingly characterized by conflict over who gets what. While portrayals of monolithic blocs were overly simplistic, the December 2012 World Conference on International Telecommunications demonstrated that Internet issues had become contentious in a way they had not previously been. Difficulty agreeing on modalities for the decennial review of the World Summit on the Information Society, as well as civil-society disappointment over the outcome document for the recent NETmundial meeting in Brazil, indicate that these discussions are likely to remain highly contentious.[8]

Generating agreement among parties with diverse interests is inherently challenging. The rapid entry of many new participants raises further difficulties associated with large numbers of players.[9] These new entrants include many developing world states, as well as firms outside the technology sector that are increasingly affected by their growing reliance on ICTs.

Dealing effectively with large numbers is only one of several challenges that ultimately stem from complexity and uncertainty. Another such problem is that processes of institutional innovation are nonlinear, dominated by unintended consequences and therefore difficult to predict.[10] Even the most powerful actors seldom get everything they want and even when they do they often find the gains realized are not what they had initially hoped. These problems are exacerbated by high levels of uncertainty.[11] This last point is critical to understanding the contemporary challenges posed by Internet governance and Internet-related aspects of public policy, since the implications of ICTs are often unclear, especially to policymakers who often lack technical knowledge.[12] Accordingly, it is hard for policymakers to determine what kind of rule-sets their states should want *ex ante*, whether they will be able to realize those preferred outcomes, and whether a theoretically preferable outcome will yield anything like the desired results.

Effective rule-making on Internet issues is also being hampered by conceptual misunderstandings. One such example is the belief that the cyber domain is an ungoverned "Wild West" where anything goes, as Jonathan Paquin suggests elsewhere in this volume. This view overlooks the legacy mechanisms of Internet governance, without which the Internet could not exist. The Internet is, and always has been, governed. However, it is governed in a decentralized and highly privatized manner. Another example is the belief that the Internet is a commons. Unlike a commons, the Internet is excludable and generally not rivalrous.[13] It is more accurately conceptualized as a set of nested clubs.[14] The commons analogy often serves the political purpose of maintaining open access. However, the trade-off is that it misdirects attention to the classic commons problem of preventing destruction by overuse. It also suggests a single resource managed in a centralized or at least unitary manner. This mental model is a poor fit to the reality of a highly decentralized Internet governance ecosystem.

Attempts to create sound Internet-related policy are also hampered by a monolithic understanding of the multi-stakeholder model of governance. This model is often conflated with ICANN, which in fact only performs a narrow set of functions related to the administration of Internet Protocol (IP) addresses and the Domain Name System (DNS). There is a presumptive norm in favour of multi-stakeholder governance, but this norm is instantiated in varying ways in different institutional contexts. ICANN is established as a non-profit corporation under California law, with a chief executive officer and an elected board, while the Internet Engineering Task Force (IETF) is governed in a much more ad hoc fashion, with much of its work done by volunteer working groups.

The final cluster of issues complicating efforts to effectively deal with Internet-related governance challenges pertains to legitimacy and trust. Such problems have two fundamental sources. The first is that interested actors have widely divergent expectations about legitimate procedural rules for dealing with Internet issues. Advanced industrial democracies generally expect to manage these issues according to a hybrid contemporary global governance framework affording significant latitude, but not complete parity, for the participation of large firms and trusted non-governmental organizations. Russia, China, and to some extent the remaining BRICS states expect deference by virtue of their claims to great power status and also remain relatively more committed to a classical notion of sovereignty that privileges states as the sole actors competent to make rules at the international level. Postcolonial states are generally also keen to preserve their sovereign privileges but more likely than the BRICS states to emphasize formal sovereign equality under international law. Because of their comfort with its procedures and their experience working in a coalition, they also prefer the United Nations as an institutional venue.

These diverse procedural perspectives are nevertheless all state-centric. Internet issues are rendered even more complex by the influence of at least two distinct classes of non-state actors with their own views about legitimate rule-making procedures. Firms, which own the vast majority of global Internet infrastructure and content distribution platforms, operate on the basis of executive decision making, accountability to shareholders, and private contracts as a means to manage external relationships. Civil society and Internet community technical bodies, in contrast, tend to value non-hierarchical, consensus decision-making procedures. These partially incommensurate ideas about legitimate rule-making procedures both help to explain and compound the effect of ambiguity about the content of multi-stakeholder governance models, as actors often apply community-specific standards by default.[15]

The second source of legitimacy and trust deficits is extensive state monitoring of online activity and communication. In foreign policy terms, perhaps the most important effect of the Snowden revelations is that they "undermine Washington's ability [and that of its Five Eyes allies] to act hypocritically and get away with it" by providing "documented confirmation ... of what the United States is actually doing and why."[16] Authoritarian states now have an easy rhetorical "get-out-of-jail-free" card when pushed on their repressive practices, and (especially non-Western) technology firms are provided with an opportunity to portray themselves as consumer champions despite widespread corporate practices that raise similar concerns about the collection, handling, and retention of data.

Implications for Canadian International Strategy

Thus far, I have argued that demographic and technological trends have indeterminate implications for policy and that crafting sound cyber-policy requires analysis of political trends. I have also argued that the dominant political trend in this issue area is a demand for institutional innovation, and that international-relations scholarship offers compelling reasons to expect that efforts to supply such innovation will be contentious. Internet and cyber issues are likely to present some of the thorniest high-stakes problems on the global agenda over the next decade, and the risk of policy failure is real.

Normally, after a survey of the policy environment, an analysis of Canada's international strategy might be expected to specify the interests that strategy should aim to secure. At one level, this is relatively straightforward even with respect to the Internet: Canada clearly has an interest in the maintenance of an open, globally interoperable and responsibly governed Internet. The problem is that such a statement is trivially true. It ignores, for example, that there is little agreement about both the meaning of "openness" and about what a "responsibly governed" Internet looks like in practice. Beyond the difficulty of countervailing values and interests even within Canadian society, there is also the problem that interests are shifting as technology evolves and in response to the actions of other actors. Further, the existence of a great deal of uncertainty about the effects of particular rule-sets on a given state of the world means that the fundamental task of strategy (matching means to desired ends, in light of the preferences and actions of other players) is incredibly difficult. At least at the present time, it is unrealistic to identify either a particular Canadian interest on a diverse and complex set of issues or the means of securing such an interest. For this reason, it is premature to recommend particular institutional responses such as Jonathan Paquin's call for a new multilateral forum to deal with cybersecurity "on the sidelines of the ITU."[17]

In such circumstances, the research surveyed in the previous section suggests that optimal policy responses should prioritize learning and flexibility. The remainder of this chapter will outline two components of an international strategy based on these priorities and will conclude by identifying two minimalist global norms essential to realizing the potential benefits of such a strategy. Canadian international strategy on Internet issues should aim to promote these baseline norms in order to ensure the success of the other strategic elements identified here and to ensure the continued functioning of the Internet in what is likely to be a contentious near-term future.

The first priority of Canadian strategy should be to ensure appropriate levels and kinds of learning. As Joseph Nye has argued, an important parallel can be drawn with the early nuclear period, when programs were created to foster dialogue among scientists, military commanders, and public officials.[18] These programs fostered understanding of a vitally important set of new technologies and their social and policy implications. As in the nuclear case, it is crucial that such learning occur rapidly and, ideally, that it take place in advance of the development of international rules. Learning can identify and remedy conceptual misunderstandings about the Internet and about how it is (and should be) governed.

It is also critical to reducing uncertainty about the implications of ICTs and about interaction effects between new technologies and particular governance models.

Government has a role to play in coordinating scientific resources and ensuring that they are brought into contact with relevant government personnel, especially among the communities of security and intelligence practitioners. Such programs might be modelled on the Minerva Initiative run by the United States Department of Defense or the Academic Centres of Excellence in Cyber Security Research created by the Engineering and Physical Sciences Research Council (EPSRC) of the United Kingdom. It is indispensable that these programs explicitly include and emphasize research on governance issues, and that they include faculty from a range of academic disciplines, including political science, law, history, and economics, in addition to computer science and engineering. Canadian universities provide crucial human-capital resources that should be leveraged in order to meet these emerging challenges. Such an effort must be adequately resourced, and must take an integrative approach rather than one based on identifying niches.

Given radically lower barriers to entry in the cyber domain relative to the nuclear one, and the interconnected nature of the Internet, it is important that learning on Internet issues be distributed as widely as possible. Accordingly, there may be a role for the Canadian Institute for Advanced Research (CIFAR), which could be called upon to convene a global research network on cybersecurity and Internet governance issues. The International Development Research Centre (IDRC) has also done important work on information technology issues; it could assist in disseminating lessons learned throughout the developing world, and ensuring that Canada learns effectively from developing-world experience.

The second element of a sound Canadian international strategy is a patient, flexible approach to rule making that recognizes and advocates for the utility of soft-law approaches in dealing with cyber challenges. Soft law encompasses an array of quasi-legal and diplomatic instruments that stop short of formal international treaties. These include voluntary codes of conduct, the development of shared regulatory approaches or interpretations, and the articulation of norms governing appropriate conduct. This approach stems from a view of the Internet as a series of nested clubs,[19] where rule-making remains decentralized and will continue to occur across levels of analysis, geographic jurisdictions, and institutional contexts. It is thus, above all, a pragmatic approach consistent with at least three reasons to believe soft law provides the best available mechanism to meet global demand for institutional innovation on Internet issues.

The first reason is that soft law helps minimize transaction costs associated with making and interpreting rules. Because it is less binding than hard law, parties have less reason to negotiate aggressively, creating more mutually acceptable bargains. Renegotiation costs are also lower in the event parties have reason to revisit rules in the future.[20]

Soft law also offers flexibility in accommodating differences among actors over legitimate rule-making procedures.[21] Such flexibility is paramount given disagreement over procedural matters at the WCIT, and with respect to the modalities for the WSIS+10 review. Because soft law is not binding, it may also be more acceptable to parties concerned about the Snowden revelations. Put simply, some governments may simply be unwilling to agree to binding legal instruments with the Five Eyes on Internet matters in the foreseeable future. In return, the Five Eyes may be unwilling to undertake international commitments on issues pertaining to espionage and online surveillance. In such a low-trust environment, soft law can provide a realistic way to sustain dialogue and make incremental progress.

The final contemporary advantage of soft law is that it buys time for learning. Experimenting with different approaches in various institutional contexts will facilitate the creation of knowledge about possible rule-sets and their relative performance in securing particular values. Soft law thus allows what John Stuart Mill referred to as "experiments of living."[22] As long as such experiments are conducted with an eye to minimizing negative externalities for the functioning of the Internet as a whole, and are consistent with the requirements of international human rights law, they can be invaluable for gradually improving governance of the Internet and of the increasing number of Internet-affected areas of public policy. Such an approach is especially important when dealing with connections between Internet governance and international trade law. The international trade regime is one of the most highly legalized components of the contemporary global governance system. Injecting Internet issues into contentious, high-stakes trade negotiations at a time when trust is at a nadir even among close allies risks creating further deadlocks and causing collateral damage the world economy can ill afford.

The feasibility of managing Internet issues at the global level in a decentralized manner reliant on soft-law instruments depends on the creation and maintenance of global facilities to minimize and remediate negative externalities created by the multitude of nested clubs that constitute the Internet governance ecosystem. Such facilities need not take the form of new international organizations or treaties; a great deal might be accomplished simply by solidifying two basic global norms of conduct. Further, these norms can be applied both to state and non-state actors. This latter point is especially important given that the vast majority of critical Internet infrastructure is privately owned and given the increasing reliance on firms and other private actors to perform governance functions. The first norm is a commitment to "do no harm" to the global interoperability of the Internet. Such a norm emphasizes a duty not to interfere with the stability and reliability of the system as a whole. Its consonance with the Hippocratic Oath is intentional; harnessing this commitment to an ancient and widely accepted set of ethical standards may frame the issue in a manner that encourages compliance. The second norm is a "responsibility to troubleshoot" analogous to the "responsibility to protect," or R2P. This norm recognizes that it will be impossible to avoid negative externalities entirely and establishes the secondary duty to act in good faith to remedy any damage caused to global Internet interoperability. Adherence to these norms is important to the continued vibrancy of the Internet as an engine for social and economic innovation, and to managing an immensely complex set of rule-making challenges.

chapter seven

Canada's International Security Agenda

JONATHAN PAQUIN

This chapter addresses the issue of Canada's role in security governance in a rapidly changing international environment. Without wishing to make a clean sweep of the past, the chapter argues that Canada could pursue a more ambitious and proactive global strategy. To this end, it should maintain its commitment to some existing multilateral initiatives that play an important role in security governance, such as the North Atlantic Treaty Organization (NATO) and collective conflict management, but it should also increase its contribution to multilateral discussions on emerging security issues that are radically transforming our relationship with security, war, and peace.

The chapter is divided into three main parts. First, I map the security landscape in which Canada must play its cards if it wishes to have a greater and more effective impact on a global scale. Second, I assess the underlying values and effects of Canada's recent diplomacy in managing pressing security issues. Third, I propose ways that could help Canada gain greater influence and better contribute to international cooperation on twenty-first-century security issues.

Mapping the Unfolding Security Landscape

The world is facing a broader spectrum of global security concerns than ever before. In addition to traditional security threats including nuclear proliferation and interstate conflict, the international community must now face new and broader security concerns such as cyberterrorism and climate change. These phenomena

---

Chapter Summary

Key Transformations
- New security concerns such as terrorism or climate change are multi-causal and do not stop at international borders.
- There has been a multiplication of non-government actors addressing these complex security issues.
- The management of international security is increasingly fragmented and decentralized.
- These transformations are occurring at a moment of rapid change in the distribution of economic and political power – a movement towards multipolarity.

Implications for Canada
- Canada will have to be more constructive (and less divisive) in the way it addresses current security concerns if it wishes to remain influential on the global stage.

Recommendations
- Canada should maintain its commitment to NATO.
- Given the complexity of the international security environment, Canada should invest more in collective conflict management (CCM).
- Canada should also invest more in multilateral initiatives dealing with new security threats, such as the use of lethal autonomous weapons systems and cyberespionage.

---

are multi-causal and do not stop at international borders. This explains why traditional interstate relations are not always well suited to tackling such crosscutting issues. It also explains why recent decades have seen the multiplication of local, national, and international non-governmental actors stepping into the international arena to address these complex security issues – so much so that we are now witnessing a fragmented and decentralized management of international security. The new world of security governance comprises actors with different backgrounds, sources of legitimacy, power attributes, and, of course, interests.

To make things even more complicated, these transformations are occurring at a time when fast-paced global change is taking place in the distribution of economic and political power, or what is sometimes called in American literature "the rise of the rest."[1] The emergence of the acronyms BRICS, MINT, and now CIVETS reflects the rise of new economic powerhouses and reminds us that the international system is increasingly multipolar.[2] This "multiplication of the 'multi'" (multi-threats, multi-actors, multi-polar) is the ecosystem within which Canada has to adjust its twenty-first-century international security strategy. The question now is whether Canada is sufficiently involved and active in this new international landscape.

In the last few years, Canada has primarily focused its energy on trade diplomacy by developing a global market strategy seeking to benefit from the rise of new economies and counter the effect of the United States' economic decline. In the last five years alone, Ottawa has diversified its trade relations by strengthening its ties with Asia, Europe, and Latin America. It signed a Comprehensive Economic and Trade Agreement (CETA) with the European Union, joined the Trans-Pacific Partnership (TPP) talks, and signed an important bilateral trade deal with South Korea, as well as smaller agreements with Honduras, Panama, Jordan, Columbia, and Peru. These trade negotiations have the potential to strengthen Canada's economic security by diversifying its trade; as Danielle Goldfarb warns in chapter 1, Canada's exports have flatlined in the last decade, while emerging economies have significantly increased their own exports. While the outcomes are still uncertain with regard to the TPP and CETA, it is clear that recent trade diplomacy has been constructive and could help resolve Canada's export problem.

However, I would argue that recent developments have not been as positive with regard to the diplomatic management of international security issues. As the next section shows, Canada has developed a penchant for "tough-talk diplomacy" that could potentially damage its ability to be a constructive and engaging actor in an increasingly complex international environment.

The Limits and Pitfalls of Tough-Talk Diplomacy

Over the years, principled diplomacy or "conviction politics," as it is often referred to, has led the Canadian government to criticize nations, international organizations, and regimes of cooperation in the name of uncompromising principles.[3] Thus Stephen Harper strongly criticized the United Nations for its ineffectiveness and moral relativism, argued that the Kyoto targets on global warming were "stupid," refused to attend a Commonwealth summit in Sri Lanka to protest against Colombo's human rights abuses, kicked Iran's diplomats out of Canada while breaking off diplomatic relations with Tehran, and went substantially further than Canada's allies in condemning President Putin's aggression against Ukraine.[4]

The fact that Canada has limited power and influence in the international system may explain why it has developed the habit of going beyond its allies in rhetoric. While the United States and other great powers are involved in intricate and sensitive negotiations on many security issues requiring restraint, nuance, and proactivity, including talks on nuclear-arsenal reduction with Russia, Israel-Palestine peace, or the P5+1 negotiations with Iran over its nuclear program, Canada is not subject to such constraints. One could argue that our government has the luxury to be so outspoken because, ultimately, war and peace are not decided by Canada, regardless of what it says, does, or stands for.[5] "We take strong, principled positions in our dealings with other nations – whether popular or not," Prime Minister Stephen Harper once declared, "and that is what the world can count on from Canada."[6] Indeed, over the last few years, Canada has fully complied with this statement, which could potentially become a problem. I would argue that since Canada does not have the means, exposure, or credibility to "walk the talk" (i.e., be consistent with its words and actions), its tough-talk diplomacy does not really have a hold in reality and is treated, at best, as a disconcerting curiosity by the rest of the world. In the process, however, one can legitimately question whether Canada has been discrediting itself as a sensible international actor that can contribute to the resolution of international issues.

Critics of this argument might respond by pointing to surveys and supporting data showing that international investors, immigrants, and tourists from all over the world see Canada as a very appealing country. International polls conducted by Gallup, the Pew Research Center, and the BBC, for instance, have all ranked

Canada as one of the most popular countries in the world, while American public opinion has consistently rated Canada as its most favoured nation.[7] These are positive indicators and a source of pride for Canadians. However, what we should be worried about is not Canada's attractiveness among foreign citizens, but rather Canada's credibility and ability to get things done in international forums, given the divisive tone of its recent diplomacy. With its uncompromising demands and harsh criticisms, Canada may be widening the rift between itself and other nations whose governments are not going to change their behaviour simply because Canada is not pleased with the way they act.

I would argue, therefore, that Canada has behaved in a paradoxical fashion with regard to the "multiplication of the multi." It has been active and constructive when it comes to trade in an increasingly multipolar world economy, but has tended to be divisive with regard to several international security issues.

A Forward-Looking Agenda

In this section, I argue that NATO continues to have great value for Canada in the twenty-first century and that we should remain committed to it. I also suggest that Ottawa should pay more attention to the objective of promoting multilateral cooperation to better tackle multiform and multilevel security issues, as described in the first section of the chapter. Investing more in collective conflict management and stressing the importance of norm setting in regulating the use of lethal autonomous weapons systems and cyberespionage may offer opportunities for Canada. These issues are transforming our relationship with security, war, and peace, but have yet to receive the international attention they deserve.

Standing by NATO

Should Canada maintain its commitment to NATO? This question is relevant given the great fluctuation in the number of NATO allies wishing to participate in "out of area" interventions as well as in the disparity in their financial and military commitment to these missions. This reality has caused resentment among some allies and angered NATO's major financial contributors (especially the United States) as well as military risk-takers in Afghanistan such as Canada.[8] With the end of the Canadian mission in Afghanistan and considering our government's fiscal constraints, some Canadian observers have legitimately questioned whether Canada should reduce its commitment to NATO.[9]

As serious as this discussion may be, it was quickly muted by Russia's invasion of Ukraine. Within a few weeks, we went from a debate on the pitfalls of NATO's "out of area" burden sharing, to a discussion focusing on the vital defence of the Atlantic realm. Indeed, in response to Russia's aggression, the Canadian government contributed Canadian Armed Forces personnel and military resources to NATO's reassurance mission in Eastern Europe.[10]

It remains to be seen if Russia's actions have settled, at least for a while, the debate on Canada's commitment to NATO. However, regardless of how Russia behaves, I maintain that Canada should remain committed to the alliance despite Ottawa's disappointment and frustration over the lack of relative parity in the collective effort deployed in Afghanistan. Yes, NATO's territorial and functional expansion has raised coordination and burden-sharing problems, but we should not forget that NATO has a rapid mobilization capacity and unmatched military skills that can significantly impact the outcome of international crises, as seen in the Balkans, Central Asia, and North Africa. Moreover, the alliance is second to none when it comes to addressing some of Canada's core security concerns such as terrorism, internal strife, and mass atrocities. This is not negligible.

Although Canada's defence budget remains well below 2 per cent of its GDP (the level targeted by the Atlantic alliance, though we are currently at 1 per cent), our government significantly invested in the Afghan ground mission and, to a lesser extent, the Libya air campaign. As a result, Canada gained credibility as a reliable ally, especially in Washington, and likely has more influence in the alliance today than fifteen years ago. This reality certainly raises a sunk-cost dilemma: Should we disengage from NATO and lose what we have recently achieved, or should we build on the reputation we acquired through hard work and sacrifice in Afghanistan? I believe Canada should (and will) choose the latter.

As for multilateral military interventions in the form of "coalitions of the willing," these can be an interesting alternative to full-fledged NATO interventions. They provide speed, broad international legitimacy, and effectiveness in tackling pressing security issues, as in the case of operations against the so-called Islamic State in Iraq and Syria (ISIS). That said, these coalitions should be used with parsimony and judgment given what recent history has shown with the 2003 US-led "coalition of the willing" in Iraq.[11] Relying on such coalitions to strengthen the international legitimacy of an intervention is one thing, but using them to work around political disagreements among the Atlantic allies is another.

The strategic shift that Canada underwent in the 1990s – which saw Canada, along with some of its allies, gradually withdrawing troops from traditional UN peacekeeping missions and increasing its participation in military interventions and stabilization missions carried out either under NATO control or by coalitions of the willing – was necessary in order for Canada to remain internationally relevant and come up to speed with post–Cold War security issues. Given the above discussion, however, I would argue that it would be premature for Ottawa to initiate a new strategic shift involving disengagement from NATO.

In addition to our commitment to NATO and given the complexity of the current security environment, Canada should invest more in so-called collective conflict management and could draw on its expertise to promote norm-building initiatives with respect to new security threats. The remainder of this chapter expands on these two propositions.

Invest More in Collective Conflict Management

Collective conflict management (CCM) is defined as "new patterns of international cooperation ... which are largely ad hoc, informal, improvised and opportunistic."[12] CCM is commonly used by state and non-state actors to prevent or resolve many types of conflicts. Some recent examples have been highly successful, including naval coordination between NATO, the EU, African coastal states and private companies to fight the endemic piracy in the Gulf of Aden.

Canada has not been a stranger to CCM. The Afganistan-Pakistan border dispute over the so-called Durand Line was mediated by Canadian representatives, with technical and working group meetings favouring constructive dialogue and cooperation between Afghan and Pakistani representatives.[13] Lately, Canada has also been an active player in the US war on drugs in Central America and the Caribbean. Canadian forces have been helping states such as Jamaica, Belize and Guatemala build their military capacity and manage their security forces in order to be more effective in this regard. Lastly, Canada's recent financial contribution to Jordan is another example of the impact of CCM. The Canadian government has provided more than $100 million in funding to Jordan to help it deal with security and infrastructure issues caused by the Syrian refugee crisis.[14]

Canada has thus been a constructive force when it comes to relying on CCM to manage multiform security issues. Yet, it should invest more in this mechanism. Over the last eight years, Canada has only invested $24 million to help with four types of mediation support: (1) conflict management, such as the Afghanistan-Pakistan cooperation process; (2) internationally-led peace processes, including the joint AU-UN mission in Darfur; (3) supporting the mediation capacity of IOs such as the OAS and the UN; and (4) the development of local-level mechanisms in the Congo, Sudan and Columbia.[15]

That said, pouring more money into these endeavours will not increase Canada's influence without greater leadership and initiative. Our government should therefore focus more on bridging differences between states, ethnic groups and military factions. However, Canada is nowhere to be seen on several security issues of current importance. While a plethora of international actors are focusing their attention on – and striving to coordinate their actions in response to – the resolution of crises, such as those in Syria, Palestine, Ukraine, the Central African Republic or Somalia, Canada has either paid little attention to them or has addressed them through tough-talk diplomacy. By investing more in CCM, Canada could better adapt its security agenda to new forms of security concerns.

Increase Canada's Contribution to High-Tech Security Issues

The current debate surrounding the emergence of Lethal Autonomous Weapons Systems (LAWS) is a crucial one. Robotized weapons are still in the early stages of development. Indeed, the combat drones that are currently used by the United States to conduct targeted killings of terrorist combatants in places such as Afghanistan, Iraq, Libya, Pakistan, and Yemen could be compared to the Model-T Ford for the auto industry.[16] Robotic experts are now predicting that fully autonomous weapons systems – military devices that are able to select targets without direct human supervision – could be operational in the very near future. This possibility blurs the issue of accountability as the ultimate decision on life and death would not be in the hands of military personnel but rather made by sophisticated machines. LAWS are therefore likely to transform the nature of conflicts and wars. The bad news is that several states, including China, Israel, Russia, and the United States, are working on developing these weapons. The good news is that fully autonomous weapons have not yet been created and that international discussions on their use are already under way. The first informal meeting organized on the issue of LAWS was held by the United Nations in Geneva in May 2014.[17] Canada, along with representatives from approximately one hundred other nations, participated in this meeting during which legal, ethical, and technical aspects of the issue were addressed by experts. This meeting could be the first step towards the establishment of an international regime that limits or even bans the use of these weapons.

Since Canada is not known to have developed fully autonomous weapons, the argument could be made that it is well positioned to participate in, or even lead, a multilateral effort to ban their production. An international campaign to stop these weapons (the

Campaign to Stop Killer Robots) is under way and has garnered the support of approximately fifty national and international NGOs, such as Human Rights Watch and Amnesty International. Representatives of this campaign have called upon the Canadian government to support the creation of a regime that would ban the development of these weapons. So far, however, their call has gone unanswered. This is unfortunate, because Canada certainly has value to add to these discussions, given its expertise as a former norm-building entrepreneur. We should not forget that Canada invested in significant multilateral initiatives in a not-so-distant past. The Arctic Council, the Commission on Intervention and State Sovereignty, and the Ottawa Mine Ban Convention all testify to the fact that, if there is sufficient political will in Ottawa, significant progress can be achieved in international security cooperation.[18]

Another area in which Canada could be more vocal and active is cyberespionage. Computer intrusions in the form of spying and interstate hacking are increasingly seen as a major global threat. This is understandable since our economic system as well as our security and transportation infrastructures depend on a safe cyber-environment. The February 2011 cyberattacks against three Canadian federal departments were an alarm bell for Ottawa.[19] Foreign hackers with Chinese IP addresses managed to get their hands on highly classified information through simple Internet connections. This event was seen as one of the biggest cyberattacks in Canadian history. More recently, the cyberattacks during the crisis in Ukraine, when Russian authorities attacked Ukrainian computer and communication networks, should remind us of the seriousness of this threat.[20]

Governments are currently pointing fingers at one another and behaving as if they are all victims and never perpetrators of cyber-spying. Canada has invested in cyber-technologies and has recently been accused of cyberespionage, notably in Brazil,[21] while facing repeated cyberattacks from China. Unless governments make progress in their discussions on such activities, insecurity and distrust will persist in the cyberworld to the detriment of all. Our government should therefore do everything in its power to promote multilateral efforts to create incentives to reduce and contain cyberespionage. This recommendation has notably been supported by Canada's former ambassador to China, David Mulroney.[22] Of course, as Mark Raymond points out in this volume, Internet governance is unlikely to change in response to an initiative carried out by a single state. However, progress can be achieved in a multilateral fashion. The UN Group of Governmental Experts on Cyber Security (GGE), which was set up by UN Secretary General Ban Ki-moon in 2012 and included Canada and 14 other states, made a noticeable breakthrough in cybercrime.[23] It recognized the importance of common norms for states' cyber-behaviour and acknowledged "the full applicability of international law to state behaviour in cyberspace."[24] It also emphasized the responsibility of national governments to pursue those who carry out cybercrime on their territory.[25] Building on the recent achievements of the UN Group of Governmental Experts, Canada could go further and make the fight against cyberespionage a central piece of its international security agenda, notably by raising its profile on this issue. Ottawa could promote the creation of a forum for discussion on cybersecurity that would include not only states but also members of the industry and civil organizations. This forum could help increase interstate trust and reduce the likelihood of cyberwarfare.

Creating such a forum would of course be a difficult task and could run up against some problems. First, the incompatibility of justice systems and disagreement on the motives to justify an international warrant against hackers could cause political deadlock. Second, despite progress achieved under the UN GGE, the balance between defending a free and open Internet space and preventing state-sponsored cyber-intrusions may be hard to achieve. The recent discussions by members of the International Telecommunication Union (ITU) led to a deadlock when the United States, Canada, and several European states rejected a Russian-sponsored treaty that would have legitimized governments' censorship of the Internet by bringing its governance under the ITU.[26] This event illustrated the profound philosophical disagreements surrounding the issue of Internet governance. However, despite these difficulties and the fact that technological developments are fast-paced, Canada could play a more active role in raising the profile of multilateral discussions on cybersecurity.[27]

Is this forward-looking agenda merely "old wine in a new bottle"? Are these options simply a return to Canada's "middle powermanship" under a different name? The answer is no. The idea of "middle powers" was a creation of the Cold War, an artefact of a bipolar world order. We are now facing a very different world that is increasingly multipolar, in which the nature of security is changing, with as many stakeholders as there are security issues. The idea should be to address these new security threats and leave our mark on international politics by better contributing to international cooperation.

Conclusion

This chapter has argued that Canada should be more entrepreneurial with regard to multilateral cooperation. Now that a security cycle has come to a close with the end of its mission in Afghanistan, Canada could seize the moment to upgrade its security objectives by investing more in multilateral initiatives in an increasingly complex and rapidly changing environment, while at the same time remaining committed to NATO. In this way, Canada could have a more durable and constructive impact on international cooperation.

chapter eight

Towards a New Canadian Human Rights Diplomacy

DAVID PETRASEK

The global power shift identified in the opening chapter of this book, alongside global social, demographic, and technological trends, are combining to create new risks and new opportunities for international efforts to promote respect for human rights. It is a pivotal moment, with some positing the "end times" of human rights and many others believing the relative decline in Western power will weaken the international human rights regime.[1] While the doomsayers are mistaken, there is no doubt that the rules of the game are changing. It is likely to be more difficult to advance human rights issues in some global forums like the United Nations – at least in ways that worked in the past. Countries like Canada that seek to promote human rights abroad will need new strategies and techniques for doing so. The purpose of this chapter is to begin a discussion on the objectives for Canadian human rights diplomacy in this shifting environment, and to do so in light of an assessment of the strengths and weaknesses Canada brings to the task.

At the outset, it is worth noting that the promotion of human rights abroad has been a *stated* priority for every Canadian government since the late 1970s. While changes in leadership and ideology have led to great variation in the priority given to other foreign-policy files, including trade, aid, the environment, and peacekeeping, for forty years Canadian governments have all claimed to take seriously the defence of human rights abroad.

That being so, it is worth asking what Canada might do to improve the impact of its efforts to promote human rights. Further, which human rights issues can Canada pursue most effectively, and in which forums? Will Canada's criticism of human rights practices in other countries make a difference? Such questions are rarely posed, perhaps precisely because the prioritization of human rights as a foreign-policy goal is largely assumed. What new foreign minister would take office *openly* abandoning this priority? This privileged position, inherited over the decades, wins broad public support. But, as there seems no need to justify the policy, there is too little critical thinking on its substance.

Chapter Summary

Key Transformations
- Global power shifts will change but not end the international discussion on human rights.
- In terms of policy, what is "foreign" is increasingly "domestic," and vice versa, especially as regards the protection of human rights.
- As the power and prestige of central state authorities declines, the role of sub-national and municipal governments in protecting human rights will grow in importance, as will the role of the private sector.

Implications for Canada
- To be effective, the Canadian promotion of human rights abroad must be an "all of Canada" effort, pursued for the long term and, to the extent possible, in a non-partisan way.
- Canada must continue to champion human rights abroad, but to do so effectively will need to show it is also acting at home, and embrace the international scrutiny it would apply to others.
- Without giving up on the UN human rights regime, Canada will need to look to regional bodies and new platforms, and engage many actors, in order to advance human rights concerns.

Recommendations
- Municipal authorities are central to the realization of human rights, but barely present in international discussions; Canada should lead an international effort championing the human rights role (and responsibilities) of cities.
- Canada should strengthen existing cross-party mechanisms or create new mechanisms to build a consensus around key, long-term priorities for Canadian human rights diplomacy.

Human Rights Diplomacy

Before turning to these questions, however, it is worth clarifying what is meant by "human rights diplomacy." Simply put, the idea is that all the tools of modern diplomacy should be used to pursue the goal of promoting human rights abroad. Human rights diplomacy should be like all serious diplomacy: it requires approaches based on principle and compromise, policies advanced in public and private, and tactics of both engagement and reproach. Above all, it requires the skill to know when the time is right for one approach or the other. This might seem obvious, but it needs to be clarified, because the moralistic (and legalistic) quality attached to universal human rights works against such a pragmatic understanding. For example, the grounding of rights in lofty principle creates doubt as to when compromise is possible, if at all, and promotes the pulpit as the preferred (and sometimes only) diplomatic tool. NGOs demand that there be no compromise in the defence of human rights abroad, and in the most egregious cases of human rights abuse this may be so. But while human rights concerns do take precedence domestically (for those whose duty it is to respect and protect the rights of the people they govern), this is not necessarily the case for those who would promote rights elsewhere via their foreign policy. There will necessarily be trade-offs and compromise; accepting this is key to setting achievable objectives.

However, there are some distinct challenges in promoting human rights abroad, not least the expansive nature of the subject. Virtually all the other foreign policy proposals covered in this book have a significant human rights element, and taking them up successfully will require attention to that dimension. No policy to promote Canada as the mining giant of the twenty-first century, as suggested in chapter 3 by Andrea Mandel-Campbell, will succeed so long as doubt persists regarding the human rights impact of Canadian companies abroad. Canadian trade and aid policy will falter if they are shown to promote inequality as well as growth. Security policies that strengthen oppressive regimes abroad will be counter-productive. But while human rights *concerns* need to permeate many areas of foreign policy, there is still a need to treat human rights *diplomacy* distinctly, on its own merits.

Another particular challenge to this field of diplomacy is that promoting rights abroad, unlike advancing trade or strengthening a military alliance, is not easily measured. The breadth of the issues makes it difficult, but there are problems, too, even for specific human rights subjects. How to properly measure progress towards religious tolerance, or ending gender discrimination? And how to assess the contribution of foreign pressure to any advances that are made? Such indeterminacy makes it easy for governments to claim success. It is easy, too, for them to point to sharply worded press releases and speeches at UN gatherings as proof of their commitment to promote human rights.

Finally, as noted above, global power shifts are impacting the ways in which human rights are debated in global forums like the United Nations. Three key differences are apparent. First, it is becomingly increasingly difficult to rely on "name and shame" approaches that single out particular countries for criticism and votes of censure. Second, making aid, trade, or other benefits or relationships conditional on a country's human rights performance is increasingly less popular and less feasible. And third, there is greater attention to the human rights issues that resonate with newly emerging powers and the global South, especially issues of global inequities and a global financial and trade architecture that appears to privilege rich countries. More than ever, developed countries are under scrutiny as regards the impact of their national legislation on human rights abroad. These developments will necessarily affect Canadian human rights diplomacy.

Opting In, Long Term

Turning to a discussion on specific objectives, these can be separated into those dealing with questions of process or "style" and those dealing with issues of substance: *how* to advance *which* human rights issues? On the first point, Canada needs to participate more fully in an international legal regime that it seeks to apply effectively to others, and it needs to move beyond the tendency to pursue issues in a faddish and partisan manner.

In the popular imagination, Canada is an enthusiastic member of the international human rights regime. In fact, we are increasingly less so; and we were not always so. While the Harper government has been criticized for being selective in which countries it names and shames, less attention has been given to the fact that Canada has stopped ratifying human rights treaties. In the past ten years, the UN has adopted two new human rights treaties (on the rights of the disabled and to prevent forced disappearances), and four protocols to existing treaties to strengthen the powers of their supervisory bodies, including those dealing with torture, children's rights, and economic and social rights. Of these six new, binding, international agreements, Canada has ratified only one – the Convention on the Rights of the Disabled – a record that compares unfavourably with all our major allies (except the United States). Moreover, unlike in the past, rather than excuse the delay, the Harper government flatly stated it has no intention of ratifying the new agreements.

This opting-out has been criticized as an aberration, but in fact it harkens back to an earlier era in Canada's approach to international human rights standards. Canada was ambivalent – even hostile – to the drafting and adoption of the Universal Declaration of Human Rights in 1948, and only reluctantly voted in favour of the Declaration at the UN General Assembly (having abstained in earlier votes).[2] This ambivalence persisted and, until the early 1970s, Canada largely stood aside from serious engagement with the UN human rights program. But even so, the reason for this reluctance to engage – that Canada would expose itself to criticism – persists today: not only in the refusal to consider ratifying new treaties, but also in the hostile attitude the Harper government has sometimes shown towards the visits and reports of UN experts operating under procedures Canada has already ratified.

No government takes up human rights issues abroad with entirely clean hands at home. Yet there is a certain immaturity apparent in the Canadian fear of UN scrutiny and criticism. All European countries are subject to the jurisdiction of the Strasbourg-based

European Court of Human Rights, which rules on hundreds of individual cases every year. Those in the European Union are additionally bound by the rulings of the European Court of Justice in Brussels, which also adjudicates human rights issues. None of the UN mechanisms that Canada has accepted, or might sign up to, has anywhere near the clout of these international courts, yet Canadian officials fret over their real or anticipated mild condemnation.

US human rights diplomacy is coloured by its exceptionalism – standing aside from international legal regimes it applies to others. However, the United States carries sufficient clout to be listened to despite the charge of hypocrisy. Canada does not enjoy that luxury. To work effectively through the UN and other intergovernmental bodies to advance human rights objectives, we must show a willingness to participate fully in their supervisory mechanisms if we are to insist they be foisted on others.

Second, and still on the question of *how* Canada advances human rights issues, there is an unhelpful tendency towards short-term approaches. Each new government, indeed each new foreign minister, feels compelled to identify a pressing human rights concern which they will devote time and resources to advancing. When he was foreign minister, John Baird prioritized the issues of child marriage and, to a lesser extent, discrimination against sexual minorities. Previous governments and ministers over the past two decades have similarly focused on children in war, violence against women, the protection of civilians, the fight against torture, and other issues. Though all of these are worthy of attention, and in most cases Canadian efforts have produced some advances, there is still much to be done, including on the files long abandoned or downgraded.

Such short-termism is understandable. Foreign ministers feel the need, pushed by politics, to "brand" their agenda and leave a legacy of action on a distinctive issue. The human rights field, with its moral overtones, offers no shortage of topics with which a minister can burnish a reputation. This erratic style, however, though often applauded at home, is distinctly unhelpful abroad. Almost all human rights problems take time to resolve, especially those grounded in inequalities, discrimination, and weak state capacity.

The current government's concern regarding early and forced marriages is a case in point. Dramatic reductions in child marriage will take decades to achieve. The governments in countries where entrenched patterns of discrimination exist may be complicit in, or indifferent to it; or, indeed, they may be genuine in their efforts to end it but lack the means to do so. Whatever the case, they are unlikely to be impressed when a foreign government, having barely spoken on the issue before, suddenly trumpets that dealing with it is a priority, only to be prioritizing some other abuse a few years later.

A key reason for such short-termism is, of course, the political cycle. Governments come and go, as do foreign ministers, and the polarization apparent in Canadian politics means there is an expectation that a new government must have a *different* approach. The very breadth of the human rights field offers endless temptation for a government to choose new human rights to emphasize, and in so doing differentiate itself from its predecessors. Indeed, the ease with which a government can assign priority to a human rights issue (child marriage), or abandon it (protecting civilians), points to a certain flippancy that would be derided in any other area of foreign policy.

Consider the decision of the Harper government to create an Office for Religious Freedom to promote tolerance and the protection of religious minorities worldwide. Though announced with great fanfare, consultations to create the office left out key constituencies, including leading human rights organizations that had been defending religious freedom for decades. There was little effort, too, on the government's part to win cross-party support. Indeed, the government appeared to go out of its way to brand it as a "Conservative" project and to suggest other parties and stakeholders who might be allies in the office's work were somehow lacking in their commitment to the issue. The result, of course, was that the office received less support at home than it might, and its impact was diminished abroad because of its narrow base. Further, the Conservative branding of the issue will make it very difficult for any new government to embrace fully the office's work.

It may sound naive to suggest it, but Canada urgently needs a cross-party approach to global human rights policies, one that identifies long-term priorities that are pursued regardless of the government in office. How could this be achieved? There is a parliamentary sub-committee on international human rights that does bring together MPs with a shared interest in the issue, but it operates in relative obscurity and with little impact on the policies either the government or opposition parties actually pursue. The status and resources of the committee could be enhanced. In addition, the foreign minister might consider establishing an ad hoc, or even standing (but extra-parliamentary), advisory committee on human rights that would be asked to draw on academic and other input to develop policy options for promoting human rights abroad. If carefully established, through consultation with all parties, and if treated as a non-partisan policy forum, such a body might help to build cross-party consensus on key human rights objectives for Canadian foreign policy. The fact that successive governments do prioritize human rights – if not the specific goals pursued – offers something to build on. The alternative is to accept that Canada's efforts in this area will always be second best.

The UN and Beyond

Related to the question of *how* is the question of *where* – in which venues should Canada be advancing its human rights objectives? The growing clout of China and the (alleged) weakening of Western power lead some to argue that issues to which the West has given prominence, such as human rights, will recede or receive diminished attention on the international agenda (a suggestion implicit in the chapter by Jennifer Welsh and Emily Paddon). This is far too simple a reading of what the global power shift will mean for human rights. Improving education levels worldwide and a growing global middle class, coupled with increasing access to information, all point to growing awareness of and interest in human rights issues.[3] Moreover, the place of human rights in global affairs is only partly attributable to support for the issue – which was rarely consistent – from Western governments. Nevertheless, the polarization on human rights issues that is already evident in UN bodies like the Human Rights Council is unlikely to improve, and raises the obvious question of whether Canada should look elsewhere to promote human rights.

The short answer is that Canada should work to strengthen the UN's independent and expert human rights monitoring bodies, even as we actively nurture other and new venues to advance human rights issues. The Human Rights Council and its system of country scrutiny and "Special Procedures" are far from perfect. But the Harper government's at times open hostility to the council and its procedures is mistaken. Ministers and Conservative MPs have derided special rapporteurs appointed by the council when they comment on Canada, and the government has taken a miserly approach to new funding for council mechanisms. Yet, despite the politics, the Human Rights Council has still proved itself able in recent years to take strong, principled action: Libya was expelled from the council when Qaddafi launched his murderous attacks on his own people; commissions of inquiry were appointed to gather evidence of the most serious human rights abuses in Libya, North Korea, and Syria; a precedent-setting resolution was passed that protected the rights of sexual minorities; a consensus was found to protect freedom of speech even as religious intolerance was condemned.

There are plenty of options for strengthening the UN's independent and expert mechanisms. None will be achieved easily. Yet, Canada has good relations with countries who might not be enthusiastic supporters of a strengthened UN human rights program. This is especially true of a number of African countries, but true also for countries in Latin America and Asia. An extra effort should be made to build new coalitions of countries that can act cross-regionally on fundamental reform issues. This should precisely engage the democracies among the emerging powers, a strategy that has advantages for many foreign policy objectives, as suggested in chapter 11 by Yves Tiberghien.

Beyond the UN, in our own hemisphere, the Organization of American States has a modest but important human rights protection regime. Sadly, there have been efforts to weaken it by Venezuela, Nicaragua, and others, even as Chile, Uruguay, and Mexico have defended the system. The fact that Canada is one of the few countries in the hemisphere that has not yet ratified the Inter-American Convention on Human Rights (IACHR) undermines our role in this struggle. A proposal to ratify was actively considered in the 1990s, but got stuck on possible conflicts between the convention and Canadian law. The fact that these are easily resolvable led a parliamentary committee to recommend ratification in 2004, but there has been no discussion of doing so since 2006. Ratification of the IACHR could be a springboard to a new and vigorous role for Canada in hemispheric human rights issues.

As argued elsewhere in this book, a truly modern diplomacy must be pursued with all the tools of a globalizing and interconnected world. In such a world, multilateral or bilateral approaches involving national governments are but one means of advancing human rights abroad. "Canada" acts internationally through many channels, not just its diplomats or even federal government officials; these other official and unofficial actors can play an enormous role in promoting rights abroad. There is a role here as well for Canadian business, which, perhaps surprisingly, lags behind many others in committing itself to respect human rights in its global operations.

Other layers of government have a part to play, too. If one considers the question of *which* human rights issues to pursue, an obvious priority is those issues arising from conflict and crisis – situations of mass atrocity and attacks on civilian populations. These are pre-eminently issues where the federal government and diplomats will lead (and are dealt with separately in chapter 9 by Jennifer Welsh and Emily Paddon). However, there are two human rights issues of growing global importance where provincial and municipal officials and institutions might play a role alongside the federal government: migration and inequitable urbanization.

Driven by labour shortages in developed countries and global wealth disparities, the number of migrants worldwide is growing rapidly, and will more than double to well over 400 million by mid-century (this excludes refugees and those fleeing war).[4] As non-citizens, migrants often do not enjoy important legal protections. Their numbers and plight will certainly raise important human rights concerns. By 2030, urbanization rates will pass 60 per cent worldwide, from 40 per cent only a few years ago.[5] But most of this urban growth will be in slums: there will be an estimated two billion slum-dwellers by 2040, double the number today.[6] This too is certain to raise numerous human rights issues.

Canada has the legitimacy and standing to take the lead in addressing both issues. It is a heavily urbanized country that still actively admits new immigrants; relatively speaking, Canada performs well in offering them citizenship and social mobility. We do not (yet) have a large pool of illegal or undocumented migrants. Canada has experience too of cooperative arrangements that allow for particular reception and integration policies to be developed at the provincial level. As Jennifer Keesmaat points out elsewhere in chapter 2, Canadian cities are among the most ethnically diverse in the world, and also perform well in global assessments for the security, social mobility, and integration they offer. It is provincial and municipal governments who design and implement most of the policies that account for this relative success – they could play a novel and useful role in promoting and sharing that experience with cities and sub-national authorities around the world.

It is unwise to go further in terms of suggestions for substantive policy areas. As I have argued, an individual wish list of human rights topics is pointless. Issues that will win broad support so as to be pursued for the long term must necessarily emerge from careful analysis and widespread consultation and debate.

Conclusion

There is a well-worn joke about a lost tourist on some forlorn back road. He asks a passing farmer for directions to the big city: "Well, I wouldn't start from here," replies the farmer. Like it or not, the road to renewing Canada's human rights diplomacy is starting from a rather lost and dismal place. Recently, the Canadian approach has been unusually selective in the criticism it levels against other countries. We have opted out of new international standards, and the government has challenged the legitimacy of UN bodies that scrutinize Canada's human rights record. All of this has undermined Canada's credibility, and hence its impact, when it seeks international action on human rights. But at least part of the problem is more deep-seated: a diminished impact that results from an ambivalence (or even immaturity) towards outside scrutiny of Canada's own human rights record and a partisan fad-dishness in advancing particular human rights issues. Overcoming both will be essential to renewing Canadian human rights diplomacy – in a way that engages multiple actors.

chapter nine

Protecting Civilians in Conflict: A Constructive Role for Canada

EMILY PADDON AND JENNIFER M. WELSH

The protection of civilians has become a central humanitarian ambition of the post–Cold War era and a consistent objective of responses to the worst of today's crises. The subsequent increase in prominence of individual security, which can in some cases stand in tension with state sovereignty, has led to the emergence of new actors engaged in civilian protection and is transforming existing international institutions and practices, particularly the United Nations. In 2013, Secretary-General Ban Ki-Moon unveiled "Human Rights Up Front," a policy that puts the imperative to protect people from serious violations of human rights and international humanitarian law at the core of the United Nations' strategy and operational activity.[1]

Canada played a formative role in bringing about this broader normative shift. Starting in 1998, it took the lead on a number of international initiatives related to the effort to prioritize individual security. Canadian officials were instrumental in getting the Security Council to adopt the first-ever protection of civilians mandate for UN peacekeepers.[2] Through the International Commission on Intervention and State Sovereignty (ICISS), Canada was pivotal in the formulation and development of the principle of the Responsibility to Protect (R2P).[3] And, in the related area of international criminal justice, Canada played an important part in the preparation of the negotiations for the Rome Statute, which established the International Criminal Court (ICC) and came into force in 2002.[4]

This period of active engagement, however, proved to be short lived. While Canada did much to help these initiatives off the ground, it took a step back under the Conservative government, elected in 2005. While in select high-profile cases, such as the international use of force in Libya in 2011, Canada did take a robust stand and offered material resources to protect civilians, its general allocation of resources shifted away from the priorities outlined above. It also ceased to lead in terms of international policy development in this area. Indeed, in some instances there was a deliberate attempt by the Harper government to distance and disassociate itself from Canada's past efforts related to the protection agenda. For example, in 2009, an internal Department of Foreign Affairs email was leaked which outlined a series of shifts in the language of Canadian foreign policy. Specifically, it banned such terms as "international humanitarian law," "human security," and "the Responsibility to Protect" from government parlance.[5]

Critics of this shift in Canada's international role charge that Canada is rapidly losing influence abroad and that it must re-engage in order to stay relevant. They call for renewed support for the norms that Canada helped institutionalize in the multilateral forums with which the country was once so closely linked.

While we agree that re-engagement is desirable, the question of *how* Canada re-engages is equally of critical importance. This is so for two reasons. First, the international landscape has changed considerably since the period of Canadian policy activism on protection. While civilian protection and related human rights norms have become more institutionalized, they have also become more politicized and inconsistently implemented in practice. The rise of non-Western states and shifts in the global balance of power away from US hegemony suggest that contestation of these humanitarian and human rights principles is likely to persist. Second, and closely related, norms by their very nature create expectations of behaviour. When peacekeepers or aid workers, for example, claim that they will protect civilians, such a pledge engenders expectations both locally and internationally. When expectations are unmet, there can be real and potentially harmful consequences. In this respect, if Canada is to re-engage, it needs to be clear about what it can honestly deliver. Failure to do so may risk even greater criticism.

Chapter Summary

Key Transformations

- While civilian protection and related humanitarian and human rights norms have become more institutionalized, they have also become more politicized, manipulated and inconsistently implemented in practice with potentially harmful consequences.
- The rise of non-Western states and shifts in the global balance of power suggest that contestation of these normative principles is likely to persist.

Implications for Canada

- If Canada is to re-engage on civilian protection, it needs to be clear about what it can honestly deliver.
- Canada should formulate and adopt a careful strategy that is principled and pragmatic, aimed at shaping implementation of civilian protection and contesting its manipulation, when warranted.

Recommendations

- Canada should pioneer evidenced-based, policy-focused research on the role of diaspora groups in responding to humanitarian emergencies and in identifying innovative channels for protection assistance.
- Canada should use its position as vice-chair of the UN's Special Committee on Peacekeeping Operations to reinvigorate and strengthen the body and its engagement on peacekeeping and civilian protection.
- Canada should assist in refining and buttressing the training of both military and civilian personnel to enhance the protection of vulnerable populations.
- Canada should re-engage on the implementation of R2P by investing in its Pillar II agenda, particularly in the realm of prevention through initiatives within the UN to address emerging crises as well as targeted forms of assistance to states under stress.

To address these issues, in what follows we illuminate the contemporary challenges surrounding civilian protection in three overlapping areas of international engagement – peacekeeping and humanitarian action, the Responsibility to Protect (R2P), and international criminal justice – and identify ways in which Canada can and should reassert itself.

Global Challenges to Civilian Protection

Peacekeeping and humanitarian action have both undergone a radical transformation over the last fifteen years. No longer tasked primarily with observing frontiers and ceasefire agreements, most peacekeeping mandates now contain an explicit mandate for peacekeepers to use force to protect civilians under chapter VII of the UN Charter. This has resulted not only in operations that are more demanding, risky, and "robust" (in terms of the mandate given to peacekeepers to use force), but also in changing perceptions about the impartiality of peacekeeping actors.[6] In the humanitarian sector, the widespread adoption of a rights-based framework has expanded the range of programs that fall under the ambit of humanitarian assistance, and placed field staff in situations where access is compromised by their advocacy efforts and principled stance. Moreover, the activities of both peacekeepers and humanitarians are increasingly coordinated through the "integrated mission" structure and "delivery as one UN" initiative.[7]

This increase in ambition has, however, not been matched by resources, which raises serious questions about the sustainability of current practices and points to deeper political tensions. The resulting significant gap between donor pledges and actual contributions hampers humanitarian responses in contexts such as Syria, and peacekeeping mission are notoriously under-resourced – both in terms of amounts pledged and in the willingness of states to actually provide what they have committed to.[8] Moreover, in contrast to the Cold War and early 1990s when Canada was last active in peacekeeping, the boots on the ground today are overwhelmingly drawn from developing states. These states increasingly resent having to carry the burden of implementing ambitious protection mandates.

Robust peacekeeping mandates, with civilian-protection objectives at their core, have also been a source of tension within the humanitarian community itself. As UN agencies and certain NGOs have worked more closely alongside blue helmets, there has arisen a concern that, by association, humanitarians will be seen as party to the conflict, thereby limiting humanitarian access and jeopardizing delivery of assistance to those most in need. More broadly, these trends raise fundamental questions about the UN's future role and, in particular, the institution's ability to act and be accepted as an arbiter and mediator. Can peacekeepers shoot to kill one day and then be accepted as impartial brokers of peace the next day? This is deeply troubling given that civilian imperilment is often the result of political conflicts that have been militarized.

Similar issues are at play with the Responsibility to Protect, the principle that every state has the responsibility to protect its populations from genocide, war crimes, ethnic cleansing, and crimes against humanity. Since the ICISS report in 2001, considerable progress has been made in institutionalizing this principle at the UN. World leaders endorsed R2P in the Outcome Document of the 2005 World Summit, a Joint Office was created in New York for the Special Adviser for the Prevention of Genocide and Special Adviser on the Responsibility to Protect, and a contact group on R2P was established to facilitate inter-departmental coordination and policy coherence. More broadly, the Security Council has now reaffirmed the principle in five thematic resolutions,[9] and has referred to the responsibility of states to protect their populations in numerous country-specific situations.[10] Nonetheless, implementation of R2P – still only a decade old within the UN system – continues to encounter resistance.

Many states are still reluctant to use the language of R2P because of its perceived politicization, and interpretations of the principle remain subject to debate. In particular, the post-Libya association of R2P with the use of military force (and by extension regime change) has been difficult to shake. The idea of a wide toolbox under Pillar III (which includes diplomatic, political, humanitarian, and military means) has not yet fully taken hold, and the question of how greater accountability of those who use military force on behalf of the UN can be achieved has still not been adequately answered.[11] In addition, the R2P agenda under Pillar II (which mandates state capacity building) is linked to other well-established policy realms (i.e., development, human rights, robust peacekeeping), so the "value-add" of an R2P lens still has to be demonstrated, and some argue that R2P's politicization may contaminate their other policy agendas.[12] Finally, international inaction on Syria demonstrates the inherent weaknesses of the UN's machinery for collective security – which is, by extension, a major part of the means for implementing R2P.

The final policy area related to humanitarian and human rights norms is international criminal justice. The ICC is unprecedented in that it is the first *permanent* international judicial body to investigate international crimes that imperil civilians and to try alleged perpetrators. It was set up in part to redress the lack of universality that tainted prior judicial mechanisms. As Louise Arbour explains, "The objective of creating a court by treaty was to eventually enlist the voluntary adherence of all UN member states."[13] However, the universality of the court is undermined by the fact that three of the permanent members of the Security Council still have yet to ratify the agreement overseeing the court. This uncomfortable fact is also problematic given that council referrals to the ICC and the threat of prosecution have increasingly been used as a "tool" of coercive diplomacy by those very same permanent members – as was the case with Darfur in 2005 and Libya in 2011 (and the failed attempt to pass a resolution on Syria in 2014). As Arbour and others have argued, such referrals go against the spirit of complementarity and could undermine the long-term credibility of the institution.[14] The credibility of the court has also been challenged by its limited geographical footprint. To date, all twenty-one cases brought before the court concern situations in Africa. This has led to charges of bias and selective justice. Tensions between African states and the court came to a head in 2013 over Kenya when Uhuru Kenyatta and William Ruto, both of whom were indicted by the ICC for international crimes, were elected respectively as president and vice-president of the country. African heads of state lobbied for the case to be dropped, and successfully managed to bring about an amendment of the court's rules of procedure and evidence to do so. The amendment allows judges to excuse high-ranking national officials in public office from the requirement of being present during their trial, and thus introduces another element of selectivity into the judicial process.

Across all three areas of international engagement, there is also a very real risk of co-option and manipulation. The instrumentalization of ICC mechanisms by local actors to prosecute political opponents, as some argue has been the case in Congo and Ivory Coast, is a prime example. So, too, are the Russian interventions in Georgia and Ukraine, which have adopted the use of protection language to mask other aims.

A Role for Canada

Given the evolution and contestation of the protection agenda, what are Canada's options? Acknowledging the challenges above is not to discredit civilian protection as an objective that Canada should seek to further. After all, the same fate has accompanied other important principles, such as the self-defence rationale for the use of force or the idea of "sustainable development." But these challenges do underscore the need for Canada to adopt an approach that is based on a careful and deliberate strategy that is principled and pragmatic, and that involves participation in shaping implementation of civilian protection and, when warranted, contesting its manipulation. Canada's approach must also be clear-sighted and realistic about Canada's own place in the world, including its limitations, and the various competing interests and dynamics that shape its involvement in situations where civilian populations are vulnerable or threatened.

To that end, in this final section we outline three areas in which Canada could have a measurable and positive impact on the evolution of policy and practice on civilian protection. The first two highlight Canada's potential contribution to and leadership of various reforms within the UN system. This avenue remains important because, while regional and international organizations as well as NGOs play a role in this domain, the UN – given its legitimacy and global character – is likely to remain the principal driver of civilian protection policy and practice for a range of activities (most notably peacekeeping). Finally, we explore how Canada's diverse and multicultural society, and specifically its diaspora population with ties to conflict-affected states, can be harnessed to shape the country's engagement abroad.

First, Canada could make a meaningful contribution to civilian protection by strengthening the role and functioning of the UN's Special Committee on Peacekeeping Operations, otherwise known as the C-34. The C-34 is mandated to conduct comprehensive reviews of peace operations in all their aspects, and together with the UN's Department of Peacekeeping Operations, works to shape and improve doctrine. Moreover, it is the primary forum for discussion and debate on peacekeeping among member states and in particular for troop and police contributing countries who criticize the council for its reluctance to engage them in the development of peacekeeping policy. Nevertheless, it is widely acknowledged that the C-34 has increasingly fallen short of its stated functions, plagued as it is by political infighting and marginalization by the Security Council.

Canada is well positioned to reinvigorate the C-34, and to help ensure it plays its rightful role in the evolution of peacekeeping that will be required over the next decade. Canada has been a member of the committee since its creation by the General Assembly in 1965 and Canadian diplomats have taken on various leadership roles within it. Since 1966, Canada has been elected annually as the committee's vice-chair and, beginning in 1990, it has served as chairman of the Working Group. Canada should use its position within the C-34 to launch and oversee a strategic review of the committee with a view to reform. The recommendations of the study could inform the global review of peace operations, called for by the Secretary-General in July 2014.[15] In addition, steps should be taken to coordinate Canadian research and expertise on peacekeeping and civilian protection following the closure of the Pearson Peacekeeping Centre in Ottawa in 2013. Established in 1994, the centre became internationally renowned for its training programs and contributions to peacekeeping research and policy development. Failure to maintain the centre's network as well as educational resources would represent a significant loss to peacekeeping – both regionally and globally. Possible initiatives that Canada could undertake include the development of a roster of peacekeeping experts, and the creation of an online database containing research as well as training and educational resources.

Second, Canada could re-engage in the implementation of R2P, by investing in its Pillar II agenda, particularly in the realm of prevention – on which there is widespread agreement among states. Since 2001, when the notion of the Responsibility to Protect was first coined, scholars and analysts have accumulated better knowledge about the dynamics that lead to atrocity crimes, and have largely converged on the risk factors for those acts.[16] In addition, in his latest report to the General Assembly, the Secretary-General identified channels through which states can be encouraged to meet their protection responsibilities, as well as a set of "inhibitors" to atrocity crimes that the international community can assist vulnerable states to create or strengthen.[17] This dimension of R2P, which is implemented in partnership with states rather than through more controversial coercive tools, offers a number of openings for Canadian expertise and capacity. For example, Canada could advance initiatives within the UN to discuss and address crises as they are emerging rather than at later stages, including through Geneva-based institutions and mechanisms such as the Human Rights Council and the Special Procedures mandate holders of the Office of the High Commissioner for Human Rights. It could also work with like-minded partners like the European Union to strengthen targeted forms of assistance to states under stress through policy experimentation with tools such as mediation or inter-communal dialogue, or law enforcement and criminal investigation. Finally, given its previous experience in peacekeeping, Canada could assist in refining and buttressing the training of both military and civilian personnel to enhance the protection of vulnerable populations, including that of women and girls.

Finally, Canada should pioneer policy-focused research on the role of diaspora groups in responding to humanitarian emergencies. A great deal of lip service is given to idea that they are an under-exploited resource in crisis response. Aid, it is frequently argued, could be made more effective by better channelling remittances, and by leveraging the political influence of national migrants and their links to affected populations.[18] To date, however, these assertions are still largely speculative. The different and in some cases divergent roles played by diaspora groups remains poorly understood by both policymakers and academics alike. And the possible risks of involving communities in protection have not been sufficiently explored.[19] In short, if diaspora groups are to be mobilized for humanitarian assistance, more evidence-based research is required.

Given its vibrant and politically active immigrant population, Canada is well placed to take a lead on this issue, and explore the involvement of diaspora groups in finding new innovative channels for protection assistance. One in five Canadians is foreign born, and there is now a large concentration of immigrants from conflict-affected regions (with the African-Canadian community constituting the fastest growing ethnic minority in the country).[20] Canada is also home to a network of leading researchers on multiculturalism and diversity, and has established institutions – most notably the Global Centre for Pluralism – that could support this kind of policy-relevant research. An agenda focused on the potential role of diaspora in humanitarian assistance could also help to divert attention away from the polarized debate on the part played by ethnic communities in shaping the Canadian government's response to particular crises, such as those in Ukraine and the Middle East.[21]

More generally, the academic and public discussion of Canada's role in the promotion of civilian protection needs to move beyond nostalgia and polemics, to a more constructive analysis of the viable options the country has to address the crises and conflicts that imperil civilian populations. The political and institutional landscape has shifted since the liberal internationalist golden age of the 1990s. Not only is the distribution and use of power changing, but the very norms associated with civilian protection, as the continuing carnage in Syria demonstrates, are also under siege. It is high time Canada re-engaged.

chapter ten

A Platform for Leadership: Building a New Generation's Role in Global Sustainable Development

JOHN W. McARTHUR

Canada is stuck in a straggler approach to global sustainable development, too often trailing the world's frontiers of both debate and implementation. This is strategically unsound for the nation's interests. A new generational approach is required, one that recognizes the complex nature and scale of global changes under way. Success will hinge on much more than government action alone. It requires active leadership from Canadian academic, corporate, and civil society communities alike.

The current problem was on vivid display during a sequence of events from late 2013 through mid-2014. December 2013 marked the multi-year replenishment deadline for the Global Fund to Fight AIDS, Tuberculosis and Malaria, one of the world's most successful modern life-saving institutions. Months earlier, the United States and the United Kingdom had made their own anchor pledges. They also offered matching grants to help motivate other countries' contributions. Nations such as Denmark, Finland, Norway, and Sweden each stepped in with commitments equivalent to $8 to $10 per citizen, per year. Canada, by contrast, left its decision to the final moment. After a flurry of last-minute internal deliberations, the government committed less than $220 million per year, or only $6 per Canadian. The lowball pledges from Canada and a few other countries meant that hundreds of millions in matching dollars were left on the table, and the Global Fund suffered a billion-dollar annual shortfall. The consequences will be measurable in terms of lives lost, and Canada will bear a share of the responsibility.

Somehow the episode passed with barely a whisper of Canadian public debate, even though the right to health care forms a pillar of our national political culture. An even worse shadow was cast on the situation when it was revealed a few months later that $290 million of Canada's official aid budget was not even spent in 2013. The general state of confusion was amplified in June 2014 when the federal government announced a five-year $3.5 billion commitment to support global child and maternal health during an international conference in Toronto. At roughly $700 million per year, the pledge was constructive but modest by global policy standards. It amounted to a tiny fraction of global health assistance and marked only a small increment on previous Canadian commitments. It also included substantive overlap with the previous Global Fund pledge and likely implied cutbacks for other priorities such as global food security.[1] Objective assessments of scale were virtually absent in public conversations. Attention around the cumulative dollar value of the announcement, including its number starting with a "B" (-illions), seemed to crowd out rigorous analysis.

Chapter Summary

Key Transformations
- Since 2000, the Millennium Development Goals have galvanized new approaches to global cooperation for results.
- Historic recent gains include at least 13 million incremental lives saved and hundreds of millions of people lifted out of extreme poverty, leading to the possibility of extreme poverty being eliminated by 2030.
- Widespread economic gains have brought significant downsides, including deep environmental strains and many interconnected social tensions.
- Achieving new sustainable development goals for 2030 will require a complex mix of public and private investments, guided by new forms of partnership and accountability across developed and emerging economies.

Implications for Canada
- Tackling the economic, social, and environmental challenges of global sustainable development constitutes a strategic imperative

for Canadians, with adequacy and leadership defined by the scale and specificity of contributions.

- The United Kingdom provides the clearest reference point for making a non-partisan leap to a global sustainable development leadership role within the span of a decade.
- Canada's success in jumping from backbencher to frontbencher on global sustainable development will hinge on rigorously informed public debate, driven by active leadership from academia, the business community, civil society, and government alike.

Recommendations
- Commit to world-class analysis and idea generation by establishing a chief scientist and research department in the Department of Foreign Affairs, Trade and Development, alongside competitive external research grants focused on specific global sustainable development priorities.
- Equip world-class Canadian professionals for the evolving frontiers of sustainable development through flagship university degree programs and incentives for ongoing skill certification.
- Establish systematic vehicles to leverage Canadian private sector resources for global sustainable development, including a prime ministerial advisory body, targeted innovation incentives, a development finance mechanism, and domestic corporate reporting on sustainable development benchmarks.
- Identify specific sustainable development goals where Canada will play an outsized global leadership role, including a long-term carbon-neutral development policy.
- Establish a growth-conditional budget for global sustainable development investments, just 2 cents of every new dollar of economic growth, up to a ceiling of 0.7 per cent of national income.

The shortcomings are not driven by partisanship. They have been consistent across recent Conservative and Liberal governments alike. We need to probe more deeply to consider other societal gaps. In fairness, large numbers of dedicated Canadians contribute across many individual fronts, ranging from the civil servants pioneering new models of support in Afghanistan to the scientists, entrepreneurs, and non-governmental organizations developing innovative technologies and initiatives around the world. Some politicians have of course dedicated significant personal efforts too. But the overall contributions remain inadequate when assessed against Canada's capacity to contribute and its ethos of global citizenship. This chapter offers ideas on how to interpret the underperformance and also how to begin to address it.

The Strategic Imperative of Global Sustainable Development

Some analysts, stuck in a bygone era, still think global development issues form the soft-hearted backwater to a hard-headed interest-based foreign policy. A deceptively alluring logic suggests that national security concerns always rank first among priorities, economic interests run a close second, and values-based approaches to helping other countries trail far behind. The implication is that only minimum effort is required towards global development, since something is better than nothing in a policy realm that is ultimately optional.

This logic falters quickly in the modern world where people, products, and problems all flow ever more freely across borders and sources of influence are quickly shifting. There is certainly a strong moral basis for investing in global development, but a purely self-interested view recognizes, for example, that a single international flight can transmit diseases like Ebola or SARS across continents within a matter of hours. All of humanity shares an interest in all countries, including the poorest, having robust health systems.

A more military-focused world view recognizes that many leading security threats now emanate from low-income economies, ranging from Afghanistan to Mali to Somalia to Yemen. Leading scientific evidence also shows that climate shocks have a direct causal role in increasing the frequency of violence. In many countries, when the temperature jumps or rains fail, crops fail too and people are more likely to fight.[2] In such cases, advanced economies are in turn more likely to deploy their own militaries, in effect tasking soldiers with climate adaptation strategies. Sustainable development shortcomings can cause global security headaches for years on end.[3]

Meanwhile, a business-oriented outlook appreciates that developing countries are now responsible for a majority of the world's annual economic growth. Their progress drives revenues for many Canadian exporters, including the natural resources sector. But one flipside of widespread economic progress is increased environmental strain, which can pose significant costs to business. As just one example, more than 300 million Asians now live at serious risk of disruptive coastal flooding.[4] Climate uncertainty is itself starting to be priced into many long-term investments. In China, leaders are acutely aware of economic and political tensions arising from different forms of pollution. In 2013, the country's Communist party leadership went so far as to call for an "ecological red line" to manage "eco-civilization."[5]

A purely geopolitical calculus also points towards the importance of global sustainable development. As emerging economies become responsible for a greater share of global economic activity, their domestic interests play a greater role in defining the global agenda. Consider the case of India, the world's largest democracy. In his 2014 Independence Day speech following a landslide national election victory, Prime Minister Narendra Modi broke with the occasion's tradition of sabre-rattling against Pakistan. Instead, he called for urgent steps in tackling open defecation, curbing violence against women, and broadening India's Internet economy, placing paramount importance on dignity and inclusion for all.

How will India pursue these priorities? Much will hinge on its domestic policy efforts. But as a lower-middle-income country with limited access to affordable capital, India also wants greater external finance to underpin its development strategy. The Bretton Woods institutional order is no longer adequate to support India's needs, so it has joined both the Asian Infrastructure Investment Bank and the BRICS' New Development Bank. China is the heavyweight source of capital for both institutions, so the old Atlantic powers are left struggling to navigate a rapid decline in a key source of their international influence.

The bottom line is that sustainable development now forms a global imperative from many angles, and Canada's success hinges on other countries' success. Canada, with its long history of helping to shape the international order, could play a central role in shaping the new global rules and systems – but only if it is seen to provide leadership aligned with emerging economies' own sustainable development interests. Basic principles of fairness, burden sharing, leadership by example, and evidence-based policymaking can help guide the nation's approach. Implementing them should form a centrepiece of our country's international grand strategy.

The Changing Global Landscape

Once sustainable development is understood as a policy imperative, the next question is how to identify objective performance standards. Fortunately, we are living amid a global transformation in cooperation for development results. Since 2000, standards have been anchored in the targets set by world leaders in the UN Millennium Declaration, guided by an overarching ambition to cut by half the many forms of extreme poverty by 2015.

The world has seen many global development breakthroughs in the years since. All regions have seen sustained economic growth, and many African development indicators have finally started to converge towards those of other regions. Hundreds of millions of people have been lifted out of poverty worldwide, and at least 40 million more children are in school. The health sphere has seen the greatest advances. As shown in figure 10.1, at least an extra 7.5 million children's lives have been saved compared to the trajectories of the late 1990s.[6] Add that to the roughly 6 million deaths averted thanks to the launch of life-saving AIDS treatment programs and a strong case can be made that well over 13 million additional lives have been saved over slightly more than a decade.[7]

In September 2015, world leaders adopted a new generation of "sustainable development goals" (SDGs) as universal objectives for 2030. Seventeen global goals have been established, linked to overarching themes of eliminating extreme poverty and social exclusion, building sustainable infrastructure to support prosperity, and protecting the planet's natural capital. The prospect of "zero" extreme poverty by 2030 is in fact tantalizingly within reach, with

Figure 10.1 Accelerated gains in child survival since 2000

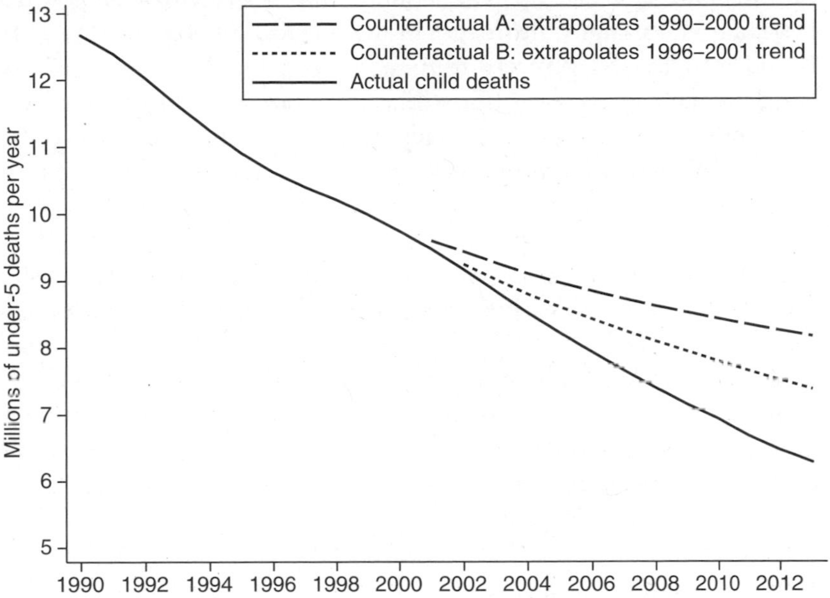

Source: John W. McArthur, "Seven Million Lives Saved: Under-5 Mortality since the Launch of the Millennium Development Goals," Brookings Global Economy and Development Working Paper, 2014

the problem already having shrunk to around 13 per cent of the developing world's population.[8]

But the broader contours of sustainable development are evolving quickly. Dichotomies between "developed" and "developing" countries are outdated, and the mix of issues and actors are more complex and universal than even a decade ago. In 2000, developing countries accounted for only 20 per cent of global economic output. As of 2013 the same countries accounted for more than 40 per cent.[9] Soon their share will be more than half, with Asia accounting for much of the shift.

Private capital has also extended its reach into many of the global economy's furthest frontiers. Fifteen years ago there was little foreign direct investment (FDI) in the poorest economies. Today it represents greater flows than official development assistance (ODA) in nearly a third of the same countries, especially those with mineral resources.[10] Public-private collaborations like Grow Africa are boosting FDI in agriculture, generally a leading vehicle for broad-based growth and poverty reduction. As a result, host countries need to manage a contentious mix of domestic interests, regional demands, macroeconomic policy trade-offs, and external pressures. New accountability mechanisms are often needed to ensure level playing fields among businesses, governments, and citizens.

Meanwhile, the bulging number of lower-middle- and upper-middle-income countries requires an enhanced blend of public and private finance to help transform their broader economies. Each economic sector has its own investment dynamics, with energy and transport systems presenting the biggest aggregate needs.[11] Many of these projects will set the planet's trajectory on climate change, so the challenge is to keep them both low-cost and low-carbon. A large share will also take shape at the level of municipalities, and so bolstering sub-sovereign financing mechanisms forms an operational imperative. Private capital will provide much of the required financing, but the needed scale of flows will only be unlocked through a blend of public incentives, guarantees, and project support mechanisms. This is why "beyond aid" development finance institutions like the International Finance Corporation can be so important.

At the same time, development assistance is still required to tackle four key priorities. The first is to support the poorest countries in delivering basic services for all. The number of low-income countries is declining, but on the current trajectory there will still be twenty-one in 2030, many of them "fragile states." A second is to help lower-middle-income countries confront their own multidimensional problems of poverty, in addition to newer challenges such as non-communicable diseases and higher levels of education for job growth. A third is to support institutional strengthening where desired. Many countries, for example, would like international support to build better tax collection systems and ensure fair royalty contracts in extractive industries. A fourth priority is to invest in common global public goods such as oceans, disease control, climate management, and agricultural research.

Another major priority for development cooperation is non-concessional lending, especially for emerging middle-income countries. This category of financing has dropped dramatically during the past decade. In the early 2000s, net flows from the World Bank's core lending arm, the International Bank for Reconstruction and Development, fell to near zero.[12] Some low-income countries like Rwanda and Senegal have moved to borrowing directly on global markets, and there are many concerns about what will happen to those countries after global interest rates rise.

The shifting finance requirements are interwoven with shifting geopolitics. Fast-growing regional democratic powers like Brazil, India, Indonesia, and Nigeria have limited say in global governance. China is becoming a major donor country and has a permanent seat on the UN Security Council, but much less formal authority in traditional multilateral economic institutions, even though it is already the world's largest economy in purchasing-power parity terms. As mentioned earlier, the emerging economies face ever stronger incentives to build parallel multilateral systems. The recently announced BRICS New Development Bank and Asian Infrastructure Investment Bank signal just one shift in this direction, as do debates over whether OECD countries should join the new institutions.

The Contrast of UK Leadership

When looking at the challenges, Canadians can draw inspiration from the United Kingdom's recent transformation into a clear global development leader. Money is not everything, but it tells a crucial story. In 1999, Canada invested 0.28 per cent of its national income in ODA and the UK invested 0.24 per cent. Fourteen years later, in 2013, the UK became the first G7 country to meet the 0.7 per cent global benchmark. Meanwhile, Canada still invested only 0.27 per cent of its income, ranking fifteenth among OECD countries. Canada's spending levels appear to be driven by inertia rather than any objective assessment of needs or share of global responsibilities.

Figure 10.2 Official development assistance as a share of national income, Canada vs. UK

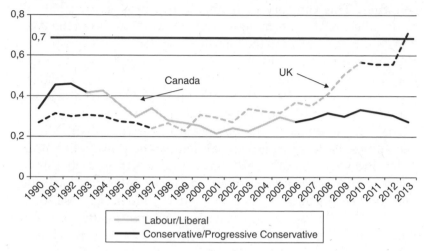

Note: Net of debt relief.

Data source: OECD-DAC online database.

In March 2015, the UK parliament went so far as to enshrine its 0.7 commitment into law. The same month the country became the first G7 economy to join the new Asian Infrastructure Investment Bank. The UK's front-footed overarching approach to new sustainable development frontiers earns it a leading role in shaping countless global policy debates. It was no coincidence, for example, that Prime Minister David Cameron was asked to co-chair the UN Secretary-General's recent high-level panel on the post-2015 global development agenda.

Figure 10.2 highlights the lack of partisan trends in either the UK or Canada. In the UK, the Conservative-led Cameron government continued its Labour predecessors' 0.7 per cent aid pledge, despite a major fiscal mess following the 2008 global financial crisis. In Canada, following the federal fiscal consolidation during the mid-1990s, there has been no clear difference between Liberal and Conservative governments' investment strategies.[13]

In recent years, the Harper government has made important advances in streamlining systems and improving impact per dollar. It has also played helpful roles in global food security and launched creative programs to support innovations in health and extractive industries, while the prime minister himself has co-chaired a global initiative on maternal and child health with the president of Tanzania. The preceding Chrétien and Martin governments made their own contributions, including debt relief in 1999, helping to launch the Global Fund in 2001, and drawing attention to sub-Saharan Africa at the 2002 Kananaskis G8 Summit. Paul Martin was probably the prime minister most fluent in global development policy circles when he entered the highest office. At a historic 2005 fork in the road, his government came very close to joining the UK in setting a 0.7 timetable to help finance the Millennium Development Goals (MDGs). At its core, this was a choice whether to be a frontbencher or backbencher on issues of primary importance for the majority of the world's countries. But in the end the Martin government demurred, a costly non-decision that still plays out today, every time the country's talented ambassadors are left to struggle for a seat at the front table.

The Role of Ideas and Public Debate

Fortunately, Canadians are open to greater engagement. Even after the global financial crisis, a 2012 survey suggested that more than two-thirds of the population believes reducing global poverty will help to fulfil human rights obligations, improve Canada's international reputation, reduce global conflict, and reduce the global HIV/AIDS pandemic.[14] A 2010 Angus Reid poll found that more than three-quarters of Canadians considered it important to be recognized as a world leader in these areas, and more than 60 per cent agreed that Canada should spend more on international aid.[15]

Some analysts argue that polling data is not important if support is "broad but thin" and does not drive voter decisions on Election Day. This is a self-defeating argument for two reasons.

First, Canadian surveys indicate similar levels of public support as in the UK, and the latter has evidently been adequate to underpin that country's generational policy leap, despite some fragility during a period of large domestic cutbacks. Canadians' support levels also appear to be much higher than corresponding measures for Americans, which commonly show wild overestimations of aid budgets and a regular desire to scale them back. So Canadian public interest should not be discounted too quickly. Second, very few foreign policy issues drive election outcomes in any case, so that is not the only test for setting policy. One doesn't hear military leaders argue not to take the nuclear Non-Proliferation Treaty seriously if it doesn't drive election results.

The difference between recent policy trajectories in Canada and the UK is likely driven, at least in part, by differing levels of public debate. Figure 10.3 suggests Canada notably trails the UK in public conversations about the MDGs. As a proxy measure, the graph shows the number of articles referencing them in the print editions of the *Globe and Mail*, the *Financial Times* of London, and *The Guardian* (UK) from 2002 through 2013. *The Guardian* has a long history of engaging on global social issues, so some analysts might be unsurprised by its relatively high level of attention to the MDGs. But the *Financial Times* also dedicated vastly more attention to the issues than the *Globe* did, notwithstanding the latter's temporary boosts in 2005, 2008, and 2010 – years with MDG-linked global summits.

The roots of media attention are complex, but they often correspond to topics raised by politicians and opinion leaders. In Canada these groups tend to have little background on issues of global sustainable development. And many NGO voices with experience in the field receive funding from the government, causing an inherent structural tension in public debates: advocates might fear retribution for questioning government policy, while officials might discount advocacy as self-interested. This is why tenured academics, business leaders, and philanthropically backed think tanks all have special roles in public debate. They need to operate at the global frontier of explaining problems and proposing solutions so that government officials, journalists, and opinion leaders can all draw from rich and rigorous debate.

Figure 10.3 Print references to Millennium Development Goals, 2001–2013

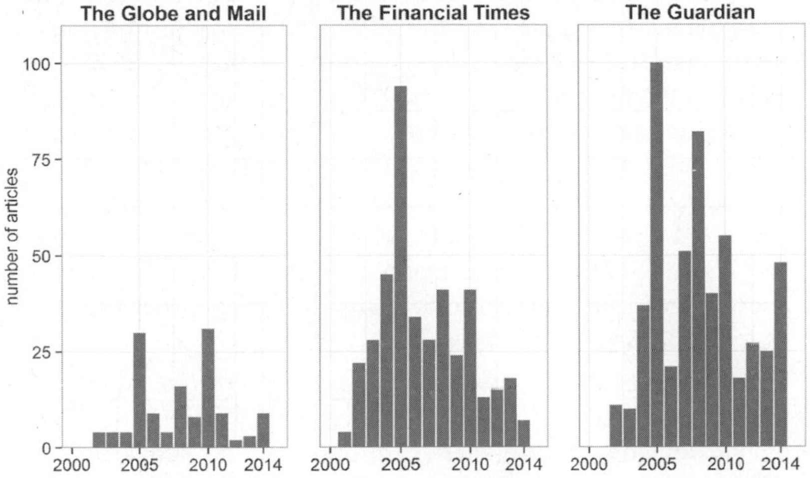

Source: John W. McArthur and Christine Zhang, "Who Talked (and Thought) about the Millennium Development Goals?" Brookings Institution, Brooke Shearer Working Paper Series no. 4, September 2015.

Three Pillars to Underpin a Platform for Global Policy Leadership

For every shortcoming in official development policy, we need to ask which gaps in ideas, expertise, and practice permitted the problem to come about. Moving forward, Canada's success will hinge on three mutually reinforcing ingredients: a commitment to world-class ideas; a commitment to equipping world-class professionals; and incentives to harness dynamic resources outside government. With those in place, Canada can pursue overarching long-term strategies that provide leadership at the scale that is desperately needed. Canada could, for example,

1. Commit to world-class analysis and ideas:

   Establish a chief scientist and research department within the Department of Foreign Affairs, Trade and Development. Rigorous analysis must set the tone both within and outside the government, and there are many gaps between the federal government and the global sustainable development research community. A prominent research department should be established within DFATD, led by a chief economist, chief scientist, or position of similar stature. The mandate should be to produce world-class analysis, including public analysis, of issues relevant to Canada's core international policy challenges. L'Agence Française de Développement, the UK Department for International Development and the US Agency for International Development already have chief economist positions, as does the US State Department.

Establish pools of major competitive research grants linked to frontier global priorities. Building on the strong legacy of the International Development Research Centre, the federal government should launch competitive pools of multiyear funding to conduct independent research on questions pertinent to forthcoming global policy goals. Grants must be anchored in academic independence so that researchers can challenge and help improve government policies based on evidence rather than opinions. Budgets of $15 or $20 million over five years can support a world-class team. Canada would gain a triple victory: its universities and think tanks would attract world-class talent, the government would have direct access to globally eminent ideas, and Canadian organizations would live at the forefront in understanding opportunities on the global horizon.

2. Commit to equipping world-class professionals:

Train practitioners for their global future. Canadian students face significant gaps in the country's university offerings for aspiring global development practitioners, especially at the graduate level. The federal government should coordinate with the provinces and national research councils to create flagship degree programs targeting the foremost sustainable development challenges. Canada needs new generations of young people who can bridge the insights of health science, social science, and natural science, with the versatility to manage across public, private, and non-profit sectors.

Grow the talents of seasoned practitioners. Advanced economies around the world are shifting towards more sophisticated divisions of labour, with increasingly fluid labour markets and even micro-certification among established professionals. Government practitioners need to be part of the trend – up-to-date, for example, on the latest scientific evidence in disease control, agriculture, environmental management, and social science. They also need to be able to operate efficiently in complex global structures that treat government, business, and civil society as equal partners. The federal government should upgrade its talent management programs to draw from emerging innovations in executive education, knowledge certification, and cross-sector collaboration. This could include incentives for offsite or online learning as qualifications for career advancement. It could also include sabbatical-type projects or field experiments conducted jointly with external entities.

3. Leverage private sector resources of all forms:

Convene structured groups to bridge insights inside and outside government. The government should convene a prime ministerial advisory body comprising top Canadian chief executives, entrepreneurs, technology leaders, academic researchers, and NGO practitioners who are operating at the forefront of global sustainable development problems. Such a body can form a vital two-way exchange. The government can draw from top-tier Canadian insight generators around the world, and the external entities can contribute to a more optimal policy environment for advancing their respective goals. Subgroups could be convened on specific priorities, similar to Prime Minister Harper's pursuits through the "Every Woman, Every Child" initiative.

Promote development-focused private finance. Canada has made important early steps to enhance the global development impact of its extractive industry firms. The long-term results will require a commitment to independent evaluation of both government policies and corporate performance. A recently announced development finance mechanism (DFM) could help mobilize private capital across broader sectors. Most other countries' bilateral DFMs were founded decades ago, and are hamstrung by outdated regulatory restrictions not suited to today's financing environment. With smart policies and top-tier talent, Canada could leapfrog to create the world's best bilateral DFM. To do so the institution needs to be adequately capitalized, have authorization to take equity positions, reinvest proceeds in itself, and adopt a tiered approach to lending concessions across countries, including grants for project preparation support where necessary.

Create goal-oriented public incentives for private innovations. The government should experiment around incentives to leverage creative assets of the Canadian business community. This should *not* be an indirect subsidy to Canadian firms or a relaunch of "tied aid." Nor should it support innovations merely for the sake of innovation. It should instead be defined by solving problems at scale, and focus on areas where explicit market-failure criteria justify public-private partnerships. For example, public instruments are needed to support climate-resilient smallholder farm credit around Africa. Canadian banks might be well suited to form a joint venture with the Canadian government, the African Development Bank, and enterprising local African banks to develop such products. Separately, digital scholarship vouchers for remote communities around the world could stimulate online educational innovations, drawing on Canada's unique mix of gaming, distance learning, and information technology enterprises.

Create incentives for low-carbon energy finance. Many of the world's commercial banks that historically financed infrastructure projects are cutting back their lending to meet the new Basel III capital requirements aimed at financial stability. Canada is home to some of the world's most respected pension funds and institutional investors, with great capacity to deploy capital in this area. To promote the major global priority of low-cost, low-carbon energy systems across emerging economies, the government should partner with similarly positioned countries like Denmark to advance multilateral incentives that improve risk-return profiles around the world.

Ensure domestic reporting against global sustainable development standards. The ever-expanding global reach of private, scientific, and NGO organizations requires standards of global responsibility across the board. The federal government should work with provincial regulators to require that all public companies above a modest threshold adopt sustainable development-consistent reporting standards as a condition of participation in stock exchanges.[16] This is particularly salient for the extractive industries, but it is equally important across all sectors. Industry-specific metrics should assess workforce conditions, energy efficiency, and ecosystem footprints, both within companies and across primary supply chains. NGOs and universities should also be encouraged to report on their performance against similar sets of standards.

4. Establish policies consistent with global scale:

Identify specific 2030 sustainable development goals where Canada will play an outsized role. As soon as the SDGs are set in late 2015, Canada should identify the priority areas where it will take on more than its fair share of responsibility, recognizing the need for coordination with other countries. Prioritizing implies mobilizing the country's political, technical, and economic resources, with intermediate benchmarks for 2020 and 2025. Top candidates could be prospective 2030 goals to (1) eliminate extreme poverty in fragile states; (2) eliminate preventable child and maternal deaths; (3) achieve "zero hunger" through sustainable food systems; (4) achieve universal access to secondary education, with a special focus on girls; and (4) achieve a minimum global standard for oceans management and preservation.

Set a long-term deadline for carbon-neutral development policy. One of Canada's trickiest strategic challenges as a major hydrocarbon exporter is to find ways to provide serious global leadership on climate change. One path with the most positive economic impact is for the government to scale up its incentives for clean energy science and technology development throughout Canada, as it already does in health. Another option would be to announce a goal of international carbon neutrality by a specific long-range date, like 2030, following the global precedent set by companies such as Microsoft and News Corp. For every ton of carbon Canada emits or exports, it would find a way to help other countries, especially developing countries, offset or sequester their emissions by an equivalent amount. Done right, such a policy would inspire Canadian creativity and boost net investments in the national economy. It would also earn positive political spillovers to other international policy priorities.

Establish a growth-conditional development budget, at 2 cents of every new dollar of income. Canada needs to increase its ODA budgets in order to align with global needs. A commitment contingent on economic growth could help make the necessary allocations in a way Canadians do not feel to be dipping in to their wallets. Specifically, the government should commit that only 2 cents of every dollar of national income will be allocated to global sustainable development challenges. Canada's national income is roughly $1.9 trillion as of 2014. Under reasonable projections of ongoing growth, it will reach $2.5 trillion by around 2025. Allocating two cents of every new dollar of income would allow Canada to reach the global 0.7 standard by that point. Such a growth-conditional commitment would only increase today's flows by around 8 per cent, but would yield disproportionate prestige and global political capital, especially for Canada as the "home of 0.7." Our ambassadors would regain their front seats at the global tables. Aid increases should not be blind resource commitments or aim to build new Canadian bureaucracies. Instead, they should finance the ground-level achievement of priority goals. Complementary research and partnerships outside government are crucial for driving high-calibre investments. These could include matching grants in partnership with other countries and private contributions, and could leverage a variety of innovative financing products, such as social impact bonds, to ensure measurability of results. Results-focused multilateral approaches deliver strong returns on investment, so the increments could be efficiently deployed by bodies like the Global Fund, the GAVI Alliance, UNICEF, the World Food Program, or a desperately needed new Global Fund for Education.

One Simple Decision

A commitment is sometimes defined as the one big upfront decision that means you don't need to worry about all the little decisions along the way. At the simplest level, Canadian leaders just need to commit to global sustainable development. That big decision will guide the many forms of needed investment along the way – measured in time, organization, financing, research, and public debate. It requires academic and business leaders as much as government and civil society leaders.

The UK experience shows how far a country can travel within a decade. Ten years from now, by 2025, Canada could easily join the same ranks as a global leader among peers. The country has long sidestepped a pivotal source of earned influence that, when done right, provides enormous direct benefits around the world. There are few issues where a mid-sized advanced economy can provide such a salient and measurable contribution to global outcomes. One upside is a stronger oar in the turbulent waters of rapid global transformation. If Canadians act decisively as a collective, they can help shape the new global order. Doing so will boost the world, and also Canada's interests.

chapter eleven

Dealing with Rapid Change and Systemic Risk: A Smart Canadian Approach to Global Institutions and Partnerships

YVES TIBERGHIEN

The world economy is in the midst of great transformation. Since the early 2000s, three major trends have combined to generate a bundle of great opportunities and great risks. First, technology, trade, and capital have continued to rise, making the world more technologically advanced and more interconnected than ever before in human history. Second, this spread of globalization has generated unprecedented systemic risks, particularly in finance, but also in cybersecurity, life-science governance, energy, food supply, climate, and the environment; rising intra-national inequality represents another growing risk. Our global governance apparatus remains poorly equipped to address these systemic risks and to generate necessary public goods, reminding us that global connectivity should not be taken for granted. It could suddenly collapse, as it did in the 1930s. Third, the last decade has witnessed the greatest change in global power in over a century: the Organisation for Economic Cooperation and Development (OECD) reports that the advanced democracies of the West (including Japan) have seen their long-stable share of the world economy drop from 60 per cent in 2000 to 49 per cent in 2011. Further, China became the world's largest economy, ahead of the United States, at the end of 2014 in terms of purchasing power parity (PPP).

We are living through a new period of intense change, technological shift, global competition, great multilevel risks, and high volatility. It is a time of opportunity and uncertainty, a time to be creative and entrepreneurial. It is a time of disruption and nonlinear change. Flexibility is the new strength. Countries that adjust to global change and play a role in shaping the future networks and institutions of tomorrow will come out on top. But many countries will face decline.

This chapter focuses on global economic and environmental institutions. The same discussion can be applied to other fields, such as health and development. Security (and human rights) institutions, however, follow a different track, with more risks and concerns for zero-sum game calculations, but improving global economic and environmental institutions should have a positive, indirect impact on the global security environment.

Many existing international institutions seem unable to cope with the pace of change today. As a result, new institutions, such as the G20, and related progress in the IMF monitory capacity, the Financial Stability Board, and associated forms of public-private partnerships, are appearing. Other advances include several new bilateral, regional, or multilateral mid-level tools, such as in the climate area or the Nagoya Protocol on Access to Genetic Resources and the Fair and Equitable Sharing of Benefits Arising from Their Utilization. In 2014 and 2015, in the face of inadequate adaptations by existing institutions such as the IMF and the World Bank, China took the lead in creating new competing institutions, including the Asian Infrastructure Investment Bank (AIIB), New Development Bank, and Silk Road Fund. By March 2015, these initiatives had divided G7 allies, particularly when the United Kingdom, France, Germany, and Italy decided to bandwagon with China and join the AIIB, against the wishes of the United States. New forms of cooperation and competition, such as cross-regional free trade agreements (FTAs), are also on the rise.

Canada is well endowed for such challenging times, but faces major risks and must be nimble. Will its economy manage to escape the twin traps of the resource curse and traditional manufacturing? Will Canada manage to build a web of new global economic partnerships that will allow its economy to adjust to global trends? Will Canada place itself at the core of rising networks and institutions that embed new rising powers in Asia/Pacific,

Chapter Summary

Key Transformations
- Global economic, environmental, and energy institutions that undergird our global economy are stretched to the limit.
- Over the last decade, global economic power has shifted more dramatically than in the previous 100 years, turning emerging powers (especially China and India) into core players in our global system.
- Yet, policy network and global institutions have not adapted to this new reality.

Implications for Canada
- Canada faces a bundle of new opportunities and risks; innovation and institutional entrepreneurship are necessary in such a period of rapid change.
- As a trading nation, Canada has a large stake in the global economic system.
- Canada faces positional and institutional risks in the face of nimble competitors; global competitiveness requires fast policy action to position Canada as a hub in the fast changing system and a shaper of global rules.

Recommendations
- Canada should take the lead in creating a new regime of global energy governance.
- Canada should take the lead in developing best practices of foreign direct investment interactions with social, indigenous, and environmental realities (social licensing) to implement the UN Global Compact.
- Canada should immediately join the Asian Infrastructure Investment Bank and support the voices of large emerging nations in global institutions.
- Canada should invest in concrete mechanisms to develop public policy networks between emerging nations of Asia and North America, including an emerging scholarship program in the policy field, and a multi-stakeholder annual policy event.
- Canada should devote maximum priority to the new Canada–China economic strategic dialogue and develop common policy innovations in trade and investment, internationalization of the Chinese currency, development norms, and academic partnerships.

or will it stick to familiar patterns and miss these opportunities? Will Canada be a catalyst in advancing global governance and addressing systemic risks, or will it free-ride on decaying old institutions?

It is time for Canada to invest further in new global and regional institutions, particularly institutions that include emerging powers in Asia. Like South Korea or Singapore, Canada can shape the trends of global networks and establish itself as a hub of global institutions. In short, Canada has the capacity and interest to be a global governance entrepreneur. Great returns on such investment are possible. This chapter offers a framework and concrete ideas to implement such a vision.

A Period of Rapid Global Change and Systemic Risk

As Roland Paris and Taylor Owen note in the introduction, the global system is characterized by increased global connectivity, expansion of markets, and acceleration of technological innovation, but also by increased systemic risks, especially in the environmental and economic spheres. These underlying trends form the foundation for new functional needs, incentives, and constraints in the realm of global cooperation and global institutions.

This means, ironically, that advances in global connectivity and global economic activity are also making us more vulnerable to sudden contagion from one spot of the world to the entire system. Apart from volatile financial markets, the world economy has a second Achilles heel: energy and commodity markets. As several of these markets move into relative scarcity, we may see a return to very competitive dynamics among countries struggling to attain security in energy or in crucial food commodities, as well as in essential metals and minerals. If even one large player lost trust in global markets, a competitive game could be unleashed. This would lead to forceful national strategies and a reassertion of power over markets. We witnessed this in the 1930s. Indeed, this dynamic lay at the origin of the Second World War in the Pacific.

As well, globalization generates more complex and multifunctional risks, such as climate change, or technological risks that can interact with natural disasters (as occurred in the Fukushima nuclear disaster). The *Global Risks Report* defines systemic risk as "the risk of breakdowns in entire systems."[1] Its Global Risk Perception Survey highlights several groups of critical systemic risks in 2014: economic risks (fiscal crises and their potential chain-reaction effects, structural unemployment, severe income inequality), environmental risks (water crises, climate change, extreme weather events, food crises), political crises, and global governance failures. Among these, global governance failure may be the most dangerous because it is connected to all other issues.

In addition to this bundle of opportunities and risks, the world is experiencing the greatest and fastest rebalancing of power in over a century. As shown in the UN Development Program's *Human Development Report* of 2013, six Western countries (the US, Canada, Germany, UK, France, Italy) accounted for 20 per cent of the world economy in 1820; this share rose to 50 per cent in 1950, but fell back below 30 per cent in 2011, in purchasing-power parity (PPP) terms. Meanwhile, the share of the three largest Southern countries (China, India, Brazil) dropped from 50 per cent in 1820 to 10 per cent in 1950, but jumped back to over 30 per cent in 2011. In nominal dollars, the size of the Chinese economy relative to the US economy rose from 6 per cent in 1990 to 12 per cent in 2000, 40 per cent in 2010, and 55 per cent in 2013, according to the World Bank.[2] China is set to pass the United States in absolute terms in 2019–20. The size of its economy relative to the US economy (again in PPP terms) was 58 per cent in 2008 at the beginning of President Obama's term and passed the 100 per cent mark in late 2014.[3]

Between 2004 and 2013, moreover, British Columbia exports to the United States dropped from 65 per cent of total exports to 46 per cent of the total, whereas BC exports to Asia increased from 24 per cent to 43 per cent of the total. Indeed, 2014 was the likely first year in which BC exports to Asia trumped its exports to the United States.[4]

Rising emerging powers can mean more business opportunities and increased connectivity. They also could mean a more multipolar world and new power realities. While in 2000 OECD countries still represented 60 per cent of the world economy in PPP terms, they fell below 50 per cent in 2011 and will be below 45 per cent in 2020.[5] It was still possible for the United States and Europe to legitimately claim unchallenged leadership at the IMF and World Bank in 2000, but not so today. Within the emerging power group, China is by far the dominant one, but other significant players include India, Brazil, Indonesia, Turkey, Mexico, South Africa, possibly Nigeria, and Korea.

Nevertheless, there is a distinct lack of policy networks linking emerging countries and established powers. G7 nations have worked with each other on global economic issues for nearly four decades. Emerging powers are relatively new to global governance and are facing a steep learning curve. Networks that include Western policy advisers, bureaucrats, and politicians with their counterparts in China, India, Indonesia, or Brazil are still weak and are prone to misperceptions and misunderstandings.

Post-war global institutions that were created to enhance cooperation between nations and manage a new global economy are overstretched and urgently need repair. The UN continues to be a useful forum for exchanges and its secretariat often has an entrepreneurial and fact-finding role. Yet, the UN's role in global economic affairs remains limited. The centres of real action in this policy domain are in Washington (International Monetary Fund, World Bank), Geneva (World Trade Organization), and Basel (Financial Stability Board, Bank for International Settlements). These Bretton Woods (and post–Bretton Woods) institutions are all in flux and transition. Their old modus vivendi, dominated by large Western powers, is no longer functional now that China, India, Brazil, and Indonesia are also top players. Paralysis at the WTO since its 2001 Cancun meeting has led to a proliferation of bilateral FTAs, followed by competitive "mega-regional" FTAs in the 2010s (such as the Trans-Pacific Partnership versus the Regional Comprehensive Economic Partnership). The outgoing WTO director-general has warned that this new competitive system may be very risky for the global trade regime.[6]

The International Monetary System (IMS) remains centred on the US dollar, but is rudderless. Most other countries are increasingly frustrated with a situation in which the currency at the core of the IMS is managed as a purely private and captive good and not as a global public good. There is currently no alternative to the US dollar; the Japanese Yen rose and declined, the Euro remains risky, and China's Renminbi still has a long way to go. Nevertheless, monopoly conditions are not sufficient for long-term stability and cooperation.

On the energy front, there is no institution to effectively monitor and undergird global markets. The International Energy Agency (IEA) remains tied to the OECD and excludes China, India, Brazil, and others – at a time when China is becoming the world's largest energy importer. Old networks and power structures are sticky. As noted by Andrew Leach and Stewart Elgie in this volume, negotiating the post-carbon transformation over the next thirty years will be a critical challenge – and not easy, partly for this reason.

All global institutions and patterns of cooperation are in flux and transition, as countries try to cope with the new global configuration of power, a configuration that has changed faster than the mindsets of policymakers. The only major institutional innovation has been the G20, a Canadian idea. This new structure has given a chance to established and emerging powers in equal numbers to discuss global issues and seek common agreements. It is the most useful arena today, although consensus on institutional solutions is mostly elusive, apparently because the sense of crisis present in the aftermath of the 2008 financial crisis has largely abated. Paralysis in US domestic politics and the return to interest-group dominance in key policy arenas (such as finance) are also major constraints among G20 members.

Canadian Risks and Opportunities

Because of its multicultural networks, high human and social capital, stable institutions, and natural resources, Canada is well positioned in the global economy. It has all the assets to grow faster than other developed countries and be at the centre of global networks and institutions. Canada can take advantage of the many global opportunities outlined above, namely, increased connectivity, technological change, and tight energy and commodity markets. It has the human capital and the wherewithal to nudge global institutions and catalyse the formation of new networks linking emerging and established powers.

Yet, Canada also faces several specific risks, which must be managed. The most serious one is the global systemic risk in finance, technological regulation, and the environment. If a chain reaction speeds through the global economy as in 1997 or 2008, Canada will not be immune. Canada has a large stake in working in the G20 and other global institutions to promote new solutions dealing with global systemic risks. Any conflict between the United States and China, for example, would likely have serious negative effects on Canada. It is in Canada's interests to build a reactive capacity to changes in one region or one sector through counter-moves in others. Canada can partly manage such risks through diversification of its commitments.

Second, Canada also faces positional risks in the global economy. Fast change and global volatility mean that nations can rise and fall very quickly. Sources of competitive advantage change quickly. Nimble and adaptable nations that are good at rapid technological upgrade, structural adjustments, and innovation will come on top. Canada must be proactive in building the institutional interface to avoid falling into the well-known "resource trap": a resource economy can quickly turn into a boom-and-bust cycle that concentrates wealth in a small enclave or group of people, while not generating public welfare. Such an economy renders the country vulnerable, rather than resilient. Canada's high dependence on carbon resources at a time of global environmental crisis makes it more vulnerable.[7] Meanwhile, Canada's manufacturing base must have the incentives to avoid decay and to adjust continuously, which will require active leadership of the government in the area of FTAs, bilateral investment treaties, and an industrial policy interface.

Third, there is also a competitive institutional risk. Several nations are now building their web of institutional links and placing themselves at the centre of such transnational webs – as hubs in global production chains, leaders in global ideas-formation, and first movers in the construction of regional and global institutions. Korea and Singapore are two good examples. Canada has been slower than some Asian countries in the 2000s in playing such roles.

Fourth, there is a need to rebalance human and policy investments towards emerging powers, particularly in Asia. This pivoting of Canada from a sheer attachment to the United States and Europe and towards emerging nations has begun. But it can be more purposeful. These could be areas in which Canada can define its future impact.

A New Canadian Approach to Global Governance: Entrepreneurship and Multi-Actor Connectivity

It is essential to recognize the value of global governance and to invest in it, including novel new forms of governance. Canada should shift its position away from a tactical short-term positioning towards a long-term-oriented institutional entrepreneurship that addresses global public good requirements. Nations that do this may bear a short-term cost and must invest in the right human capital, but will reap the rewards of enhanced reputation, soft power, influence in multi-actor global networks, and long-term competitive advantages.

To what ends should Canada pursue such entrepreneurship and connectivity? The primary purpose should be to ensure the long-term survival and stability of the post-war liberal economic order through the right combination of enlargement and reform. Canada has an enormous stake in this system. Yet, great-power rivalry and a lack of creativity and innovation could cripple it. The secondary goal should be to ensure that reforms in the global financial architecture fit Canadian values and support Canada's economic interests. Positioning Canada at the core of new networks is a good way to advance these goals.

Canada should invest more in the G20 process and play a role in upgrading its institutional basis and its agenda, turning it into a "thinking box" for cooperation between established and emerging powers. Canada should continue to support the Mutual Assessment Process (MAP) and reforms of the global financial architecture, including measures that can decrease systemic risk, such as a smartly designed small tax on speculative currency transactions (the so-called Tobin tax), while recognizing that this requires complex global cooperation.

Many other institutions should be incubated, in areas such as global energy governance, global investment governance, the international monetary system, global food production, and environmental regulation. All Canadian stakeholders should be involved in taking the lead in such institutional innovation, including government at all levels, universities, think tanks, private actors, and civil society. Countries that manage to be entrepreneurial first movers will be able to upload their ideas into the global matrix – and will benefit greatly. As noted, this strategy has been pursued by countries such as Korea and Singapore. Canada could take the lead in a serious rethinking of global energy governance (where global markets don't function efficiently, given the presence of cartels and oligopolies). Unless a truly global energy governance institution is established, emerging powers will soon develop their own separate system, which would not serve Canada's interest. In addition:

- Canada should set up a Canadian-led global task force to incubate new global rules and a global institution to govern global energy and commodity markets – targeting a global Achilles heel where Canada has a tremendous comparative advantage.
- Canada should develop a long-term strategic vision of its position as a hub of FTAs and investment treaties, with a more aggressive action plan to implement such a strategy. The aim should be to make Canada a trade and investment entrepreneur with the ability to shape future rules of the game at the global level.
- Canada should play a leading role in reinvigorating the G20 process beyond its current coasting phase and turn it into a group with the ability to shapes rules and markets over the longer term.

Canada should also pursue closer direct links with emerging powers. Any investment in human and policy networks with China, India, Indonesia, Brazil, Vietnam, Myanmar, Turkey, or South Africa and Nigeria will pay huge dividends in the future. The world is in the midst of a major power rebalancing towards these countries. Becoming an effective and trusted partner of theirs will generate great business opportunities and guarantee Canadian prosperity and relevance. Such engagement requires joint action by governments, universities, business, civil society, and individuals. In particular, Canada should engage China, India, Korea, Indonesia, and Brazil as core partners at the G20 and go beyond its traditional reliance on G7 networks. Canada could incubate proposals at the G20 in cooperation with such key emerging powers. In particular:

- Canada should immediately support and, where appropriate, join new global and regional institutions led by emerging powers, such as the China-led AIIB, while also supporting the internationalization of the Renminbi. The more that rising powers have a stake in global institutions, the more stable the global system will be. Canada could play a positive role in promoting compatibility between such new institutions and existing ones. Canada should also support major innovation in the global development infrastructure, as suggested by McArthur in this volume.
- Canada should play a supportive role in making the TPP China-compatible, with the aim of having China join the TPP over time.
- Canada should give top priority to the Canada–China strategic economic dialogue, which the Canadian prime minister and Chinese president established in early November 2014. By investing in this dialogue, Canada can ensure that China's top leaders will take it seriously and that the dialogue becomes an effective tool to deliver powerful benefits to the relationship and externalities for the global system.

A third priority involves multi-actor and multi-stakeholder partnerships. All effective foreign and domestic policy today relies on leveraging and partnership between the public sector, private sector, and civil society sector, in addition to universities and think tanks. The more ideas, networks, and people move across these boundaries and support each other, the more effective Canada will be on the global scene. The government can sometimes play the role of catalyst, sometimes hub, sometimes partner. The times call for a nimble and entrepreneurial smart state. In particular:

- Canada should establish a scholarship fund targeting future elites of emerging nations to be trained in Canada, similar to the Fulbright scholarship. This fund could be strategically aimed at a few key nations and a few sectors to ensure maximum impact and Canadian soft power in such fields.
- Canada could establish a top-level short-term annual forum on targeted global policy issues (rotating issues over years) that is geared towards an innovative dialogue between elites of emerging nations and Canadian societal actors (private sector, NGOs, universities, government actors at various levels, etc.)
- Canada could establish competitions for multi-stakeholder projects that involve the private sector, NGOs, and universities to address one particular policy issue at the global or a national level.

Fourth, successful foreign investment projects require active engagement of social, labour, and environmental rules to ensure that benefits spread to larger communities and generate win-win feedback loops. Absent such an institutional interface, foreign direct investment (FDI) projects can provide quick returns for some individuals and corporations without generating more widely shared benefits. Canada should play a leading role, through a partnership among government, civil society, the private sector, and universities, in identifying and supporting institutional tools that turn FDI flows into win-win instruments for host societies, particularly poorer countries. This remains a domain in its infancy, and Canada could help develop global best practices.

Will other large players welcome an increased Canadian presence in multilateralism and network building? By and large, Canada has built and retained a reputation as a country with credible know-how, a "public good" orientation, and support for global human networks. This reputation makes it easier for Canada to play the role of agenda-setter and catalyst of cooperation.

We are living through interesting times of great opportunities, change, and global risks. Since 2008, it has become clear that the governance infrastructure of the global economy is insufficient. As a mid-sized trading nation, Canada depends on a stable, functioning, open global economy. Yet, the future health and stability of the global economy depend on the upgrading of the institutional infrastructure that sustains it. At a time of a new power configuration, such upgrading can only happen through creative cooperation between emerging powers and established powers. This is the new reality.

With its human endowments, diplomatic skills, and non-threatening reputation, Canada could play an important role in efforts to renew and strengthen global governance. Doing so would serve the public good, but it would also put Canada at the core of the future infrastructure of the global economy. This would, in turn, benefit all Canadian players, including business, policy-makers, and universities.

The world is moving fast. Canada must be nimble and energetic, and join the handful of nations that are able to read and anticipate future global trends through proactive leadership. This is a time for Canada to demonstrate institutional and global governance entrepreneurship.

Imagining a More Ambitious Canada

ROLAND PARIS AND TAYLOR OWEN

The contributors to this book were each assigned three tasks: first, to evaluate major global trends in their respective areas of focus; second, to describe the implications of these changes for Canada; and third, to propose strategies that would position Canada to succeed not in the world that *was*, but in the world that is in the process of *emerging*. In this chapter, we summarize common elements in their analyses and draw out nine general conclusions for the future direction of Canada's international strategy – and we then add a tenth of our own (see text box).

Ten Lessons and Prescriptions
1. Don't underestimate the scale and speed of global transformation.
2. Recognize that Canadian policy isn't adapting quickly enough.
3. Creatively reframe policy issues and break down old "silos."
4. Mobilize coalitions around Canadian goals.
5. Strengthen international rules and norms.
6. Use knowledge as a comparative advantage.
7. Focus on practical solutions to concrete problems.
8. Identify long-term strategic objectives – and stick with them.
9. Don't succumb to a "small Canada" syndrome.
10. Update liberal internationalism for a new era.

---

1. Don't underestimate the scale and speed of global transformation

The central premise of this book is that the world is changing so rapidly that a fundamental rethinking of Canadian international policy is required. In the introduction we identified several "global shifts," or broad transformations cutting across individual policy domains, including the rapid diffusion of power to rising states and non-state actors, the waning of US leadership, the expansion of the global middle class, the changing pattern of global energy sources and flows, mounting pressure on the natural environment, greater volatility and turbulence in global politics, and an increasingly strained system of global governance.

Many of these trends are also visible in the individual chapters of this volume, which describe profound changes under way in their respective areas. Patterns of trade and investment are undergoing dramatic change. In energy and extractive industries the global markets are more competitive than ever. New technologies, emerging powers, and non-state actors are gaining importance in the international security environment, giving rise to new conventional and unconventional threats. Global governance is not keeping pace with these changes; many of our international institutions and regimes were built for an earlier era. Questions of Internet management and cybersecurity are increasingly difficult for traditional state-based actors to manage. Old assumptions about international development, including the very distinction "developed" and "developing" states, are rapidly falling out of date. Climate change proceeds apace, human rights norms are facing intensified pressure, and there are mounting demands for more effective humanitarian action.

The upshot is clear: any consideration of Canadian foreign policy that does not begin by recognizing the scale and speed of global transformation is likely to be based on old – and increasingly false – premises.

2. Recognize that Canadian policy isn't adapting quickly enough

All the chapters argue unambiguously that Canada is failing to keep up with these global changes. This perspective is striking and consistent. Danielle Goldfarb, for example, observes that other countries are well ahead of Canada in thinking strategically about their trade and investment policies. Andrew Leach and Andrew Mandel-Campbell both point to inadequate innovation and efficiency in Canada's natural resource industries, which face intense international competition. Although his recommendations focus more on the environmental effects of these industries, Stewart Elgie also contends that Canada could be a leader, rather than a laggard, in promoting solutions to global climate change.

According to Yves Tiberghien, Canada is well positioned to bridge the growing divide between established and emerging powers, particularly in Asia, but is not yet doing so. John McArthur writes that Canada "is stuck in a straggler approach to global sustainable development." Jennifer Keesmaat argues that Canada should be doing much more to address urbanization problems at home and abroad, noting that "the world's poorest, most vulnerable, and least resilient cities are also the fastest growing."

Jonathan Paquin contends that Ottawa's recent penchant for "tough-talk diplomacy" has been regarded as largely empty rhetoric by the rest of the world, and that Canada should be play a more active and constructive role in addressing international security challenges from cybersecurity to robotic weapons. Similarly, David Petrasek notes that Canada has offered a heavy dose of moralizing, but has failed to pursue a sustained international human rights policy.

This is a long list of shortcomings. While the authors recognized that Canada has recently been active on certain issues, including child and maternal health, most suggest that Canada is becoming increasingly marginal in world affairs – and, worse, that it has been marginalizing *itself* by failing to adapt to global shifts. This poses a problem. Canada's core interests, including its prosperity, are at stake.

Indeed, there is a sense of urgency in all the chapters. Canada cannot afford to stand still. The world in which we once engaged as a "middle power" no longer exists. Simply stating our desire to be relevant is not enough. In many areas in which we once engaged, the international policy conversation has moved on. Re-engagement will require assertive, strategic, ambitious, and sustained involvement in an increasingly crowded and complex global field.

3. Creatively reframe policy issues and break down old "silos"

Many contributors also suggested that thinking strategically about today's cross-cutting global challenges will require breaking down boundaries between foreign and domestic policy, including the traditional silos of trade, the military, diplomacy, and development. Taking this suggestion seriously could have far-reaching implications for existing academic disciplines, practitioner communities, methods of engagement, and the "scale" of policy. For example, framing an international policy conversation around the challenges faced by cities and urbanization, as Keesmaat and Petrasek both recommend, would require analysis and action across local, regional, and national scales, addressing a mix of issues, from sustainability, security, and poverty to human rights and innovation. Leach offers a different example of this kind of reframing when he argues for breaking down the conceptual and regulatory barriers separating production, manufacturing, and extraction. This would allow us to think of Canada's resource sector as something to be "manufactured" and not just extracted or consumed.

The same is true for many of our pressing global challenges, including climate change, terrorism, growing inequality, and cybersecurity. Goldfarb argues that making Canada more competitive in the rapidly changing global economy will require a whole-of-Canada approach. "Domestic policy actions," she writes, "may not draw as much public attention as signing trade deals or sending trade missions, but they are no less critical, and perhaps even more so." From this perspective, domestic policy concerns such as regulatory differences between the provinces, education and skills programs, and infrastructure development projects, need to be seen through a foreign policy lens. When Jennifer Welsh and Emily Paddon recommend involving diaspora groups in Canada in humanitarian emergency-response initiatives, they are also calling for a breaking down of divisions between what are often considered separate domestic and international issues.

These arguments suggest that more strategic approaches to Canada's international policy require not only understanding that the world has changed and that complacency in the face of that change is disadvantageous, but also that traditional definitions of policy domains serve to inhibit strategic thinking.

4. Mobilize coalitions around Canadian goals

The proliferation of actors in international affairs, including rising states and non-governmental organizations, will make it harder for individual countries to pursue policy agendas by themselves. Increasingly, global effectiveness will require the ability to assemble and mobilize broad "action coalitions" of diverse actors who share an interest in specific policy objectives.[1] Several of the contributors to this volume suggest that Canada is well equipped to perform this role, but doing so will require a conscious strategy on the part of the Government of Canada and the collaboration of other levels of government and non-state groups: in short, a pan-Canadian effort. This has been done in a more limited way in the past, including, for example, in the campaign to ban anti-personnel landmines that resulted in the Ottawa Convention of 1998, or Ottawa's more recent leadership on the issue of child and maternal health. But these instances remain the exceptions, and the range of capabilities of global actors is now far more disparate.

Over the last hundred years, Canada has played an important role in the development of the current international architecture, be it the UN, international legal bodies, or the large network of international development organizations. But many of these institutions face crises of legitimacy and effectiveness. For some issue areas, authors argued that we need to work within this system to promote and modernize ideas and practices that are still vital. Welsh and Paddon argue that we need to re-engage with the implementation of the Responsibility to Protect, focusing in particular on civilian protection. Tiberghien maintains that Canada has a stake in the post-war liberal economic order, and that we therefore need to work to enhance the global financial architecture in a way that fits our values and supports our economic interests. This involves, he suggests, further investing in the G20 and imagining it as a place to develop an institutional agenda that "deeply and proactively engages emerging powers."

Others go further, arguing that new policy challenges may require entirely new international architecture. Raymond points out that while there are a wide range of emerging international institutions to regulate the Internet, many are decisively state-centric and don't adequately incorporate the business and civil society communities that both have significant power and that also "tend to value non-hierarchical, consensus decision-making procedures." Petrasek argues that in the field of human rights we need to move beyond the UN to the much broader objective of human rights diplomacy, which empowers the wide range of non-state actors who ultimately shape how Canada "acts" in the world. Paquin would like to see Canada invest in new forms of collaborative conflict management that would prioritize ad hoc, informal, and improvised processes, while Keesmaat sees a largely informal network of cities serving as a platform for addressing big transnational problems such as poverty, migration, crime, climate change, and pluralist tolerance. In all these areas, the authors underline the importance of building networks, coalitions, and institutions in order to advance Canada's international goals.

5. Strengthen international rules and norms

Likewise, many authors pointed out that Canada has in the past proven effective at developing norms and laws in the international system. As a moderately-sized country that is open to the world,

Canada has always had a direct interest in helping to maintain the rules-based international order that is now under strain. Norms and rules are not equivalent to organizations; rather, they are the "operating system" of global politics that regulate the behaviour of states and other international actors in myriad domains. Canada benefits when this operating system supports an open international economy and a peaceful world. In this vein, Petrasek, Welsh, and Paddon all argue that Canada needs to build on its role as a norm entrepreneur in relation to human rights, for example, and Paquin maintains that Canada should be a leader in norm setting and regulating in relation to cyberespionage and the use of lethal autonomous weapons systems.

However, as new kinds of actors from ISIS to Anonymous gain prominence, and as states with different ideas about justice and sovereignty also come to the fore, we will need to devise new methods of rule building. In the realm of cybersecurity and Internet governance, for example, Raymond argues for what he calls "soft law," which "encompasses an array of quasi-legal and diplomatic instruments that stop short of formal international treaties." This is important because, he points out, the Internet functions as "a series of nested clubs, where rule-making remains decentralized and will continue to occur across levels of analysis, geographic jurisdictions, and institutional contexts."

6. Use knowledge as a comparative advantage

Another thread running through most of this volume is the importance of Canadian expertise, knowledge, and technical know-how in any forward-looking international policy strategy. For Goldfarb, Mandel-Campbell, and Leach, innovation is a key to our competitiveness. McArthur recommends establishing a chief scientist and research department within DFATD, emulating a model used in France, the UK, and the US to ensure rigorous analysis and research innovation in development policy. Tiberghien sees Canada's multicultural networks and human capital as a source of creativity for developing new forms of international institutional collaboration.

Technical expertise is similarly central to Elgie's vision of Canada as a global leader in the environmentally responsible production of natural resources.

For Keesmaat, too, sharing Canadian experiences and knowledge of urbanism with developing countries should be part of a multilayered cities agenda. Raymond also emphasizes know-how, arguing that the challenges of Internet governance are so complex and changing so rapidly that the most sensible approach for Ottawa would be to "prioritize learning and flexibility" in this area. Canada, he maintains, should bring together practitioners and researchers to understand the social and policy implications of new communications technologies, and aim to be a world leader by building Canadian-based expertise in the requirements and possible methods of governing the Internet. In short, most of our contributors regard expertise as a critical comparative advantage for Canada. Building and leveraging knowledge should be an integral part of any forward-looking international strategy.

7. Focus on practical solutions to concrete problems

While theories of world politics and foreign policy can shed light on patterns of international relations, the contributors to this volume focus relentlessly on the need for practical solutions to specific problems, recognizing that a shifting international environment is changing both the type and scope of the challenges facing Canada, and the utility of various policy tools and strategies for addressing these problems. We could take this a step further: Canada's greatest contributions to global order – our contribution to Allied efforts during the world wars, the creative and committed diplomacy of Canadians after the Second World War, and their assistance in creating the United Nations, NATO, and a system of rules to govern international trade, as well as the innovation of peace operations, Canada's contribution to the campaign against South African apartheid, our advocacy for and welcoming of refugees, our leading role in efforts to establish the International Criminal Court and to ban anti-personnel landmines, and most recently our leadership on the issue of maternal, newborn, and child health in the world – have all been driven by a spirit of public-mindedness, yet they have all been relentlessly pragmatic and problem-focused.

Yet, while this has always been a part of Canada's international policy tradition, it has not always been fully appreciated. Debates about whether Canada is a "middle" or "principal" power, for example, sometimes seem to obscure more than they reveal. Perhaps the pragmatic bent of this volume reflects a generational change in the ranks of Canadian foreign-policy thinkers, with the newer generation having less interest in paradigmatic debates. None of the authors seems interested in debating the value of "soft" versus "hard" power, for example. Rather, they appear to recognize that both types of power – indeed, *all* the instruments at Canada's disposal – should be mobilized to advance Canadian interests and to contribute to global public goods. Their emphasis on problem solving also suggests that the success of Canada's international policy should be judged on the basis of demonstrated results. We welcome this approach.

8. Identify long-term strategic objectives – and stick with them

Given the pace of global change and the fact that new governments come to power with different views and priorities, long-term international policy planning can be difficult. But many of our authors stressed the importance of moving away from short-term policy making. Too often, they lamented, foreign policy seems to be driven by election-cycle political calculations and the desire of governments to place their own stamp on foreign policy.

Many of the recommendations in this volume require long-term commitments, including the building of coalitions and networks on global topics of importance to Canada, and the cultivation of expertise within Canada on key issues. Expanding Canadian economic involvement in the rapidly growing markets of the

Asia-Pacific region demands a sustained effort to deepen commercial and diplomatic relationships. Working on the problems of cities at home and abroad is a long-term endeavour. So is boosting the productivity, innovativeness, and environmental soundness of Canada's extractive sectors. The same is true of improving human rights. As Petrasek points out, the Harper government's initiative on child and forced marriage will take decades to achieve; such projects should not simply flutter in the political winds.

Tiberghien similarly urges that Canada pivot from its "tactical short-term positioning toward a long-term-oriented institutional entrepreneurship that addresses global public good requirements." And as John McArthur notes, both global sustainable development goals and carbon policy are by definition long-term initiatives that require us to develop policies that are firmly grounded in research, and then to stick with them across changes in government.

9. Don't succumb to a "small Canada" syndrome

Ultimately, we were struck by both the ambition and the optimism of our contributors. The dominant message to emerge from these chapters is that Canada can and must pursue a more comprehensive, constructive, and ambitious international strategy: more comprehensive in involving private actors and civil society groups in the conception and implementation of policy; more constructive in working with other countries, non-government organizations, and multilateral institutions towards common goals; and more ambitious in placing Canada at the forefront of efforts to make the world safer, more prosperous, and healthier.

None of the authors believed that Canada was achieving its potential or using all of the policy levers, international and domestic, at its disposal. On the contrary, the impression one gets from reading these chapters is that Canada has neglected its international policy for too long, and that the price for doing so will continue to rise over time.

Indeed, while each of the authors emphasized different objectives, they all reject what Daniel Livermore has called a "small

Canada" approach to international policy, one based on resigna-
tion that Canada's international role is destined to fade, and that
consequently treats foreign affairs as a matter of secondary importance.[2] This type of thinking is counterproductive and can become
a self-fulfilling prophecy. Neglecting international policy would
reduce Canada's influence and capacity to shape international
events. More importantly, it would fail to recognize that positioning Canada for success in a rapidly changing world will demand
initiatives at both the domestic and international level – and approaches that transcend the conceptual and policy boundaries of
traditionally defined "foreign policy."

10. Update liberal internationalism for a new era

We would take this observation further. Speaking only for ourselves and not necessarily for the other authors of this book, we believe that Canada has experienced a period of weak international
policy leadership in recent years. Although some observers have
objected to the Harper government's brash style and bald state-
ments on a number of international issues, our objection is that our
leaders have paid *too little* attention to foreign affairs. Nor should
Canada turn its back on a tradition of diplomacy that has served
this country well liberal internationalism.[3]

This approach is a blend of realist and liberal elements of foreign policy. Among other things, it emphasizes multilateral cooperation and international rule building, not solely because doing
so reflects Canada's own domestic values and success as a multicultural, bilingual country, but perhaps even more importantly
because energetic multilateral diplomacy provides Canada with
opportunities for international influence that it would have otherwise lacked. This approach has never prevented Ottawa from
taking strong stands on important issues, from nuclear arms control to South African apartheid. Nor has it precluded participation in close military alliances, including NATO and the North
American Aerospace Defense Command (NORAD). In short, it
was not necessary to choose between hard and soft power because

they reinforced each other, just as effective multilateral diplomacy made it easier to pursue closer bilateral relationships with key partners, and vice versa. As Louis St Laurent once said, by contributing to multilateral efforts to improve the world, Canadians could be "useful to ourselves through being useful to others."[4]

This is not to suggest that liberal internationalism has always worked as intended, or that Canadian foreign policy has always been successful. There were moments of both great achievement and outright failure. Nevertheless, liberal internationalism provided a largely non-partisan basis for Canada's global policy for more than six decades, because it was believed to serve our interests and values. As we noted in the introduction, one of the most effective practitioners of liberal internationalism in recent years was Brian Mulroney.

After coming into office in 2006, the Harper government dismissed and disparaged many elements of liberal internationalism, portraying it as more Liberal than liberal, rather than as an approach that has historically made sense to all parties because it made sense for Canada as a whole. Instead of maintaining the virtuous circle of effective bilateral and multilateral diplomacy, Canada began marginalizing itself. The result – a very unfortunate one, in our view – was a shift towards a "small Canada" approach to foreign affairs.

Given the changes now under way in the world, Canada cannot afford to continue treating its international policy as an afterthought, or as an instrument of domestic electoral politics. We believe that an updated version of liberal internationalism would provide a sound basis for an ambitious policy that responds to these new conditions. Energetic and creative multilateralism and coalition building; promoting an open international economy, peace and stability, and a rules-based international order; investing in the tools of international policy, including robust diplomatic and military capabilities and a well-funded development program; and cultivating and maintaining a broad array of relationships with international actors, including established and emerging states and non-governmental organizations – these are all elements of the liberal internationalist approach, and they are more important now than ever.

To put it simply, Canada needs an updated version of liberal internationalism, based on clear-eyed analysis of how the world is changing and how these changes will affect Canada, and in recognition of the fact that the security, prosperity, and well-being of the current and future generations of Canadians will depend, in part, on how effectively we respond to these challenges. We hope that this book provides some useful ideas on how such a policy could be conceived and pursued.

Notes

Preface

1 Robert Greenhill has served as a managing director and chief business officer of the World Economic Forum, president of the Canadian International Development Agency, and president and chief operating officer of Bombardier International.
2 To watch Greenhill's presentation at the Ottawa Forum 2014 and the other sessions, visit http://cips.uottawa.ca/the-ottawa-forum.

Introduction

1 Recent books examining the strategic directions of Canadian foreign policy include Derek H. Burney and Fen Osler Hampson, *Brave New Canada: Meeting the Challenge of a Changing World* (Montreal and Kingston: McGill-Queen's University Press, 2014); Joe Clark, *How We Lead: Canada in a Century of Change* (Toronto: Random House Canada, 2013); and Paul Heinbecker, *Getting Back in the Game: A Foreign Policy Playbook for Canada* (Toronto: Dundurn Press, 2011).
2 Some of the more active and productive Canadian think tanks that do work on international affairs include the Canadian International Council, the Asia-Pacific Foundation, the Canadian Global Affairs Institute, the Fraser Institute, and the Conference Board of Canada. Several have shut down in recent years, including the North-South Institute, while others, such as the Centre for International Governance Innovation, do work on international affairs but devote little attention to Canadian foreign policy.
3 OpenCanada.Org and the Centre for International Policy Studies (http://cips.uottawa.ca) both maintain active international affairs blogs that have a Canadian policy focus.

4 For example: Brian W. Tomlin, Fen Osler Hampson, and Norman Hillmer, *Canada's International Policies: Agendas, Alternatives, and Politics* (Oxford: Oxford University Press, 2007).

5 Charles Kupchan, "No One's World," *Huffington Post*, 3 February 2014, http://www.huffingtonpost.com/charles-kupchan/transforming-world-power_b_4703784.html.

6 "Catching the Eagle," *The Economist*, 22 August 2014, http://www.economist.com/blogs/graphicdetail/2014/08/chinese-and-american-gdp-forecasts

7 National Intelligence Council, *Global Trends 2030: Alternative Worlds* (Washington, DC: United States Government, 2012), 128.

8 See poll results in "Public Sees U.S. Power Declining as Support for Global Engagement Slips," Pew Research Centre for the People and the Press, 3 December 2013, http://www.people-press.org/2013/12/03/public-sees-u-s-power-declining-as-support-for-global-engagement-slips.

9 Robert Samuelson, "Humanity Is Actually Making Progress, Believe It or Not," *Washington Post*, 8 October 2014, http://www.washingtonpost.com/opinions/robert-samuelson-were-making-progress-believe-it-or-not/2014/10/08/3efe2648-4efc-11e4-babe-e91da079cb8a_story.html.

10 Ernst and Young, "Hitting the Sweet Spot," http://www.ey.com/Publication/vwLUAssets/Hitting_the_sweet_spot/$FILE/Hitting_the_sweet_spot.pdf, 4.

11 David Mulroney and Janet De Silva, "Canada's Asia Challenge: Creating Competence for the Next Generation of Canadians," research report, Asia Pacific Foundation of Canada (2013).

12 International Energy Agency, *World Energy Outlook 2013*, July 2013, http://www.worldenergyoutlook.org/publications/weo-2013.

13 James Parker, "A Global Energy Shift," *The Diplomat*, 28 November 2012, http://thediplomat.com/2012/11/a-global-energy-shift-2; and Grant Smith, "U.S. Seen as Biggest Oil Producer after Overtaking Saudi," *Bloomberg Business*, 4 July 2014, http://www.bloomberg.com/news/2014-07-04/u-s-seen-as-biggest-oil-producer-after-overtaking-saudi.html.

14 Joseph S. Nye, Jr, "Shale Gas Is America's Geopolitical Trump Card," *Wall Street Journal*, 8 June 2014, http://www.wsj.com/articles/joseph-nye-shale-gas-is-americas-geopolitical-trump-card-1402266357.

15 Intergovernmental Panel on Climate Change, *Climate Change 2014: Mitigation of Climate Change*, Working Group III Contribution to the Fifth Assessment Report of the IPCC (New York: Cambridge University Press, 2014), 6.

16 Intergovernmental Panel on Climate Change, *Climate Change 2014: Impacts, Adaptation, and Vulnerability*, Working Group II Contribution to the Fifth Assessment Report of the IPCC, Summary for Policymakers (2014), http://ipcc-wg2.gov/AR5/images/uploads/WG2AR5_SPM_FINAL.pdf, 6.

17 Intergovernmental Panel on Climate Change, *Climate Change 2014: The Physical Science Basis*, Working Group I Contribution to the Fifth Assessment Report of the IPCC, Summary for Policymakers (2014), http://www.climatechange2013.org/images/report/WG1AR5_SPM_FINAL.pdf, 24.

1. Why Canada's Global Commerce Policy Needs to Lean In

1 See Mike Burt and Lin Ai, *Walking the Silk Road: Understanding Canada's Changing Trade Patterns* (Ottawa: Conference Board of Canada, 2012)

2 Measured in purchasing-power terms.

3 United Nations Conference on Trade and Development, *World Investment Report 2014* (Geneva: UNCTAD, 2014).

4 Ibid.

5 For a list of Canada's most important future markets based on factors related to economic growth potential, see Danielle Goldfarb, *Canada's Next Top Markets* (Ottawa: Conference Board of Canada, 2013).

6 Kip Beckman, *What Might Canada's Future Exports Look Like?* (Ottawa: Conference Board of Canada, 2012).

7 See, for example, the World Bank's Ease of Doing Business index (http://www.doingbusiness.org/rankings) or Transparency International's Corruption Perceptions Index (http://cpi.transparency.org/cpi2013/).

8 Danielle Goldfarb and Sui Sui, *Not for Beginners: Should SMEs Go to Fast-Growth Markets?* (Ottawa: Conference Board of Canada, 2014).

9 The world now has a massive excess supply of oil, in large part due to dramatic change in the US energy landscape. The United States' energy demand dropped at the same time that it experienced a dramatic acceleration of its shale gas production.

10 Pedro Antunes and Kip Beckman, *Regional Shakeup: The Impact of Lower Oil Prices on Canada's Economy* (Ottawa: Conference Board of Canada, 2015).

11 See Danielle Goldfarb, "Integrative Trade Can Pull Us Down and Up," in *Crisis and Intervention: Lessons from the Financial Meltdown and Recession* (Ottawa: Conference Board of Canada, 2010).

12 Jacqueline Palladini, *Spotlight on Services in Canada's Global Commerce* (Ottawa: Conference Board of Canada, 2015).

13 For more on Mexico's recent reforms and the best opportunities in Mexico for Canadian companies, see Joseph Haimowitz, *"Sweet Spots" for Canadian Businesses in Mexico* (Ottawa: Conference Board of Canada, 2014).

14 Canada has in recent years introduced new tariffs to protect domestic dairy production, and as of 2015 no longer exempts imports from countries such as China from tariffs (on the basis that these countries have advanced economically and should no longer qualify for special treatment aimed at poor countries).

15 Laura Dawson, *Skills in Motion: U.S. Workers May Hold the Key to Canada's Skills Shortage* (Ottawa: Conference Board of Canada, 2013).

2. Towards an International Strategy for Liveable Cities

1 *State of the World's Cities 2010/2011 – Cities for All: Bridging the Urban Divide.* See United Nations Human Settlements Programme (UN-HABITAT)/Earthscan, 2010, http://mirror.unhabitat.org/pmss/listItemDetails .aspx?publicationID=2917.

2 Grosvenor, *Resilient Cities: A Grosvenor Research Report,* http://www .grosvenor.com/Grosvenor/files/19/194bb2f9-d778-4701-a0ed-5cb451044ab1.pdf.

3 UNICEF and World Health Organization, *Progress on Drinking Water and Sanitation, 2012 Update,* http://www.sswm.info/sites/default/files/reference_attachments/UNICEF%20and%20WHO%202012%20Progress%20on%20Drinking%20Water%20and%20Sanitation%20Update%20 2012.pdf.

4 United Nations Development Programme, *The Energy Access Situation in Developing Countries: A Review Focusing on the Least Developed Countries and Sub-Saharan Africa,* 2009, http://content.undp.org/go/cms-service/stream/asset/?asset_id=2205620.

5 "Lagos, the Mega-City of Slums," *IRIN News,* 5 September 2006, http://www.irinnews.org/report/60811/nigeria-lagos-the-mega-city-of-slums.

6 World Bank and International Monetary Fund, *Global Monitoring Report 2013: Rural-Urban Dynamics and the Millennium Development Goals,* 2013, http://issuu.com/world.bank.publications/docs/9780821398067.

7 Tiiu Paas and Vivika Halapuu, "Attitudes towards Immigrants and the Integration of Ethnically Diverse Societies," *NORFACE Migration Discussion Paper* no. 2012-23, 2012), http://www.norface-migration.org/publ_uploads/NDP_23_12.pdf.

8 UN Habitat, *State of World's Cities 2012/2013: Prosperity of Cities*, 2012, https://sustainabledevelopment.un.org/content/documents/745habitat .pdf.

9 Economist Intelligence Unit, "Global Liveability Ranking and Report," August 2013, http://www.eiu.com/public/topical_report.aspx?campaig nid=Liveability2013.

10 YouthfulCities, 2014 Global Index, http://www.youthfulcities.com/ #!2014results/c24u3.

11 Grosvenor, *Resilient Cities*.

12 fDi Magazine, *American Cities of the Future 2013/14*, 2013, http:// www.fdiintelligence.com/Locations/Americas/American-Cities-of-the-Future-2013-14?ct=true.

13 2012 Canadian Infrastructure Report Card, http://www.canada infrastructure.ca/en/report.html.

14 City of Toronto, Immigration Portal, http://www1.toronto.ca/wps/ portal/contentonly?vgnextoid=6fa6ba2ae8b1e310VgnVCM10000071d60 f89RCRD.

15 Doug Saunders, *Arrival City: How the Largest Migration in History Is Re-shaping Our World* (New York: Pantheon, 2010).

16 UN Habitat Climate Change webpage, http://unhabitat.org/urban-themes/climate-change.

17 Economist Intelligence Unit, "Hot Spots 2025: Benchmarking the Future Competitiveness of Cities," 2013, http://www.citigroup.com/citi/ citiforcities/pdfs/hotspots2025.pdf.

3. Make Canada the World Leader in Mining Innovation

1 HSBC Global Research, "The World in 2015," January 2012.

2 Mark Cutifani, "A Critical Imperative – Innovation and a Sustainable Future," World Mining Congress, Montreal, August 2013.

3 Canada's Public Policy Forum, "Towards a More Innovative Future: Insights from Canada's Natural Resources Sector," 21 March 2012.

4 Ibid.

5 Interview with the author, April 2014.

6 Mining Association of Canada, "Facts and Figures of the Canadian Mining Industry 2013," http://mining.ca/documents/facts-figures-2013.

7 Ibid.

8 Canadian Chamber of Commerce, "Mining Capital: How Canada Has Transformed Its Resource Endowment into a Global Competitive Advantage," 30 January 2013.

9   Interview with the author, April 2014.
10 Mining Association of Canada, "Facts and Figures."
11 Ibid.
12 Conference Board of Canada, "Measuring the Mining Supply and Services Sector," May 2011.
13 Mining Association of Canada, "Facts and Figures."
14 Ibid.
15 Canadian Chamber of Commerce, "Mining Capital."
16 In March 2015, Barrick won a major victory when Chile's Environmental Court found the company had not damaged glaciers in Pascua-Lama's area of influence. See Cecilia Jamasmie, "Chile's Court Says Barrick's Pascua Lama Has Not Damaged Glaciers," *Mining.com*, 23 March 2015, http://www.mining.com/chiles-court-says-barricks-pascua-lama-not-damaged-glaciers.
17 Marcus Leroux, "Miners at Turning Point after Paying for Greenfield Excesses," *The Times*, 5 June 2014, http://www.thetimes.co.uk/tto/business/industries/naturalresources/article4109595.ece.
18 Cutifani, "A Critical Imperative."
19 Ibid.
20 Leroux, "Miners at Turning Point."
21 Interview with the author, June 2014.
22 South African-based Anglo American, Brazil's Vale, Swiss-based Glencore, and the two Anglo-Australians, Rio Tinto and BHP Billiton.
23 Interview with the author, March 2014.
24 Both companies are dual-listed in London and Australia and have head offices in both countries under merger conditions established by the Australian Foreign Investment Review Board. In the case of the merger between Australia's BHP and Anglo-Dutch Billiton, the Australian government insisted the CEO and CFO of the merged company be based in Australia and the majority of board meetings be held in Australia.
25 Canadian Chamber of Commerce, "Mining Capital," 36.
26 Interview with the author, March and June 2014.
27 Interview with the author, July 2014.
28 Interview with the author, April 2014.
29 Interview with the author, March and June 2014.
30 Robert Benzie, "Ontario government bails out MaRS building for $309m," *Toronto Star*, 23 September 2014.
31 Interview with the author, July 2014.
32 Interview with the author, July 2014.
33 Interview with the author, July 2014.

34 Interview with the author, July 2014.
35 Interview with the author, July 2014.
36 Interview with the author, July 2014.
37 Vancouver-based Teck merged with Cominco in 2001.
38 Canadian Chamber of Commerce, "Mining Capital."
39 There are other chairs in related fields such as in earth and environmental sciences; however, taken together they do not reflect mining's known contribution to GDP (4 per cent), which would be equivalent to 80 chairs.
40 GeoScience BC is a non-profit organization with seed funding from the BC government which generates earth science information in partnership with First Nations, industry, universities, and government.
41 Interview with the author, July 2014.
42 Report of the Standing Committee on Foreign Affairs and International Development, "Driving Inclusive Growth: The Role of the Private Sector in International Development," House of Commons Canada, November 2012.
43 Department of Foreign Affairs, Trade and Development Canada, "Harper Government Announces Enhanced Corporate Social Responsibility Strategy to Strengthen Canada's Extractive Sector Abroad," 14 November 2014.
44 Interview with the author, May 2014.
45 CIIEID is a joint venture between UBC, Simon Fraser University and the École Polytechnique in Montreal.
46 See stoptheinstitute.ca.
47 Interview with the author, June 2014.
48 Interview with the author, July 2014.
49 Interview with the author, July 2014.

4. Canadian Hydrocarbon Resources in an Era of Manufactured Energy

1 Statistics Canada, CANSIM table 303-0051.
2 Alberta Energy Regulator, *Alberta's Energy Reserves 2012 and Supply/Demand Outlook 2013–2022*, ST98-2013.
3 US Energy Information Administration, "International Energy Statistics" (Washington, DC, 2014).
4 A play is a geographic deposit of hydrocarbons.
5 For example, the January 2006 forecast from Sproule Associates, used to value oil reserves of publicly traded companies, saw oil prices for West Texas Intermediate crude of $US65 per barrel for 2006, declining to $US53 per barrel by 2017.

6 National Energy Board, "Market Outlook for Oil Sands" (Calgary, Alberta, 2000).
7 NEB, "Oil Sands Opportunities and Challenges to 2015" (Calgary, 2006).
8 See International Energy Agency, "World Energy Outlook 2014" (Paris, 2014).
9 Energy Information Administration, "2006 International Energy Outlook" (Washington, 2006).
10 EIA, "2014 International Energy Outlook" (Washington, 2014).
11 Canadian Energy Research Institute, "Global LNG: Now, Never, or Later?" (Calgary, 2013).

5. Canada's Resource-Intensive Economy in a Low-Carbon World

1 OECD, *Towards Green Growth* (2011), http://www.oecd.org/greengrowth/48224539.pdf.
2 The World Bank, *Inclusive Green Growth: The Pathway to Sustainable Development* (May 2012), http://siteresources.worldbank.org/EXTSDNET/Resources/Inclusive_Green_Growth_May_2012.pdf.
3 International Energy Agency, *Ensuring Green Growth in a Time of Economic Crisis: The Role of Energy Technology* (April 2009), http://www.iea.org/publications/freepublications/publication/ensuring_green_growth.pdf.
4 McKinsey Global Institute, *Resource Revolution: Meeting the World's Energy, Materials, Food, and Water Needs* (2011), http://www.mckinsey.com/insights/energy_resources_materials/resource_revolution.
5 Canadian Council of Chief Executives, "Clean Growth 2.0: How Canada Can Be a Leader in Energy and Environmental Innovation" (2010), http://www.ceocouncil.ca/wp-content/uploads/archives/Clean_Growth_2_0_November_8_2010_with_cover_page.pdf .
6 The UN Global Compact-Accenture CEO Study on Sustainability 2013, http://www.accenture.com/SiteCollectionDocuments/PDF/Accenture-UN-Global-Compact-Acn-CEO-Study-Sustainability-2013.PDF.
7 World Business Council for Sustainable Development, *Vision 2050: The New Agenda for Business* (2010), http://www.infosys.com/newsroom/features/Documents/2050-agenda-business.pdf.
8 S. Hastings-Simon et al., "Myths and Realities of Clean Technologies" (McKinsey and Company, April 2014), http://www.mckinsey.com/insights/energy_resources_materials/myths_and_realities_of_clean_technologies.
9 World Resources Institute, *Millennium Ecosystem Assessment, 2005. Ecosystems and Human Well-being: Synthesis* (Washington, DC: Island Press, 2005).

10 Organisation for Economic Cooperation and Development, *OECD Environment Statistics* (2014). Available at http://www.oecd-ilibrary.org/environment/data/oecd-environment-statistics_env-data-en;jsessionid=63s83bqprhhim.x-oecd-live-01.

11 See, for example, Clean Energy Canada, http://cleanenergycanada.org/about/mission.

12 Associated Press, "Rebranding Part of Push to Streamline Environmental Reviews," *CBC News*, 28 March 2012, http://www.cbc.ca/news/politics/rebranding-part-of-push-to-streamline-environmental-reviews-1.1141562.

13 E. Greenspon et al., "How Keystone XL Soured the 'Special Relationship' between Stephen Harper and Barack Obama," *National Post*, 24 April 2014, http://news.nationalpost.com/news/canada/canadian-politics/how-keystone-xl-soured-the-special-relationship-between-stephen-harper-and-barack-obama.

14 TransAlta, *Report on Sustainability* (2012), http://www.transalta.com/sites/default/files/2012-Report-on-Sustainability.pdf.

15 S. McCarthy, "The Tree Whisperer, " *Corporate Knights*, Summer 2012, 22–3, http://static.corporateknights.com/CK40.pdf

16 OECD data, above, 2013.

17 Government of Canada, *National Inventory Report: Greenhouse Gas Sources and Sinks in Canada 1990–2012 (Part 3)* (2014), http://unfccc.int/national_reports/annex_i_ghg_inventories/national_inventories_submissions/items/8108.php.

18 United Nations Environment Programme, *Decoupling 2 Technologies, Opportunities and Policy Options* (2014), http://www.unep.org/resourcepanel/Portals/24102/PDFs/IRP_DECOUPLING_2_REPORT.pdf.

19 European Environment Agency, *Environmental Indicator Report 2012* (2012), http://www.eea.europa.eu/publications/environmental-indicator-report-2012.

20 For example, World Bank, "Putting a Price on Carbon," 3 June 2014, http://www.worldbank.org/content/dam/Worldbank/document/Carbon-Pricing-Statement-060314.pdf.

21 International Monetary Fund, *Climate, Environment, and the IMF Factsheet* (September 2014), 1, http://www.imf.org/external/np/exr/facts/pdf/enviro.pdf.

22 Canada's Ecofiscal Commission, *Smart, Practical, Possible – Canadian Options for Greater Economic and Environmental Prosperity* (2014), http://ecofiscal.ca/wp-content/uploads/2014/11/Ecofiscal-Report-November-2014.pdf.

23 S. Raush and V.J. Karplus, "Market versus Regulation: The Efficiency and Distributional Impacts of U.S. Climate Policy Proposals," in *MIT Joint Program on the Science and Policy of Global Change*, Report no. 263 (2013), 10, http://globalchange.mit.edu/files/document/MITJPSPGC_Rpt263.pdf.

24 The following results all come from Stewart Elgie, "Just the Facts: What's Behind B.C.'s Whopping Fuel Use Drop?" 9 July 2014, http://www.sustainableprosperity.ca/blogpost97.

25 T. Barker et al., "The Effects of Environmental Tax Reform on International Competitiveness in the European Union: Modelling with E3ME," in *Carbon-Energy Taxation: Lessons from Europe*, ed. M.S. Andersen and P. Ekins (Oxford: Oxford University Press, 2009), 147–214.

26 S. Elgie, "Carbon Offset Trading: A Leaky Sieve or Smart Step?" *Journal of Environmental Law and Practice* 17 (2007), 247.

27 R. Newell, W. Pizer, and D. Raimi, "Carbon Markets 15 Years after Kyoto: Lessons Learned, New Challenges," *Journal of Economic Perspectives* 27.1 (Winter 2013), 123–46.

28 M. Purdon, D. Houle, and E. Lachapelle, "The Political Economy of California and Québec's Cap-and-Trade Systems" (2014), http://www.sustainableprosperity.ca/article3877.

29 OECD, *OECD Economic Surveys – Canada – June 2014 – Overview* (2014), http://www.oecd.org/eco/surveys/Overview%20_CANADA_2014.pdf.

30 The Environics Institute and David Suzuki Foundation, "Canadian Public Opinion about Climate Change" (2014), http://www.environicsinstitute.org/news-events/news-events/environics-institute-and-david-suzuki-foundation-release-new-survey-on-climate-change.

31 Ibid.

32 Canada's Ecofiscal Commission, *Smart, Practical, Possible – Canadian Options for Greater Economic and Environmental Prosperity* (2014), http://ecofiscal.ca/wp-content/uploads/2014/11/Ecofiscal-Report-November-2014.pdf.

33 CNW Group, "220+ of Canada's Leading Economists Call for Action on Climate Change" (2008), http://www.newswire.ca/en/story/271633/220-of-canada-s-leading-economists-call-for-action-on-climate-change.

34 Environment Canada, *Turning the Corner: An Action Plan to Reduce Greenhouse Gases and Air Pollution* (n.d.), http://www.ripplegroup.ca/siteDown/index.html.

35 L. Whittington, "Stephen Harper Says Economy Trumps Climate Action,"*Toronto Star*, 9 June 2014, http://www.thestar.com/news/

canada/2014/06/09/stephen_harper_says_economy_trumps_climate_
action.html.

36 K. Leslie, "Ontario and Quebec Sign Deals on Climate Change, Energy
Projects," *CTV News*, 21 November 2014, http://www.ctvnews.ca/
politics/ontario-and-quebec-sign-deals-on-climate-change-energy-
projects-1.2113673.

37 S. Mass, "Premiers Agree to Move Forward with a National Energy
Strategy," *CBC News*, 29 August 2014, http://www.cbc.ca/news/politics/
premiers-agree-to-move-forward-with-a-national-energy-strategy-
1.2750537.

38 One could add transportation systems to this list. To some extent, this
also falls under changing the energy system (electric vehicles), but it also
involves vehicle efficiency standards, public transit, and other policy
areas.

6. Global Demand for Institutional Innovation in Internet Governance

1 Taylor Casti, "Who Will the Next Billion Internet Users Be?" *Mashable*,
30 August 2013, http://mashable.com/2013/08/30/next-billion-internet-
users/; Richard Dobbs et al., *Urban World: Cities and the Rise of the Con-
suming Class* (McKinsey Global Institute, 2012), http://www.mckinsey
.com/insights/urbanization/urban_world_cities_and_the_rise_of_the_
consuming_class.

2 On the Internet's economic impact, see Matthieu Pélissié du Rausas et al.,
Internet Matters: The Net's Sweeping Impact on Growth, Jobs, and Prosperity
(McKinsey Global Institute, 2011), http://www.mckinsey.com/insights/
high_tech_telecoms_internet/internet_matters; for its public safety and
human rights applications, see www.ushahidi.com. On global economic
trends, see also Yves Tiberghien's chapter (11) in this volume.

3 NETmundial Multistakeholder Statement, 24 April 2014, http://
netmundial.br/wp-content/uploads/2014/04/NETmundial-
Multistakeholder-Document.pdf.

4 Robert D. Putnam, "Diplomacy and Domestic Politics: The Logic of Two-
Level Games," *International Organization* 42.3 (1988), 427–60.

5 The distinction here is between coordination problems and cooperation problems. See Lisa L. Martin and Beth A. Simmons, "Theories and
Empirical Studies of International Institutions," *International Organization*
52.4 (1998), 729–57.

6 Peter M. Haas, "Epistemic Communities and International Policy Coordination," *International Organization* 46.1 (1992), 1–35.

7   Mark Raymond and Gordon Smith, *Reimagining the Internet: The Need for a High-Level Strategic Vision for Internet Governance* (Waterloo, ON: Centre for International Governance Innovation, 2013), http://www.cigionline.org/publications/2013/7/reimagining-internet-need-high-level-strategic-vision-internet-governance.

8   On the importance of nuance in analysis of diplomacy pertaining to Internet governance, see Tim Maurer and Robert Morgus, *Tipping the Scale: An Analysis of Global Swing States in the Internet Governance Debate* (Waterloo, ON: Centre for International Governance Innovation, 2014), http://www.cigionline.org/sites/default/files/no7_2.pdf; on NETmundial, see Angela Mari, "Brazil Internet Governance Event Disappoints Activists," *ZDNet*, 25 April 2014, http://www.zdnet.com/brazil-internet-governance-event-disappoints-activists-7000028797/.

9   Mancur Olson, Jr, *The Logic of Collective Action: Public Goods and the Theory of Groups*, 2nd ed. (Cambridge, MA: Harvard University Press, 1971).

10   Alexander Wendt, "Driving with the Rearview Mirror: On the Rational Science of Institutional Design," *International Organization* 55.4 (2001), 1019–49.

11   Kenneth W. Abbott and Duncan Snidal, "Hard and Soft Law in International Governance," *International Organization* 54.3 (2000), 421–56.

12   Joseph S. Nye, Jr, "Nuclear Lessons for Cyber Security?" *Strategic Studies Quarterly* 5.4 (2011), 18–38.

13   These terms are drawn from the literature on public goods. Consumption of an *excludable* good can be prevented – whether by private property rights, by a price mechanism, or by social allocation rules. A *rivalrous* good is either consumed by use or incapable of being used simultaneously by multiple parties. See Inge Kaul, Isabelle Grunberg and Marc A. Stern, "Defining Global Public Goods," in *Global Public Goods*, ed. Kaul, Grunberg, and Stern (Oxford: Oxford University Press, 1999).

14   Mark Raymond, "Puncturing the Myth of the Internet as a Commons," *Georgetown Journal of International Affairs*, International Engagement on Cyber 2013, 5–16.

15   Laura DeNardis and Mark Raymond, "Thinking Clearly about Multistakeholder Internet Governance," paper presented at the 8th Annual GigaNet Symposium, Bali, Indonesia, 21 October 2013, http://papers.ssrn.com/sol3/papers.cfm?abstract_id=2354377.

16   Henry Farrell and Martha Finnemore, "The End of Hypocrisy: American Foreign Policy in the Age of Leaks," *Foreign Affairs*, November/December 2013, http://www.foreignaffairs.com/articles/140155/henry-farrell-and-martha-finnemore/the-end-of-hypocrisy.

17 See Paquin's chapter (7) in this volume.
18 Nye, "Nuclear Lessons."
19 Raymond, "Puncturing the Myth."
20 Abbott and Snidal, "Hard and Soft Law."
21 Mark Raymond, "Renovating the Procedural Architecture of International Law," *Canadian Foreign Policy Journal* 19.3 (2013), 268–87.
22 John Stuart Mill, "On Liberty," in *On Liberty and Other Essays*, ed. John Gray (Oxford: Oxford University Press, 1991), 63.

7. Canada's International Security Agenda

The author would like to thank Stéphane Leman-Langlois, Justin Massie, Robert McRae, Taylor Owen, and Roland Paris for their helpful and constructive comments on an earlier draft of this chapter.

1 Fareed Zakaria, *The Post-American World* (New York: W.W. Norton & Co., 2009).
2 BRICS stands for Brazil, Russia, India, China, and South Africa. MINT stands for Mexico, Indonesia, Nigeria, and Turkey. CIVETS stands for Colombia, Indonesia, Vietnam, Egypt, Turkey, and South Africa. These neologisms define either newly advanced economies, as in the case of BRIC, or emerging markets, as in the case of MINT and CIVETS.
3 L. Ian MacDonald, "Q&A: A Conversation with John Baird, 'We Promote Canadian Values,'" *Policy: Canadian Politics and Public Policy* 1.2 (2014), 4–9.
4 Bruce Campion-Smith, "Doughnuts over Diplomacy," *Toronto Star*, 24 September 2009, http://www.thestar.com/business/2009/09/24/doughnuts_over_diplomacy.html.
5 See Tim Harper, "Stephen Harper Has Harsh Words for Putin on Historic Visit to Ukraine," *Toronto Star*, 22 March 2014.
6 Colin Robertson, "Harper's World View," *Policy Options*, October 2011, 76.
7 Reputation Institute, "Canada Has the World's Best Reputation according to Reputation Institute's 2013 Country RepTrack Study," New York/Copenhagen, 27 June 2013. *BBC News*, "BBC poll: Germany Most Popular Country in the World," 23 May 2013, http://www.bbc.com/news/world-europe-22624104 (under "Risers and Fallers"). Jay Loschky and Rebecca Riffkin, "Canada, Great Britain Are Americans' Most Favored Nations," *Gallup*, 15 March 2015, http://www.gallup.com/poll/181961/canada-great-britain-americans-favored-nations.aspx.
8 David P. Auerswald and Stephen M. Saideman, *NATO in Afghanistan: Fighting Together, Fighting Alone* (Princeton: Princeton University Press,

2014). Robert Gates, "The Security and Defense Agenda (Future of NATO)," Brussels, 10 June 2011, www.defense.gov/speeches/speech.aspx?speechid=1581.

9   Jack L. Granatstein, "Is NATO Still Necessary for Canada?" Canadian Defence & Foreign Affairs Institute (March 2013), http://www.operationspaix.net/DATA/DOCUMENT/7804~v~Is_NATO_Still_Necessary_for_Canada_.pdf

10 Government of Canada, "Minister Nicholson Meets with Counterparts at NATO Defence Ministerial Meeting," 5 February 2015, http://news.gc.ca/web/article-en.do?nid=928519.

11 Philip Gordon and Jeremy Shapiro, *Allies at War: America, Europe and the Crisis over Iraq* (Washington, DC: Brookings Institution, McGraw-Hill, 2004). See also Ivo H. Daalder and James M. Lindsay, *America Unbound: The Bush Revolution in Foreign Policy* (Hoboken, NJ: Wiley Editions, 2005).

12 Chester A. Crocker, Fen Osler Hampson, and Pamela Aall, "Collective Conflict Management: A New Formula for Global Peace and Security Cooperation," *International Affairs* 87.1 (2011), 39–58; and Lepgold, who defines this mechanism as "a pattern of group action, usually but not necessarily sanctioned by a global or regional body, in anticipation of or in response to the outbreak of intra- or interstate armed conflict." Joseph Lepgold, "Regionalism in the Post-Cold War Era: Incentives for Conflict Management," in *Regional Conflict Management*, ed. Paul F. Diehl and Joseph Lepgold (Oxford: Oxford University Press, 2003), 12.

13 Crocker, Hampson, and Aall, "Collective Conflict Management," 46.

14 Campbell Clark, "Harper Pledges $105-Million to Help Jordan Handle Influx of Syrian Refugees," *Globe and Mail*, 23 January 2014, http://www.theglobeandmail.com/news/politics/harper-kicks-off-first-visit-to-jordan/article16462478.

15 Department of Foreign Affairs, Trade and Development Canada, *Conflict Prevention and Mediation*, 2014, http://www.international.gc.ca/start-gtsr/prevention-mediation.aspx?lang=eng. I thank Justin Massie for raising this important issue during one of our numerous discussions on Canadian foreign policy.

16 Drew F. Cohen, "Autonomous Drones and the Ethics of Future Warfare," *Huffington Post*, 15 December 2013, http://www.huffingtonpost.com/drew-f-cohen/autonomous-drones-and-the_b_4428112.html.

17 United Nations Office in Geneva (UNOG), "Report of the 2014 Informal Meeting of Experts on Lethal Autonomous Weapons Systems (LAWS)," 13–16 May 2014, http://www.unog.ch/80256EDD006B8954/

(httpAssets)/350D9ABED1AFA515C1257CF30047A8C7/$file/Report_
AdvancedVersion_10June.pdf.

18 For more on Canada's past norm-building initiatives, see the chapter
in this volume (9) by Emily Paddon and Jennifer Welsh.

19 CBC, "Foreign Hackers Attack Canadian Government," *CBC News*,
17 February 2011, http://www.cbc.ca/news/politics/foreign-hackers-
attack-canadian-government-1.982618.

20 Security and Defence Agenda, "Crimea Crisis Cyber Attacks Spike in
March," 20 March 2014, http://www.securitydefenceagenda.org/
Contentnavigation/Library/Libraryoverview/tabid/1299/articleType/
ArticleView/articleId/3667/Crimea-crisis-cyberattacks-spike-in-March
.aspx.

21 It was revealed that Communications Security Establishment Canada
(CSEC) has been spying on Brazil's energy and mining sectors in order
to lend a hand to Canadian companies. See Susan Ormiston, "Canada's
Spying Touches Nerve in Brazil," *CBC News*, 15 October 2013, http://
www.cbc.ca/news/world/canada-s-spying-touches-nerve-in-brazil-
susan-ormiston-1.2054334.

22 David Mulroney, "China Will Keep Spying. Canada Must Respond with
Skill, not Rhetoric," *Globe and Mail*, 31 July 2014, http://www
.theglobeandmail.com/globe-debate/china-will-keep-spying-canada-
must-repond-with-skill-not-rhetoric/article19872035/.

23 The GGE included the five permanent members of the UN Security
Council as well as Argentina, Australia, Belarus, Canada, Egypt, Estonia,
Germany, India, Indonesia, and Japan.

24 Detlev Wolter, "The UN Takes a Big Step Forward on Cybersecurity,"
Arms Control Association, 4 September 2013, http://www.armscontrol.
org/act/2013_09/The-UN-Takes-a-Big-Step-Forward-on-Cybersecurity.

25 Government of Canada, "Developments in the Field of Information and
Telecommunications in the Context of International Security," https://
unoda-web.s3.amazonaws.com/wp-content/uploads/2014/10/Canada.pdf.

26 This proposition was notably supported by China and the United
Arab Emirates. See Eric Pfanner, "U.S. Rejects Telecommunications
Treaty," *New York Times*, 13 December 2012, http://www.nytimes.
com/2012/12/14/technology/14iht-treaty14.html?_r=0.

27 Of course, critics could argue that, because of its status as a spying
nation (through the Communications Security Establishment Canada –
CSEC), Canada has little interest in establishing a rule-based governing
system in this area.

8. Towards a New Canadian Human Rights Diplomacy

1 The best articulation of this argument is in Stephen Hopgood, *The End-times of Human Rights* (Ithaca: Cornell University Press, 2013).
2 The full story is told in William Schabas, "Canada and the Adoption of the Universal Declaration of Human Rights," *McGill Law Journal* 43 (1998), 403–42.
3 A fuller discussion on this point is found in David Petrasek, "Global Trends and the Future of Human Rights Advocacy," *International Journal of Human Rights* 11.20 (2014).
4 International Organization for Migration, *World Migration Report 2010. The Future of Migration: Building Capacities for Change* (Geneva: IOM, 2010), 1.
5 National Intelligence Council, *Global Trends 2030: Alternative Worlds* (Washington: NIC, 2012), 26. http://www.dni.gov/files/documents/GlobalTrends_2030.pdf.
6 European Strategy and Policy Analysis System (ESPAS), *Global Trends 2030: Citizens in an Interconnected and Polycentric World* (Paris: European Union, Institute for Security Studies, 2012), 46. http://www.iss.europa.eu/uploads/media/ESPAS_report_01.pdf.

9. Protecting Civilians in Conflict

1 The initiative was a direct response to the assessment of the UN's "systematic failure" to protect populations in the final phase of the Sri Lankan conflict in 2009. See *Report of the Secretary-General's Internal Review Panel on United Nations Action in Sri Lanka*, November 2012.
2 United Nations, S/RES/1270 (1999).
3 International Commission on Intervention and State Sovereignty, *The Responsibility to Protect: Research, Bibliography, Background. Supplementary Volume* (Ottawa: International Development Research Council, 2001).
4 Philippe Kirsch and John Holmes, "The Rome Conference on an International Criminal Court: The Negotiating Process," *American Journal of International Law* 93.2 (1999), 2–12.
5 See Jeff Davis, "Liberal-Era Diplomatic Language Killed Off," *Embassy*, July 2009.
6 Emily Paddon, *Taking Sides in Peacekeeping: Impartiality and the Future of the United Nations* (Oxford: Oxford University Press, forthcoming).
7 See Victoria Metcalfe, Alison Giffen, and Samir Elhawary, *UN Integration and Humanitarian Space: An Independent Study Commissioned by the UN Integration Steering Group* (London: Overseas Development Institute, 2011).

8 See data produced by the Financial Tracking Service (FTS) of the United Nations Office for the Coordination of Humanitarian Affairs (OCHA) at https://fts.unocha.org/.

9 See S/RES/1674 (2006), 1894 (2009), 2117 (2013), 2150 (2014), and 2171 (2014). The two resolutions from 2014 also explicitly support the work of the Joint Office in providing an early warning function for states.

10 In relation to some situations, the council has also authorized action to assist a state to protect its populations from atrocity crimes. See S/RES/2085 (2012) on Mali, 1996 (2011) on South Sudan, and 1975 (2011) on Côte d'Ivoire.

11 *Pillar I* of R2P stresses that states have the primary responsibility to protect their populations from genocide, war crimes, ethnic cleansing, and crimes against humanity. *Pillar II* addresses the commitment of the international community to provide assistance to states in building the capacity to protect their populations. *Pillar III* focuses on the responsibility of the international community to take timely and decisive action when a state is manifestly failing to protect its populations.

12 Jennifer M. Welsh, "Implementing the 'Responsibility to Protect': Catalyzing Debate and Building Capacity," in *Implementation in World Politics: How Norms Change Practice*, ed. Alex Betts and Phil Orchard (Oxford: Oxford University Press, 2014), 124–43.

13 Louise Arbour, *The Inaugural Roland Berger Lecture on Human Rights and Human Dignity*, University of Oxford, 7 February 2014, available at http://www.crisisgroup.org.

14 Ibid.

15 "Secretary-General's Remarks at the Security Council Open Debate on Trends in United Nations Peacekeeping, June 11, 2014." www.un.org/sg/statements/index.asp?nid=7773.

16 *Responsibility to Protect: State Responsibility and Prevention*, Report of the Secretary-General, A/67/929, 9 July 92013, paras. 12–29.

17 *Fulfilling our Collective Responsibility: International Assistance and the Responsibility to Protect*, Report of the Secretary-General, A/68/947, 11 July 2014, paras. 43–58. These inhibitors include a professional and accountable security sector, impartial institutions for overseeing political transitions, independent judicial and human rights institutions, a capacity to assess risk and mobilize early response, local capacity to resolve conflicts, media capacity to counteract prejudice and hate speech, and effective and legitimate transitional justice.

18 E.g., Dennis King and Hermes Grullon, "Diaspora Communities as Aid Providers," *Migration Policy Practice* 3:4 (August–September 2013).

19 For two studies that set out some of the core issues and policy options, see The Mosaic Institute and the Walter and Duncan Gordon Foundation, *Tapping Our Potential: Diaspora Communities and Canadian Foreign Policy*, Toronto, 11 July 2011; and Manuelle Chanoine, Meredith Giel, and Tamara Simao, *Effectively Engaging Diasporas under the New Canadian Department of Foreign Affairs, Trade and Development*, CIGI Junior Fellows Policy Brief, No. 6, July 2013.

20 David Hornsby, "Turning Perception into Reality: Canada in Africa," *Opencanada.org*, 7 November 2013, available at http://opencanada.org/features/the-think-tank/essays/turning-perception-into-reality-canada-in-africa/.

21 E.g., See John Ibbitson, "Harper's Foreign Policy: Ukraine and the Diaspora Vote," 19 March 2014, https://www.cigionline.org/blogs/john-ibbitsons-blog/harpers-foreign-policy-ukraine-and-diaspora-vote; and David Carment and Yiagadeesan Samy, "The Dangerous Game of Diaspora Politics," *Globe and Mail*, 10 February 2012, http://www.theglobeandmail.com/globe-debate/the-dangerous-game-of-diaspora-politics/article544912.

10. A New Generation's Role in Global Sustainable Development

I thank Julie Biau, Sinead Mowlds, and Christine Zhang for excellent research assistance. I also thank Laurence Chandy, Brett House, George Ingram, Homi Kharas, the editors, and anonymous peer reviewers for many helpful comments and suggestions.

 1 As one reference point, the pledge was equivalent to slightly more than 2 per cent of global development assistance for health. John W. McArthur, "Taking Stock of Canada's New Global Health Pledge," *Ottawa Citizen*, 5 June 2014.

 2 See Solomon M. Hsiang, Marshall Burke, and Edward Miguel, "Quantifying the Influence of Climate on Human Conflict," *Science* 341.6151 (September 2013), DOI: 10.1126/science.1235367; and Edward Miguel, Shanker Satyanath, and Ernest Sergenti, "Economic Shocks and Civil Conflict: An Instrumental Variables Approach," *Journal of Political Economy* 112.4 (2004), 725–53.

 3 The seminal 2004 UN High-level Panel on Threats, Challenges and Change argued that there can be no security without development, and no development without security. High-level Panel on Threats, Challenges and Change, *A More Secure World: Our Shared Responsibility* (New York: United Nations, 2004).

4 Asian Development Bank, *Key Indicators for Asia and the Pacific 2012* (Manila: ADB, 2012).

5 Zhu Ningzhu, "Ecological 'Red Line' Great Breakthrough in Environment Protection: Expert," *Xinhua News*, 25 November 2013, http://news.xinhuanet.com/english/indepth/2013-11/25/c_132915115.htm.

6 John W. McArthur, "Seven Million Lives Saved: Under-5 Mortality since the Launch of the Millennium Development Goals," Brookings Global Economy and Development Working Paper 78, September 2014.

7 The figure for deaths averted thanks to antiretroviral therapy (ART) only includes developing countries. As of the end of 2013, ART is estimated to have averted 7.6 million deaths globally since 1995. UNAIDS, *The Gap Report* (Geneva: UNAIDS, 2014).

8 Note that while there is broad agreement regarding the rapid decline in the share of humanity living in extreme poverty, estimates of the absolute number of people still living in extreme poverty remain imprecise. The 13 per cent figure is based on the World Bank's extreme poverty estimate for 2015, available as of August 2015 at http://www.worldbank.org/en/publication/global-monitoring-report/poverty-forecasts. That figure will likely be updated in late 2015 based on recent revisions to global purchasing-power parity benchmarks. In 2014, Chandy and Kharas independently estimated that the extreme poverty headcount has fallen to 870 million people. See Laurence Chandy and Homi Kharas, "What Do New Price Data Mean for the Goal of Ending Extreme Poverty?" Brookings Institution blog, 5 May 2014, http://www.brookings.edu/blogs/up-front/posts/2014/05/05-data-extreme-poverty-chandy-kharas.

9 The OECD further estimates that 18 developing countries are already on track to graduate from the official development assistance (ODA) eligibility threshold by 2024. Simon Scott, "Enhancing the Development Impact of ODA," OECD-DAC presentation to retreat organized by Independent Research Forum on Post-2015 Sustainable Development Agenda, New York, 3 May 2014.

10 Homi Kharas, "Financing for Development: International Financial Flows after 2015," Brookings Institution, 8 July 2014, http://www.brookings.edu/research/papers/2014/07/08-financing-development-international-financial-flows-kharas

11 My colleague Homi Kharas and I have previously described five main categories for private investment: agriculture, social sectors, extractives, services (e.g., finance, retail, digital), and infrastructure and decarbonization. Homi Kharas and John W. McArthur, "Mobilizing Private Investment for Post-2015 Sustainable Development," Brookings briefing note, 27 May

2014, http://www.brookings.edu/research/papers/2014/07/mobilizing-private-investment-post-2015-develoment-kharas-mcarthur.

12 Homi Kharas, "Time to Boost IBRD as well as IDA," World Bank Future Development blog, 19 February 2014, http://blogs.worldbank.org/futuredevelopment/time-boost-ibrd-well-ida.

13 The non-partisan pattern extends south of the border too. US ODA hit its all-time low in 1997 under President Bill Clinton, before George W. Bush initiated transformative increases in the 2000s, especially for global health.

14 Inter-Council Network of Provincial and Regional Councils for International Cooperation (ICN), "Canadian Engagement on Global Poverty Issues: Report of Results," 2012.

15 See http://www.makepovertyhistory.ca/story/poll-shows-canadians-support-increasing-foreign-aid-and-want-canada-to-show-leadership-on-chil.

16 This strategy builds on the recommendation of the 2012 UN High-Level Panel on Global Sustainability and the 2013 UN High-Level Panel on the Post-2015 Development Agenda that companies must face "comply or explain" requirements on social and environmental standards. See High-Level Panel of Eminent Persons on the Post-2015 Development Agenda, *A New Global Partnership: Eradicate Poverty and Transform Economies through Sustainable Development* (New York: United Nations, 2013).

11. Dealing with Rapid Change and Systemic Risk

1 World Economic Forum, *Global Risks 2014*, 9th ed., p. 12, http://www3.weforum.org/docs/WEF_GlobalRisks_Report_2014.pdf.

2 Percentages calculated by the author.

3 Chris Giles, "The New World Economy in Four Charts," Alphaville, *Financial Times*, 7 October 2014, http://ftalphaville.ft.com/2014/10/07/1998332/moneysupply-the-new-world-economy-in-four-charts/.

4 BC Stats, available at http://www.bcstats.gov.bc.ca/StatisticsBySubject/ExportsImports/Data.aspx.

5 Organisation for Economic Cooperation and Development, *Looking to 2060: Long-term Global Growth Prospects* (Paris: OECD, 2012).

6 Remarks given at the opening of the Third Global Think Tank Summit at the China World Hotel, Beijing, China, on 28 June 2013 (event organized by the China Center for International Economic Exchanges).

7 See the chapters by Elgie (5) and Leach (4).

Conclusion

1 Thomas Hale, David Held, and Kevin Young, "Gridlock: From Self-Reinforcing Interdependence to Second-order Cooperation Problems," *Global Policy* 4:3 (September 2013), 223–35.
2 Daniel Livermore, "Harper, Baird and Multilateral Cooperation," Centre for International Policy Studies Blog, University of Ottawa, 5 October 2013, http://cips.uottawa.ca/harper-baird-and-multilateral-cooperation.
3 Roland Paris, "Are Canadians Still Liberal Internationalists? Foreign Policy and Public Opinion in the Harper Era," *International Journal* 69:3 (September 2014), 274–307.
4 Louis St Laurent, "The Foundations of Canadian Policy in World Affairs," Duncan and John Gray Memorial Lecture, 13 January 1947, in J.L. Granatstein, *Canadian Foreign Policy: Historical Readings* (Toronto: Copp Clark Pitman, 1986), 33.

Contributors

Stewart Elgie is a professor of law and economics at the University of Ottawa, and director of the university's interdisciplinary Environment Institute. He received his masters of law from Harvard and his doctorate (JSD) from Yale. He is also the founder and chair of Sustainable Prosperity, Canada's major green-economy think tank and policy-research network. His research involves many aspects of environmental and economic sustainability, with a particular focus on market-based approaches. Elgie started his career as an environmental lawyer in Alaska, litigating over the Valdez oil spill. He returned to Canada and founded Ecojustice, now Canada's largest non-profit environmental law organization. He was later hired by Pew Trusts as founding executive director of the multi-stakeholder Canadian Boreal Initiative. Prior to his faculty position at University of Ottawa (2004), Elgie held faculty appointments (part-time) at several Canadian universities (UBC, Alberta, York). He has served on or chaired many advisory bodies in the environment/sustainability area. In 2001, Elgie was awarded the Law Society of Upper Canada medal for exceptional lifetime contributions to law – the youngest man ever to receive the profession's highest honour.

Danielle Goldfarb leads the Conference Board of Canada's Global Commerce Centre, where she heads up research delving into underexplored and emerging areas critical for evidence-based policymaking. Ongoing topics of interest include responding to rapid global economic change, selling Canada's high-value services in global markets, and improving the links between Canada's multicultural population and global trade. She speaks regularly to government, media, academic, and business audiences, and her articles and commentaries have been published by several Canadian think tanks and by most major Canadian media, including the *Globe and Mail* and *Maclean's* magazine. Her most recent (co-authored) publications include "Not for Beginners: Should Canada's SMEs Go to Fast-Growth Markets?" and "For Innovators Only: Canadian Companies' EU Export Experience." Goldfarb has been part of Statistics Canada's advisory committee on trade, Georgetown University's leadership seminar, the Department of Foreign Affairs Academic Advisory Group on trade, and the US International Visitor Program on trade. She has an MPhil in international relations from Cambridge University and a BComm in honours economics from McGill University.

Jennifer Keesmaat is chief planner for the City of Toronto. Over the past decade she has been repeatedly recognized by the Canadian Institute of Planners and Ontario Professional Planners Institute for her innovative work in Canadian municipalities. Most recently, she was named as one of the most influential people in Toronto by *Toronto Life* magazine and one of the most powerful people in Canada by *Maclean's* magazine. Her planning practice is characterized by an emphasis on collaborations across sectors, and broad engagement with municipal staff, councils, developers, business leaders, NGOs, and residents' associations. Her priorities include implementing a divisional strategic plan, leading an official plan review process, refining public consultation to provide more access to city-building conversations, transit planning, midrise development on the City of Toronto's many avenues, and overseeing development review for over 4000 applications annually. Keesmaat is the founder of Project Walk, which premiered its first short film in 2011 as an official selection at the Toronto International Film Festival. In 2012, she debuted her first TED talk, "Walk to School," and in 2013 delivered her second, "Own Your City." She is a graduate of Western University (combined honours

English and philosophy) and has a master's degree in environmental studies (politics and planning) from York University.

Andrew Leach is an energy and environmental economist and associate professor of energy policy at the Alberta School of Business, University of Alberta. He has a PhD in economics from Queen's University, and a BSc (environmental sciences) and MA (economics) from the University of Guelph. Leach was previously assistant professor at HEC Montréal. His academic research interests span climate and energy economics and policy. He has also consulted for a variety of federal and Alberta government departments and recently spent a year on leave from the University of Alberta as a visiting scholar at Environment Canada, where he worked mostly on greenhouse gas policy for the oil and gas sector.

Andrea Mandel-Campbell is vice-president of corporate communications for Kinross Gold Corporation, a leading global gold producer. She was previously director of communications for the Honourable Tony Clement, president of the Treasury Board. A veteran journalist, broadcaster, and author, Andrea was an anchor on CTV's Business News Network and was a correspondent for the *Financial Times* of London in Latin America for close to a decade. She is the author of *Why Mexicans Don't Drink Molson*, the most comprehensive analysis to date of why Canadian companies fail to go global and why they must.

John W. McArthur is a senior fellow in the Brookings Institution's Global Economy and Development Program, where he focuses on interrelated issues of economic growth, sustainability, health, agriculture, poverty reduction, and global collaboration. He is also a senior fellow with the United Nations Foundation and senior fellow with the Hong Kong–based Fung Global Institute. He was previously the CEO of Millennium Promise and prior to that managed the UN Millennium Project, the advisory body to then-Secretary-General Kofi Annan. He was a faculty member at Columbia's School of International and Public Affairs and policy director at the university's Earth Institute. Earlier, he was a research fellow at the Harvard Center for International Development, where he co-authored the Global Competitiveness Report. In 2007–8, McArthur co-chaired the International Commission on Education for Sustainable Development Practice, which led to the launch of a new global network of master in development practice programs. He has chaired the World Economic Forum's Global Agenda Councils on Benchmarking Progress (2011–12) and on Poverty and Sustainable Development (2013–14). In 2009, the forum recognized him as a Young Global Leader. He completed a DPhil and MPhil in economics at Oxford University, which he attended as a Rhodes Scholar, a master's in public policy at Harvard's Kennedy School of Government, and a BA (honours) at the University of British Columbia.

Taylor Owen is assistant professor of digital media and global affairs at the University of British Columbia and a senior fellow at the Columbia Graduate School of Journalism. He was previously the research director of the Tow Center for Digital Journalism at Columbia University, where he designed and led a program studying the impact of digital technology on the practice of journalism. He is the founder and editor of OpenCanada.org, an award-winning international affairs website, and the director of the International Relations and Digital Technology Projects, an international research project exploring the intersection of information technology and international affairs. He has previously held positions at Yale University, the London School of Economics, and the International Peace Research Institute, Oslo. His PhD is from the University of Oxford, where he was a Trudeau Scholar. He is the author of *Disruptive Power: The Crisis of the State in the Digital Age* (Oxford University Press, 2015).

Emily Paddon is the Rose Research Fellow in International Relations at the University of Oxford and a European Research Council postdoctoral fellow on the "Individualization of War" project. Previously, she was an associate faculty member of the Blavatnik School of Government and a lecturer at Wadham College, both at Oxford. Her research analyses the impact of the increased prominence of human rights in the theory and practice of armed conflict. Specifically, she focuses on the politics and practices of United Nations peacekeeping, humanitarianism, and military action, with a geographical emphasis on sub-Saharan Africa. Paddon is an elected fellow of the Rift Valley Institute and co-founder of the Oxford Central Africa Forum (OCAF). She has served as an Action Canada public policy fellow, a visiting scholar at the International Peace Institute, Columbia University, and the Sauvé Foundation. She holds a BA from Brown University and an MPhil and DPhil in international relations from St Antony's College, Oxford, where she was a Trudeau Scholar.

Jonathan Paquin is an associate professor of political science and director of the International Peace and Security Program at Université Laval. He is also the editor of the peer-reviewed journal *Études internationales*. Paquin is the co-editor (with Patrick James) of *Game Changer: The Impact of 9/11 on North American Security* (UBC Press, 2014) and the author of *A Stability-Seeking Power: US Foreign Policy and Secessionist Conflicts* (McGill-Queen's, 2010). He has written articles in numerous academic journals including *Cooperation and Conflict, Foreign Policy Analysis*, and the *Canadian Journal of Political Science*. He has been a visiting researcher in the Department of Government at Georgetown University and a Fulbright visiting scholar and resident fellow at the School of Advanced International Studies (SAIS) at Johns Hopkins University in Washington, DC. He received a PhD in political science from McGill University.

Roland Paris is founding director of the Centre for International Policy Studies (CIPS) at the University of Ottawa. He is also University Research Chair in International Security and Governance, and associate professor in the Graduate School of Public and International Affairs. He was previously director of research at the Conference Board of Canada; policy adviser in the Privy Council Office and in the Department of Foreign Affairs; and assistant professor of political science at the University of Colorado Boulder. He has also been a visiting researcher at the Johns Hopkins School of Advanced International Studies in Washington, DC, and the Centre d'études et de recherches internationales at Sciences Po in Paris.

His research on international security, civil wars, and post-conflict peace building has appeared in leading academic publications and has won several awards. He has also received four prizes for university teaching and two awards for public service. In 2012 he was appointed a Global Ethics Fellow by the Carnegie Council on Ethics and International Affairs in New York. In 2014 the secretary-general of NATO appointed him to a ten-member international panel of experts to provide advice on the future of the transatlantic partnership.

David Petrasek is associate professor at the University of Ottawa's Graduate School of Public and International Affairs and former special adviser to the secretary-general of Amnesty International. He has worked extensively on human rights, humanitarian, and conflict resolution issues, including for Amnesty International (1990–6), the Office of the UN High Commissioner for Human Rights (1997–8), and the International Council on Human Rights Policy (1998–2002), and as director of policy at the Centre for Humanitarian Dialogue (2003–7). He has taught international human rights and humanitarian law courses at the Osgoode Hall Law School, the Raoul Wallenberg Institute at Lund University, Sweden, and at the University of Oxford. David has also worked as a consultant or adviser to several NGOs and UN agencies.

Mark Raymond is the Wick Cary Assistant Professor of International Security in the Department of International and Area Studies at the University of Oklahoma. His research interests include international relations theory, international law and organization, and international security. His work has appeared or is forthcoming in *International Theory*, the *Georgetown Journal of International Affairs*, and the *Canadian Foreign Policy Journal*. He is also the co-editor, with Gordon Smith, of *Organized Chaos: Reimagining the Internet* (CIGI, 2014). Raymond was formerly a research fellow at the Centre for International Governance Innovation (CIGI). He has testified or delivered invited presentations on Internet governance and cybersecurity to the UN Commission on Science and Technology for Development (CSTD), the Institute of Electrical and Electronics

Engineers (IEEE), and the Royal Institute of International Affairs (Chatham House). He holds a PhD in political science from the University of Toronto.

Yves Tiberghien is the director of the Institute of Asian Research at the University of British Columbia, executive director of the UBC China Council, and co-director of the UBC Master of Public Policy and Global Affairs (MPPGA) program, and associate professor of political science. He was an Academy Scholar at Harvard University in 2004–6. He specializes in East Asian comparative political economy, international political economy, and global governance, with an empirical focus on China, Japan, and Korea. In 2007 he published *Entrepreneurial States: Reforming Corporate Governance in France, Japan, and Korea* (Cornell University Press). Tiberghien has also published many articles and book chapters on Japan's and China's political economy, global governance, global-climate-change politics, and the governance of agricultural biotechnology in China and Japan. His most recent publications include *L'Asie et le futur du monde* (Science Po Press, 2012; Chinese expanded version published by the Chinese Academy of Social Sciences, 2015) and *Leadership in Global Institution-Building: Minerva's Rule* (edited volume, Palgrave McMillan, 2013). He is currently working on articles and a book on China's role in global governance. He is also scheduled to publish *The Political Economy of East Asia: Regional Transformation and Global Impact* (Palgrave, 2016). Tiberghien has published several articles on the G20 geopolitical chessboard and on the Chinese role in the G20. As a senior fellow with the Global Summitry Project at the Munk School of Global Affairs, he regularly attends G20 meetings.

Jennifer M. Welsh is professor and chair in international relations at the European University Institute (Florence, Italy) and a fellow of Somerville College, University of Oxford. She is co-director of the Oxford Institute for Ethics, Law and Armed Conflict, and the principal investigator of a European Research Council five-year grant on the "Individualization of War." Welsh is the author and editor of numerous publications on humanitarian intervention, the evolution of the "responsibility to protect" principle, the United Nations Security Council, and Canadian foreign policy. She sits on the editorial boards of the journals *Ethics and International Affairs* and *Global Responsibility to Protect*, and of the Cambridge University Press book series in international relations. She is also a steering committee member of the American Academy of Sciences project on ethics, technology, and war. In 2013, UN Secretary General Ban Ki-moon appointed Welsh to be his special adviser on the responsibility to protect.

Index